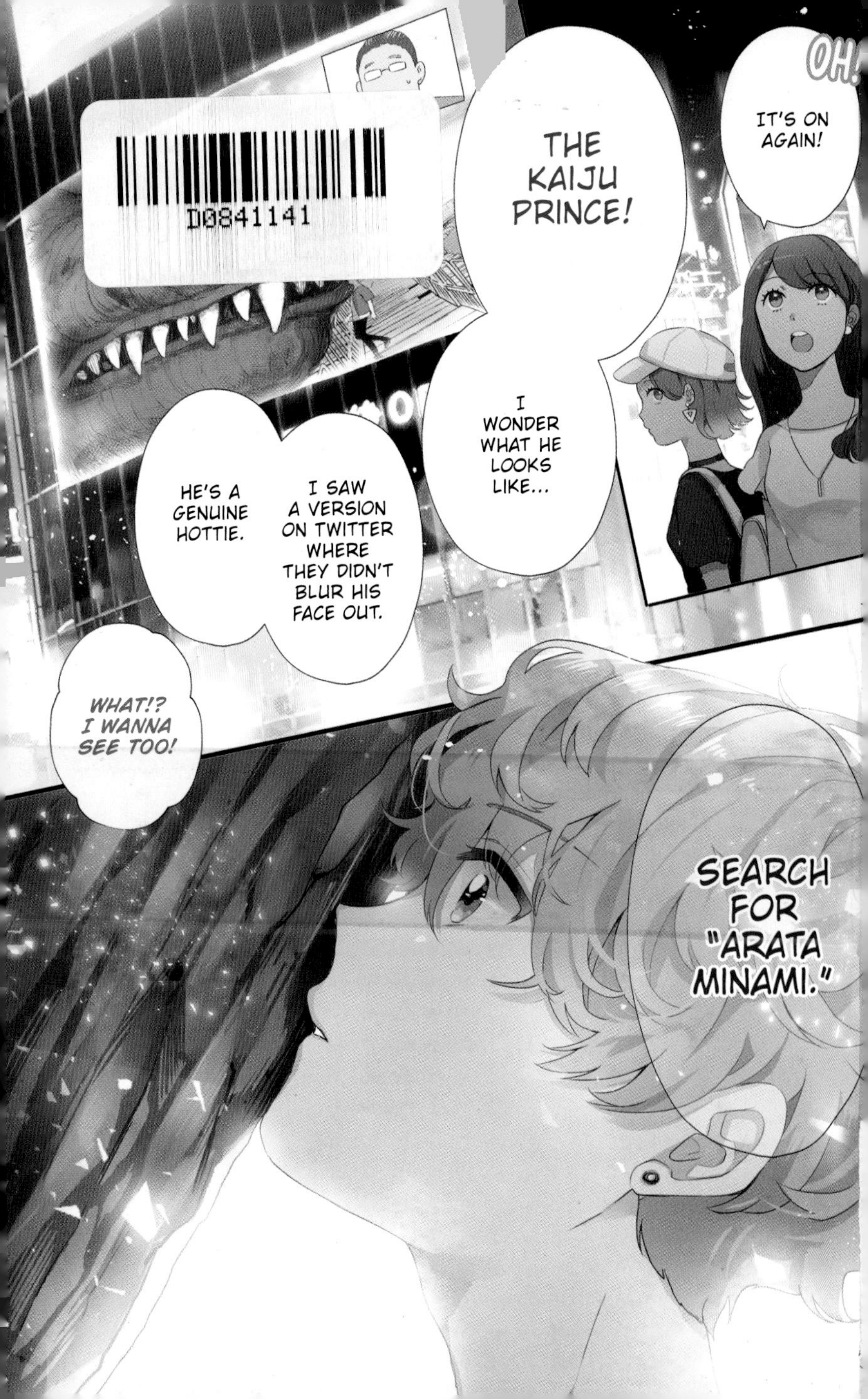
OH!
IT'S ON AGAIN!
THE KAIJU PRINCE!
I WONDER WHAT HE LOOKS LIKE...
I SAW A VERSION ON TWITTER WHERE THEY DIDN'T BLUR HIS FACE OUT.
HE'S A GENUINE HOTTIE.
WHAT!? I WANNA SEE TOO!
SEARCH FOR "ARATA MINAMI."

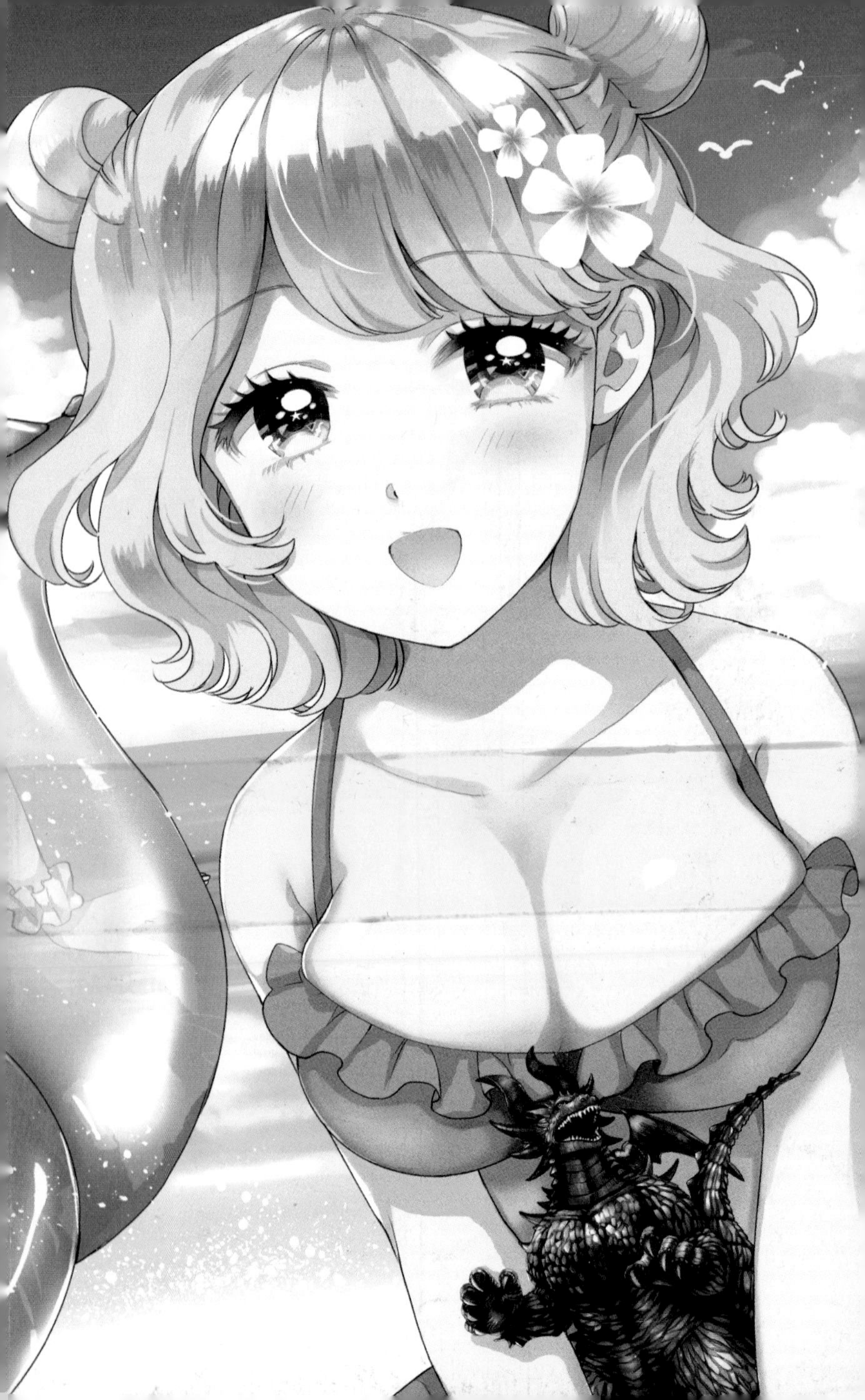

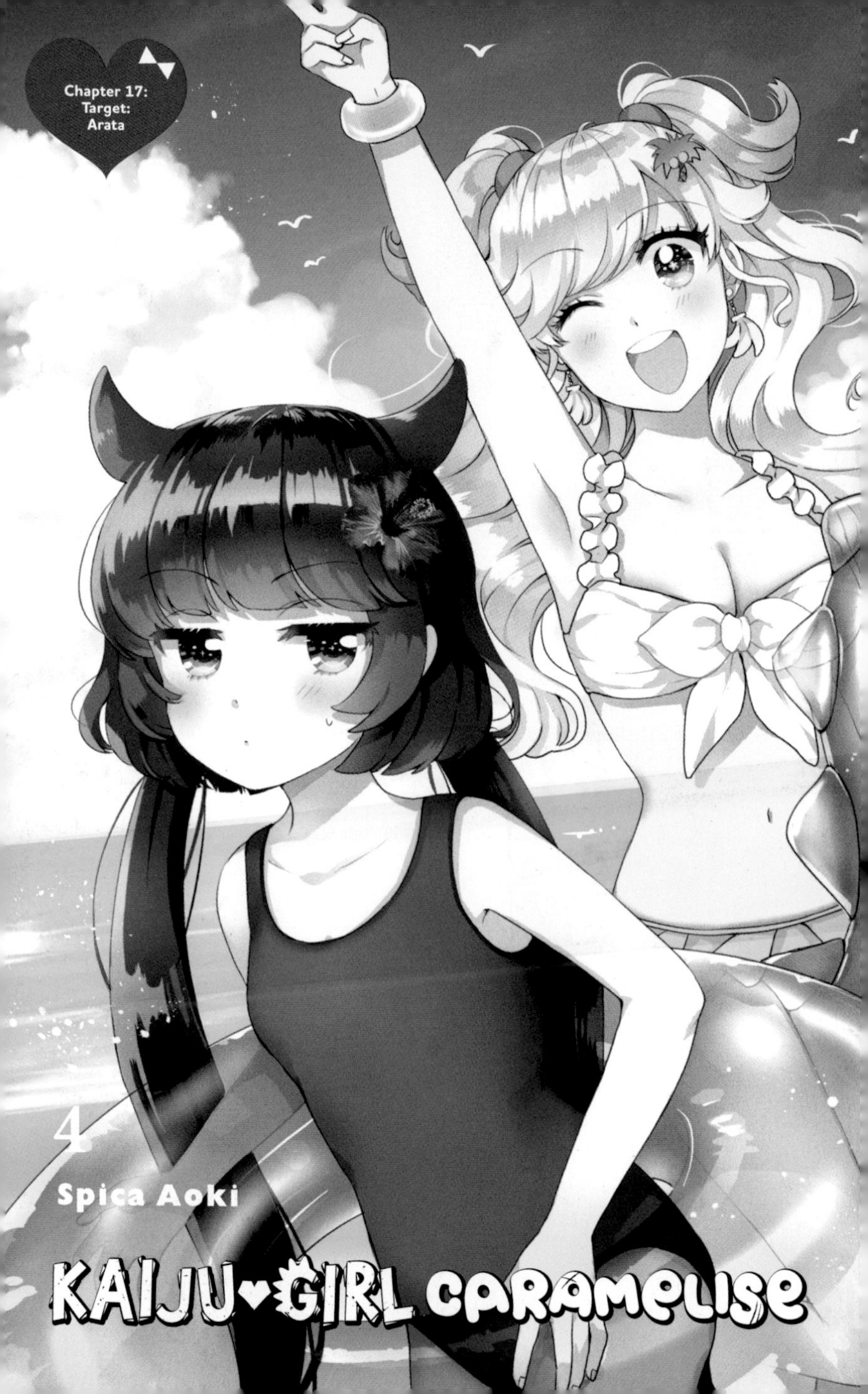
Chapter 17:
Target:
Arata
4
Spica Aoki
KAIJU♥GIRL CARAMELISE

contents

Chapter 17 Target: Arata - 001

Chapter 18 Midsummer Trip to Kaiju Island!! Part 1 - - - - - - 023

Chapter 19 Midsummer Trip to Kaiju Island!! Part 2 - - - - - - 049

Chapter 20 Japan Is Waiting for Me? - - - - - - - - - - - - - - - - 083

Chapter 21 Emergency! Mom's Gone! - - - - - - - - - - - - - - - - 107

Chapter 22 Gripe Away, Kaiju Girl! - - - - - - - - - - - - - - - - - 123

Afterword   - 162

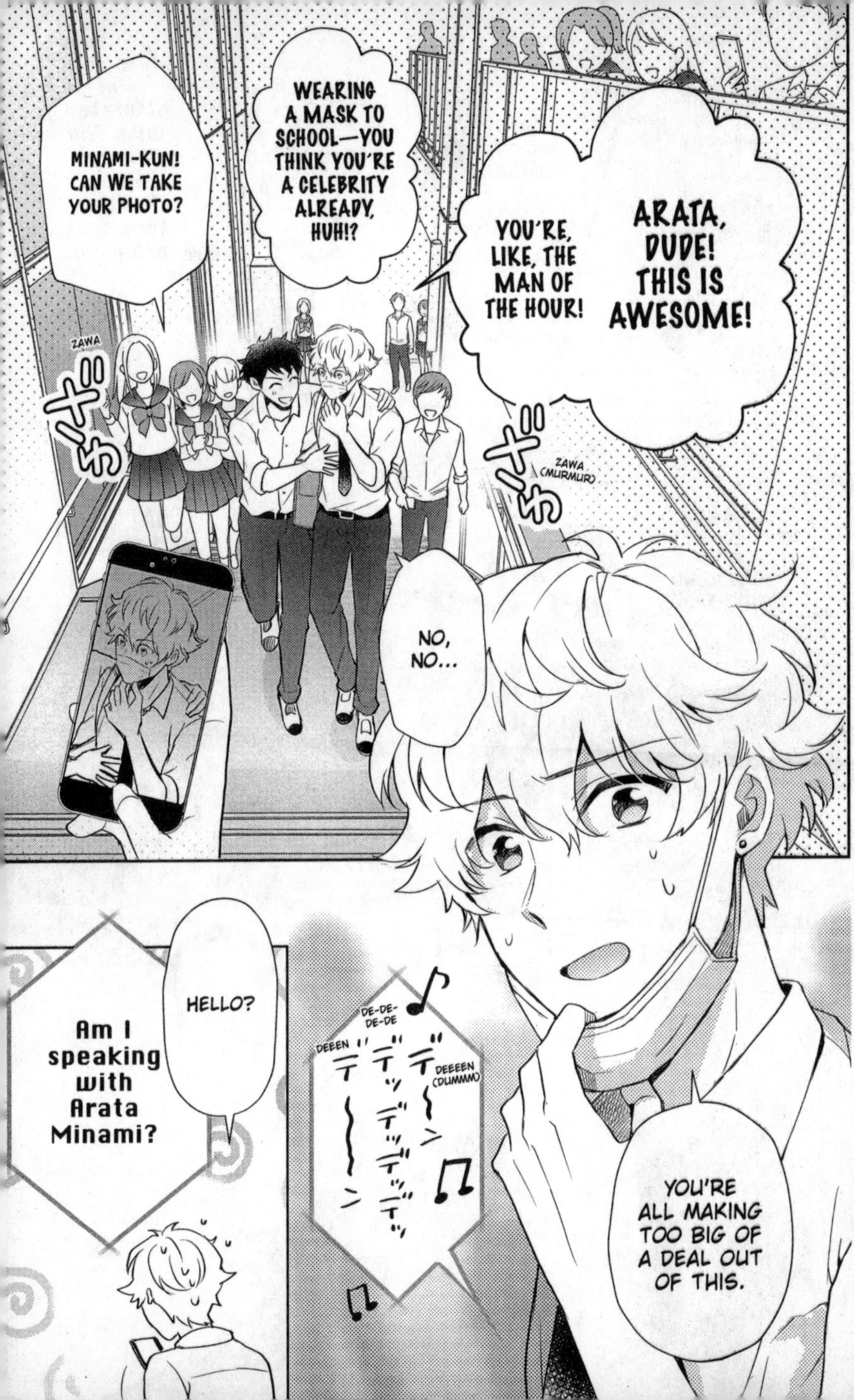
ARATA, DUDE! THIS IS AWESOME!
YOU'RE, LIKE, THE MAN OF THE HOUR!
ZAWA (MURMUR)
WEARING A MASK TO SCHOOL—YOU THINK YOU'RE A CELEBRITY ALREADY, HUH!?
MINAMI-KUN! CAN WE TAKE YOUR PHOTO?
ZAWA
NO, NO...
YOU'RE ALL MAKING TOO BIG OF A DEAL OUT OF THIS.
DEEEEN (DUMMM)
DE-DE-DE-DE
DEEEN
HELLO?
Am I speaking with Arata Minami?

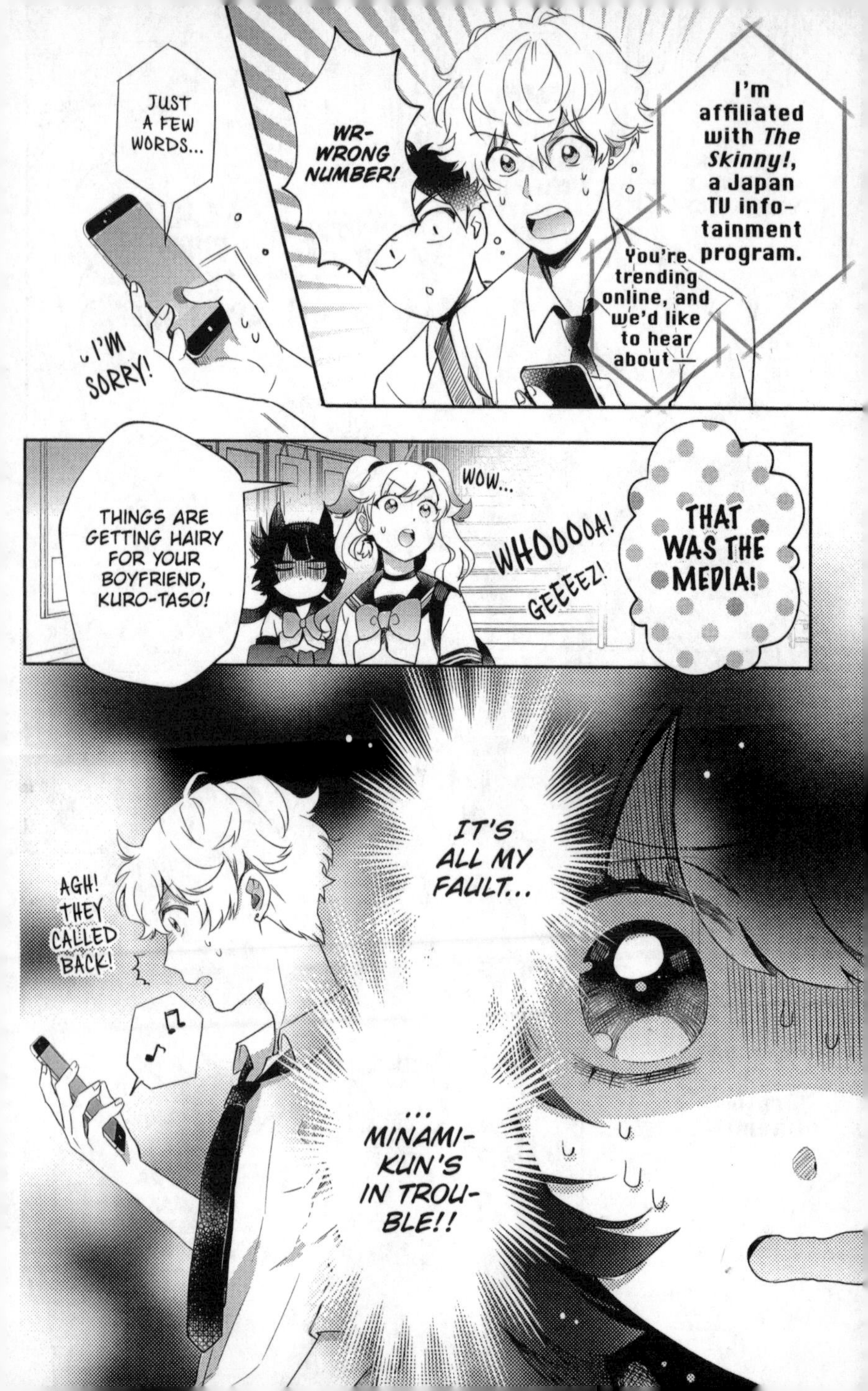
I'm affiliated with *The Skinny!*, a Japan TV info-tainment program.
You're trending online, and we'd like to hear about—
WR-WRONG NUMBER!
JUST A FEW WORDS...
I'M SORRY!
THAT WAS THE MEDIA!
WHOOOOA!
GEEEEZ!
WOW...
THINGS ARE GETTING HAIRY FOR YOUR BOYFRIEND, KURO-TASO!
IT'S ALL MY FAULT...
...MINAMI-KUN'S IN TROU-BLE!!
AGH! THEY CALLED BACK!

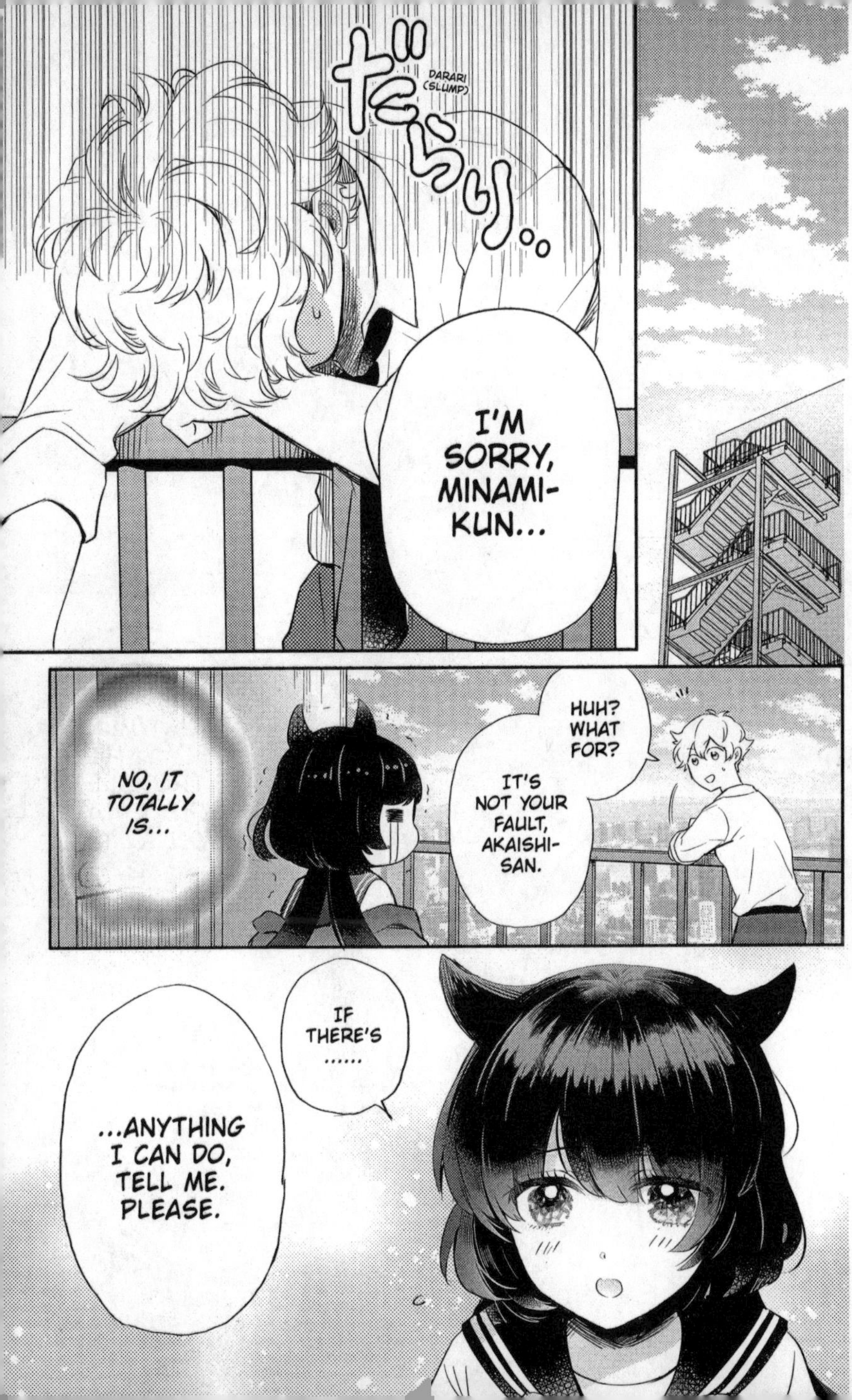
だらり。。
DARARI (SLUMP)
I'M SORRY, MINAMI-KUN...
HUH? WHAT FOR?
IT'S NOT YOUR FAULT, AKAISHI-SAN.
NO, IT TOTALLY IS...
IF THERE'S ......
...ANYTHING I CAN DO, TELL ME. PLEASE.

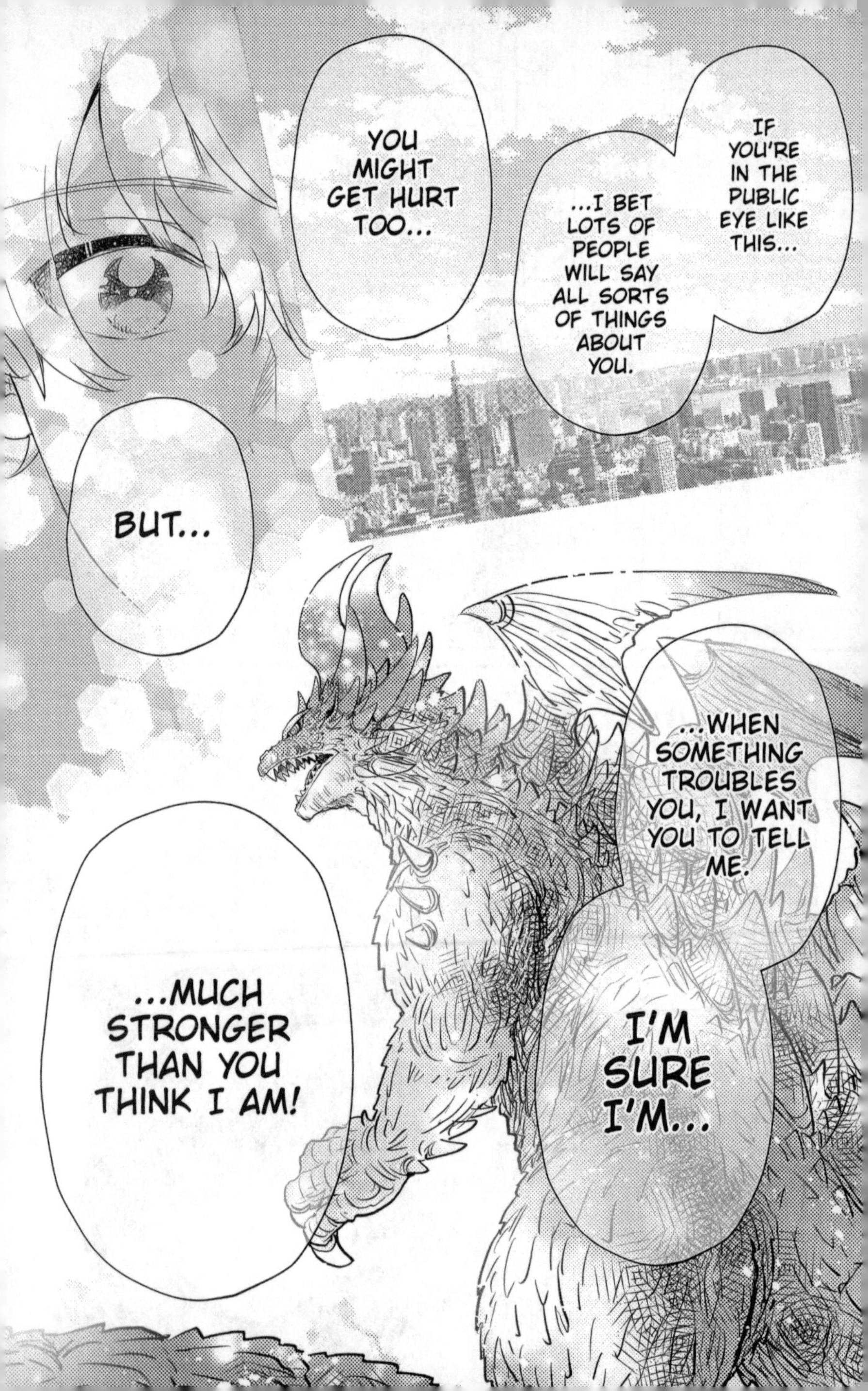
IF YOU'RE IN THE PUBLIC EYE LIKE THIS...
...I BET LOTS OF PEOPLE WILL SAY ALL SORTS OF THINGS ABOUT YOU.
YOU MIGHT GET HURT TOO...
BUT...
...WHEN SOMETHING TROUBLES YOU, I WANT YOU TO TELL ME.
I'M SURE I'M...
...MUCH STRONGER THAN YOU THINK I AM!

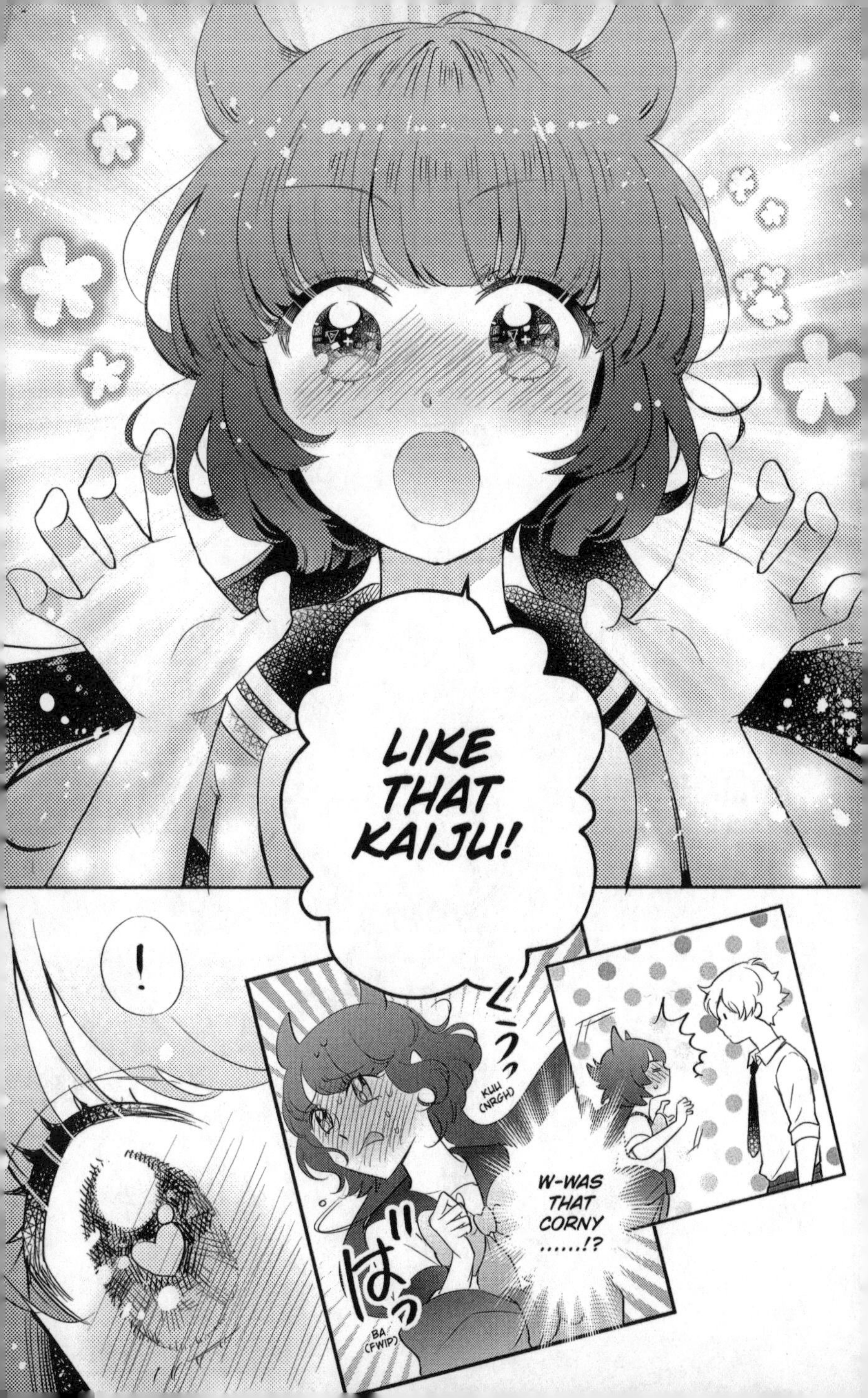
LIKE THAT KAIJU!
くぅっ
KUU (NRGH)
W-WAS THAT CORNY ......!?
ばっ
BA (FWIP)
!

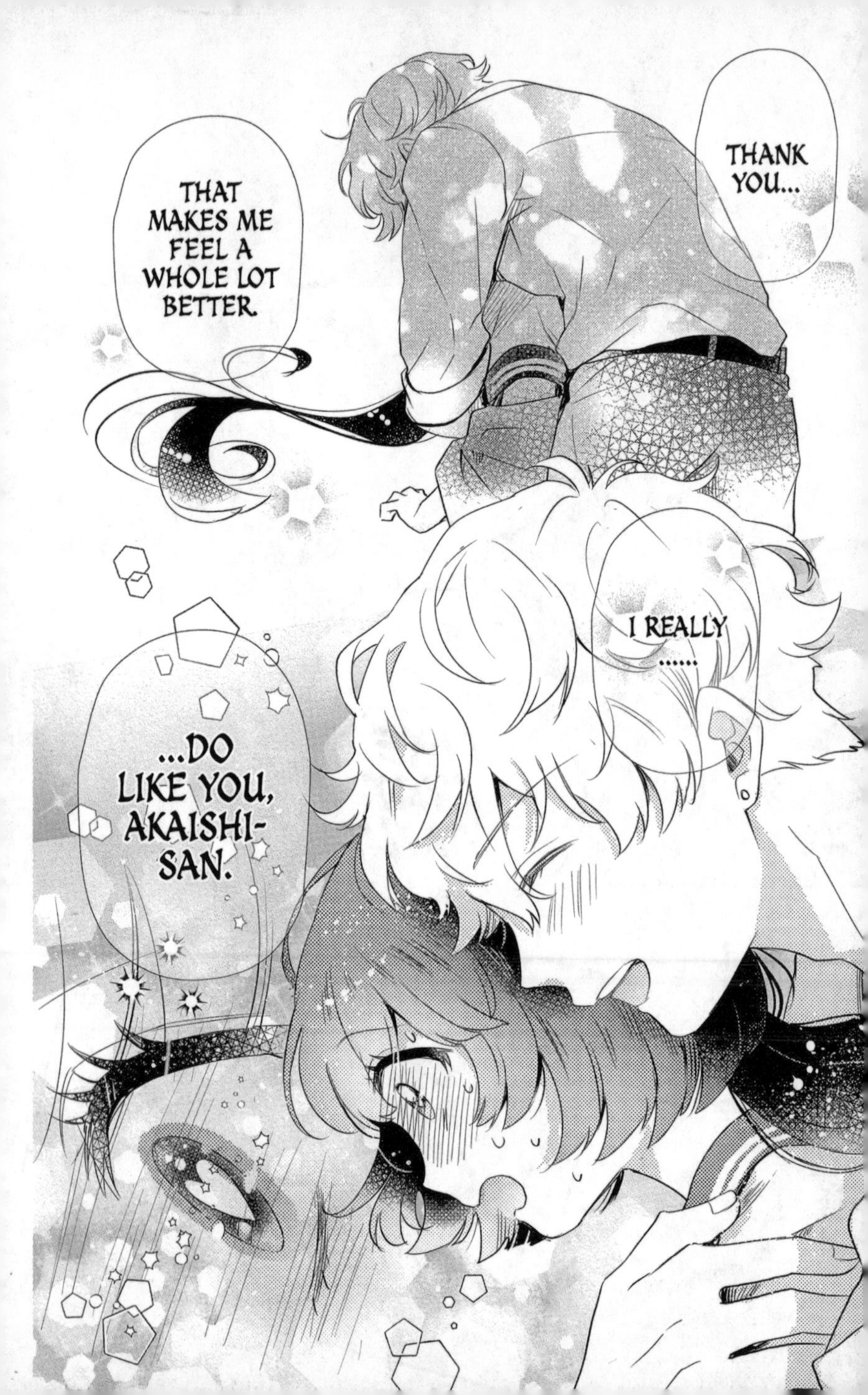
THANK YOU...
THAT MAKES ME FEEL A WHOLE LOT BETTER.
I REALLY ......
...DO LIKE YOU, AKAISHI-SAN.

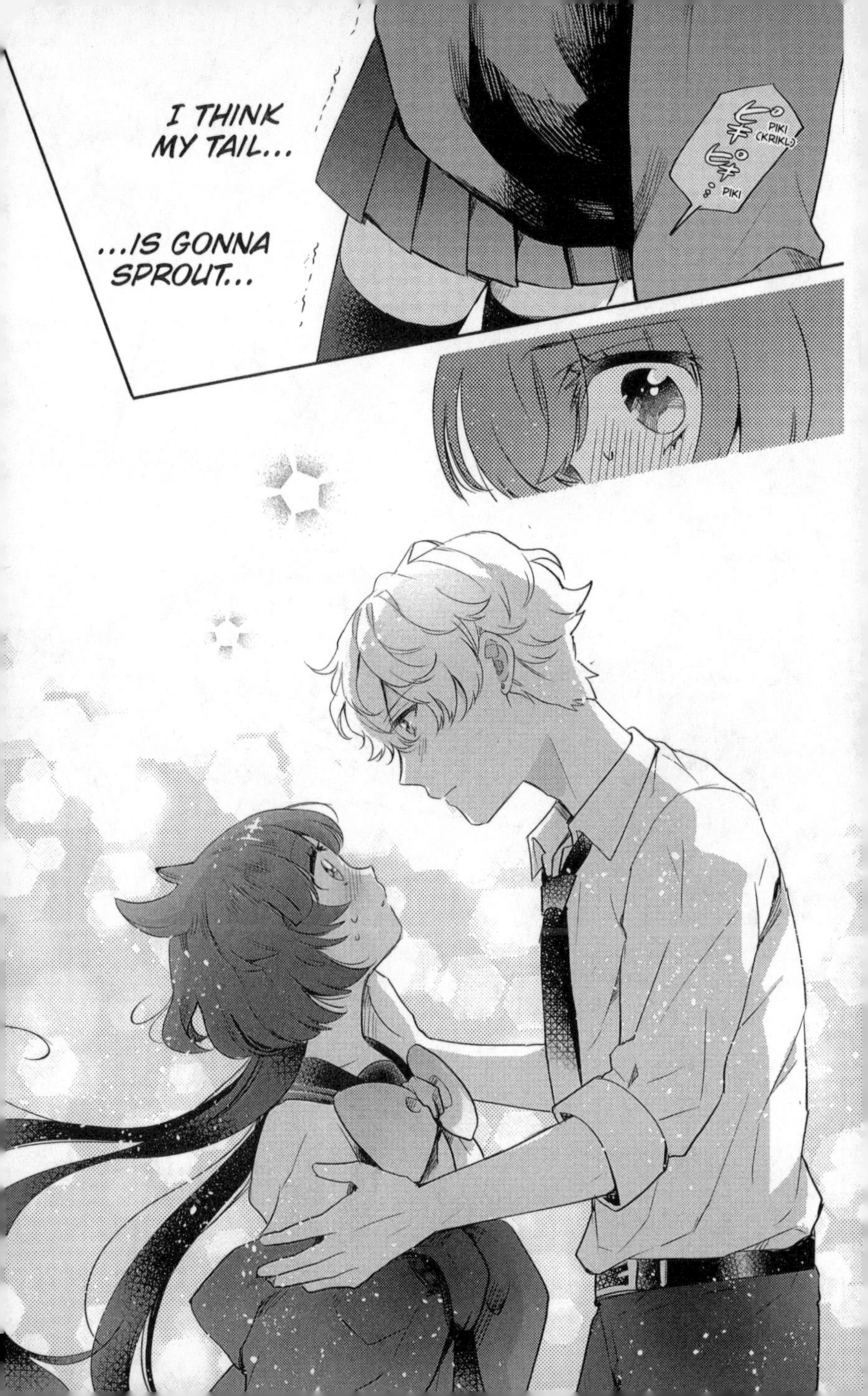

I THINK MY TAIL...
...IS GONNA SPROUT...
ピキ PIKI (KRIKL)
ピキ PIKI

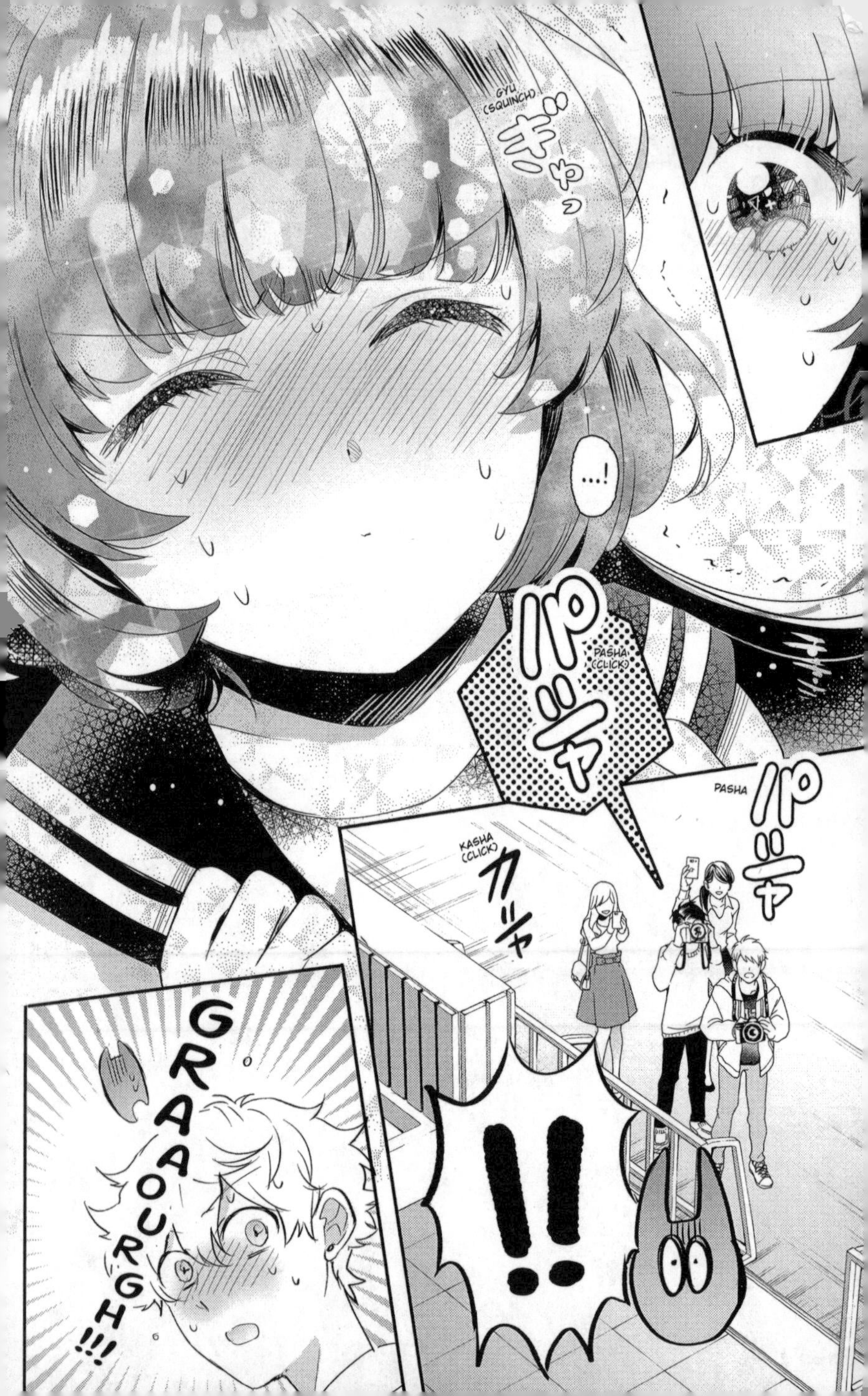
GYU (SQUINCH)
ぎゅっ
...!
PASHA (CLICK)
パシャ
PASHA
パシャ
KASHA (CLICK)
カシャ
!!
GRAAAOURGH!!!

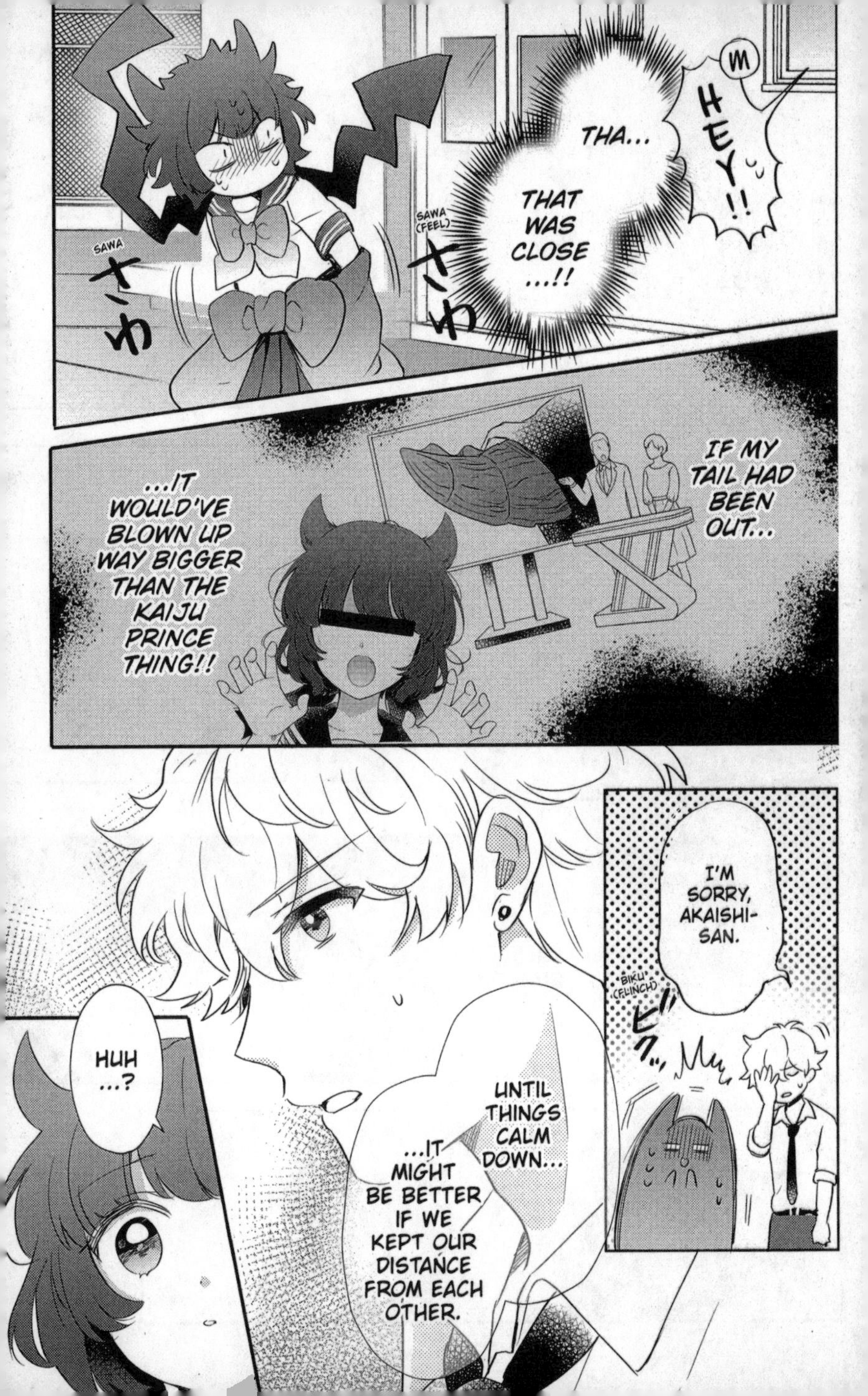
HEY!!
THA...
THAT WAS CLOSE ...!!
SAWA (FEEL)
さわ
SAWA
さわ
IF MY TAIL HAD BEEN OUT...
...IT WOULD'VE BLOWN UP WAY BIGGER THAN THE KAIJU PRINCE THING!!
I'M SORRY, AKAISHI-SAN.
BIKU (FLINCH)
ビクッ
UNTIL THINGS CALM DOWN...
...IT MIGHT BE BETTER IF WE KEPT OUR DISTANCE FROM EACH OTHER.
HUH ...?

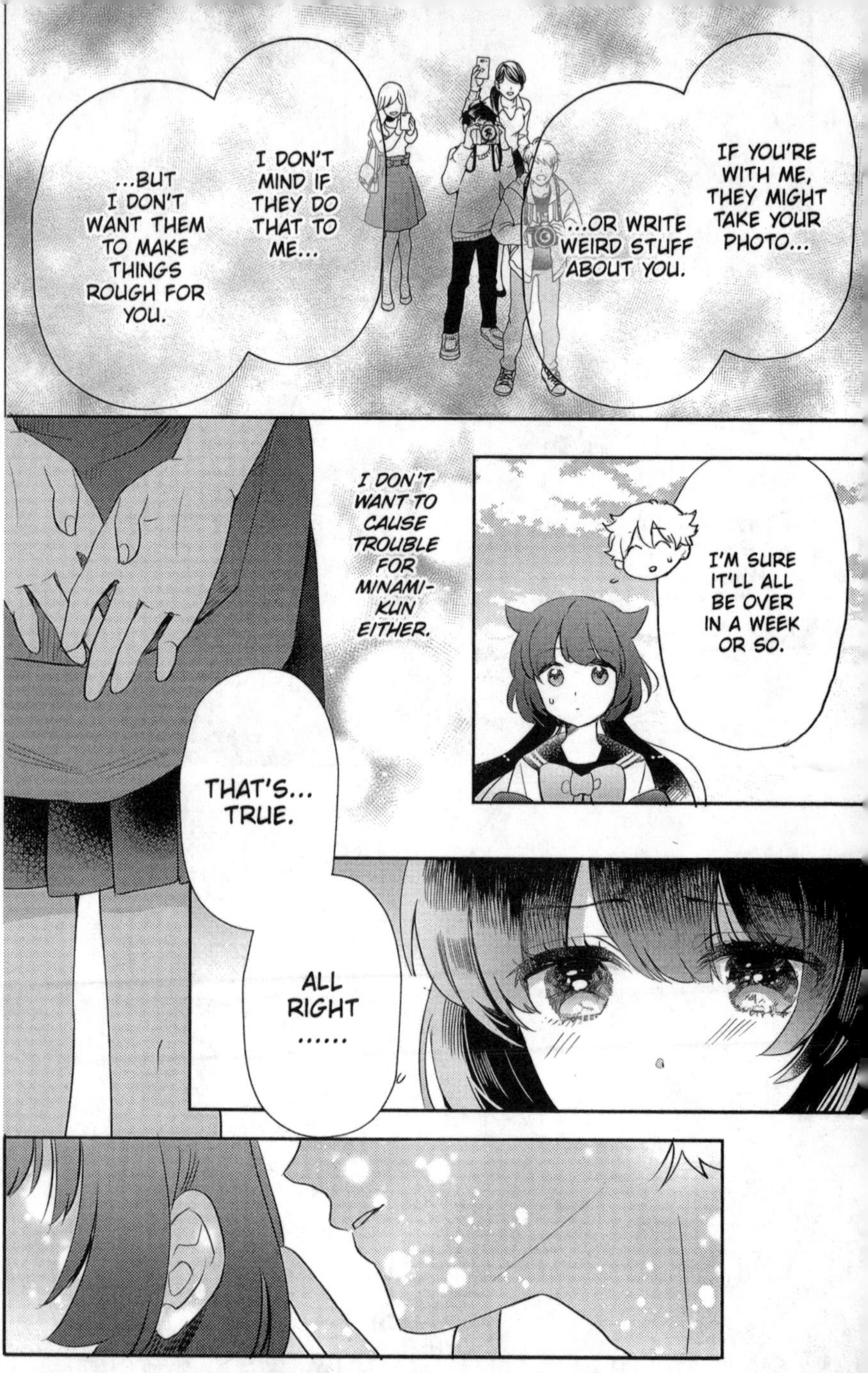
IF YOU'RE WITH ME, THEY MIGHT TAKE YOUR PHOTO...
...OR WRITE WEIRD STUFF ABOUT YOU.
I DON'T MIND IF THEY DO THAT TO ME...
...BUT I DON'T WANT THEM TO MAKE THINGS ROUGH FOR YOU.
I'M SURE IT'LL ALL BE OVER IN A WEEK OR SO.
I DON'T WANT TO CAUSE TROUBLE FOR MINAMI-KUN EITHER.
THAT'S... TRUE.
ALL RIGHT ......

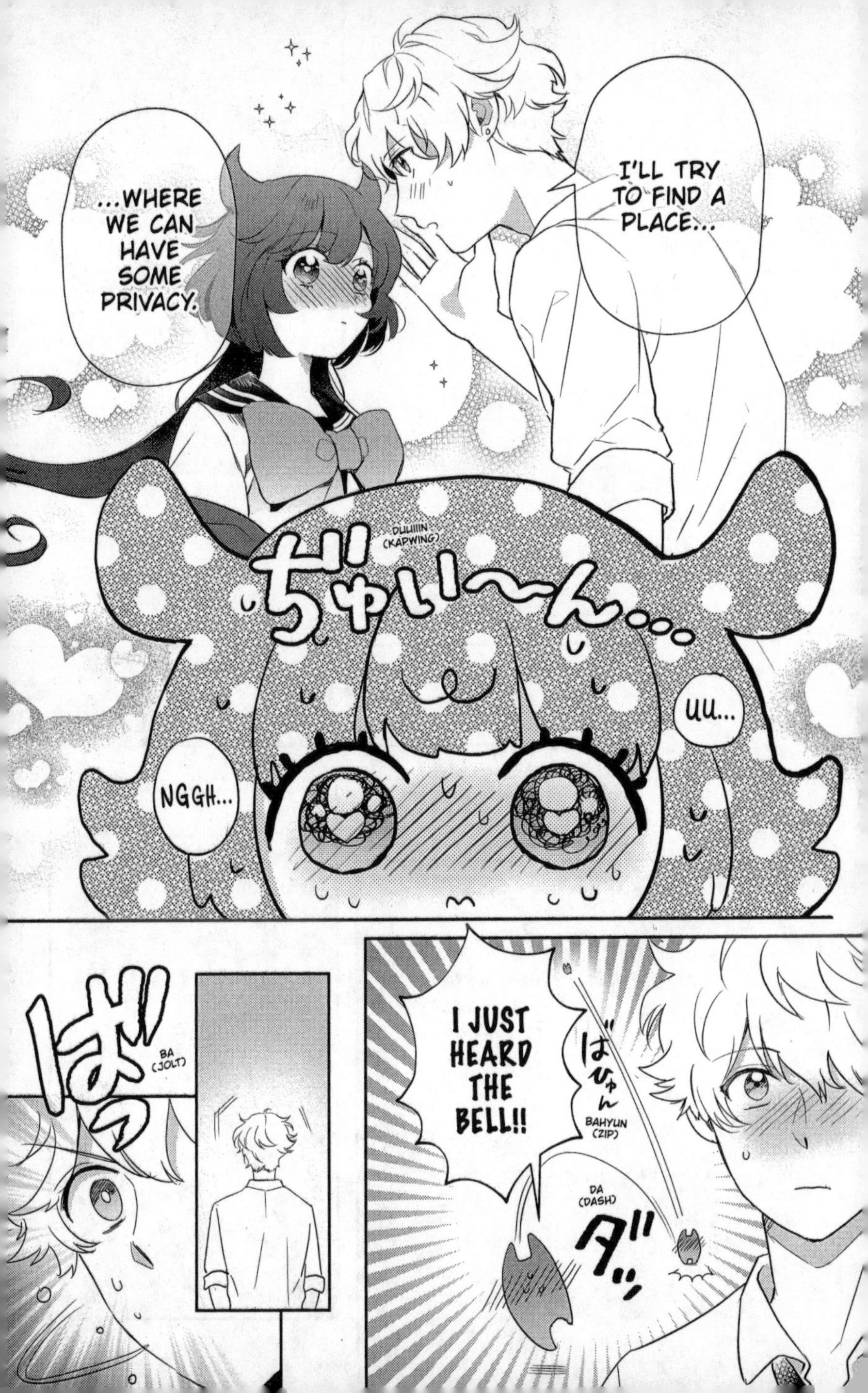
I'LL TRY TO FIND A PLACE...
...WHERE WE CAN HAVE SOME PRIVACY.
ぢゅい〜ん…
DUUIIIN (KAPWING)
UU...
NGGH...
I JUST HEARD THE BELL!!
ばひゅん
BAHYUN (ZIP)
ダッ
DA (DASH)
ばっ
BA (JOLT)

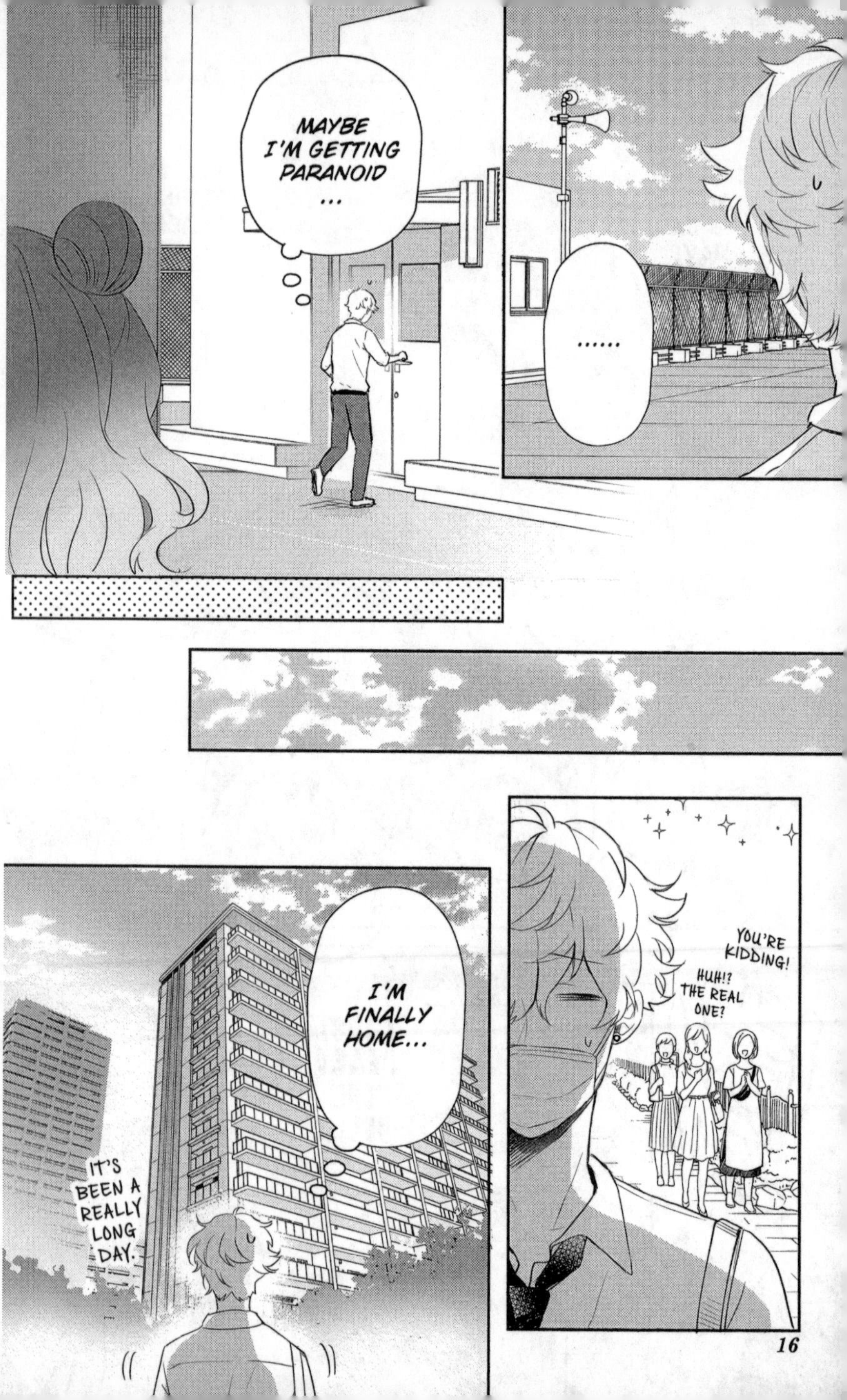

......
MAYBE I'M GETTING PARANOID ...
YOU'RE KIDDING!
HUH!? THE REAL ONE?
I'M FINALLY HOME...
IT'S BEEN A REALLY LONG DAY.

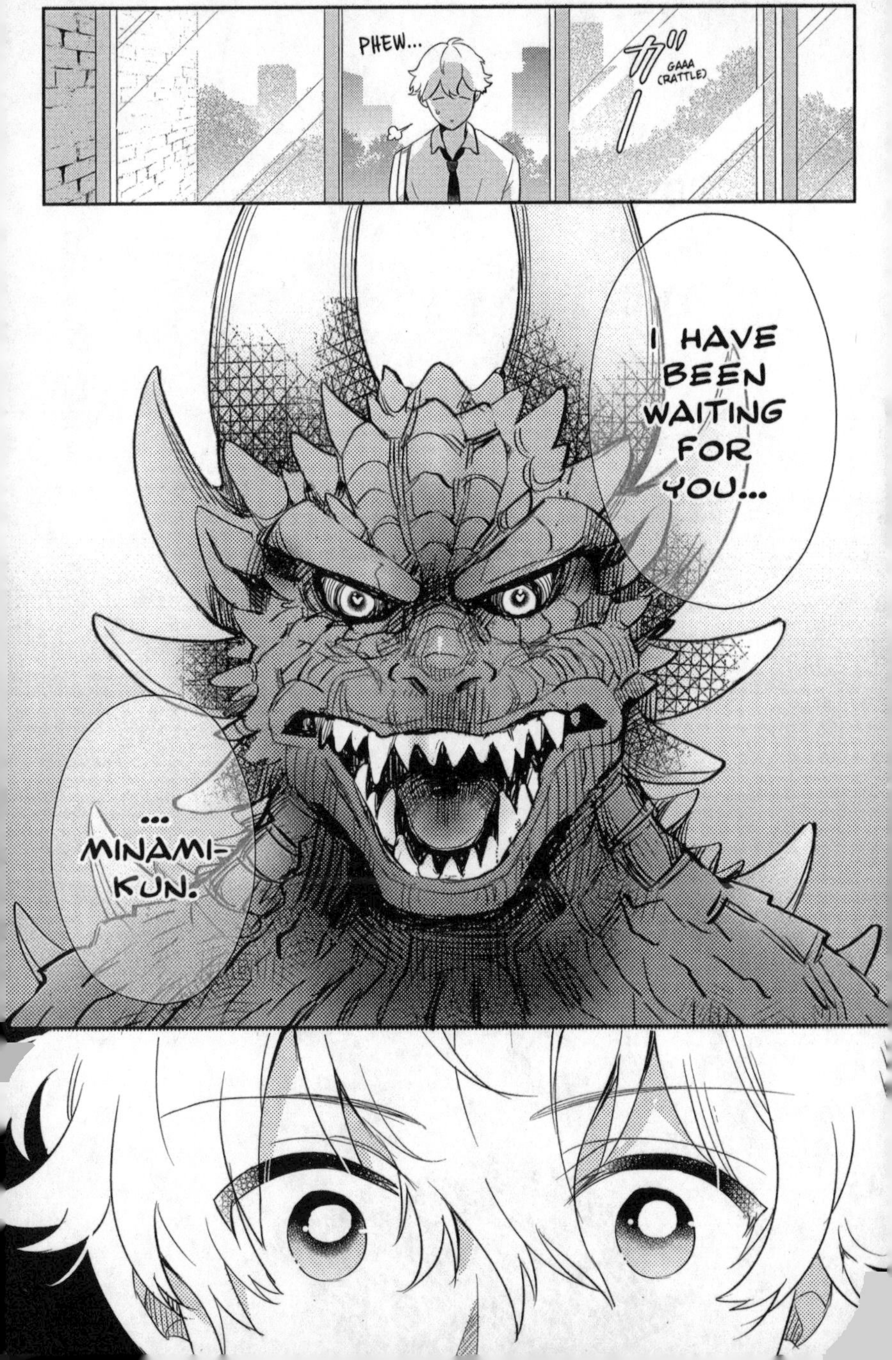
GAAA (RATTLE)
PHEW...
I HAVE BEEN WAITING FOR YOU...
...MINAMI-KUN.

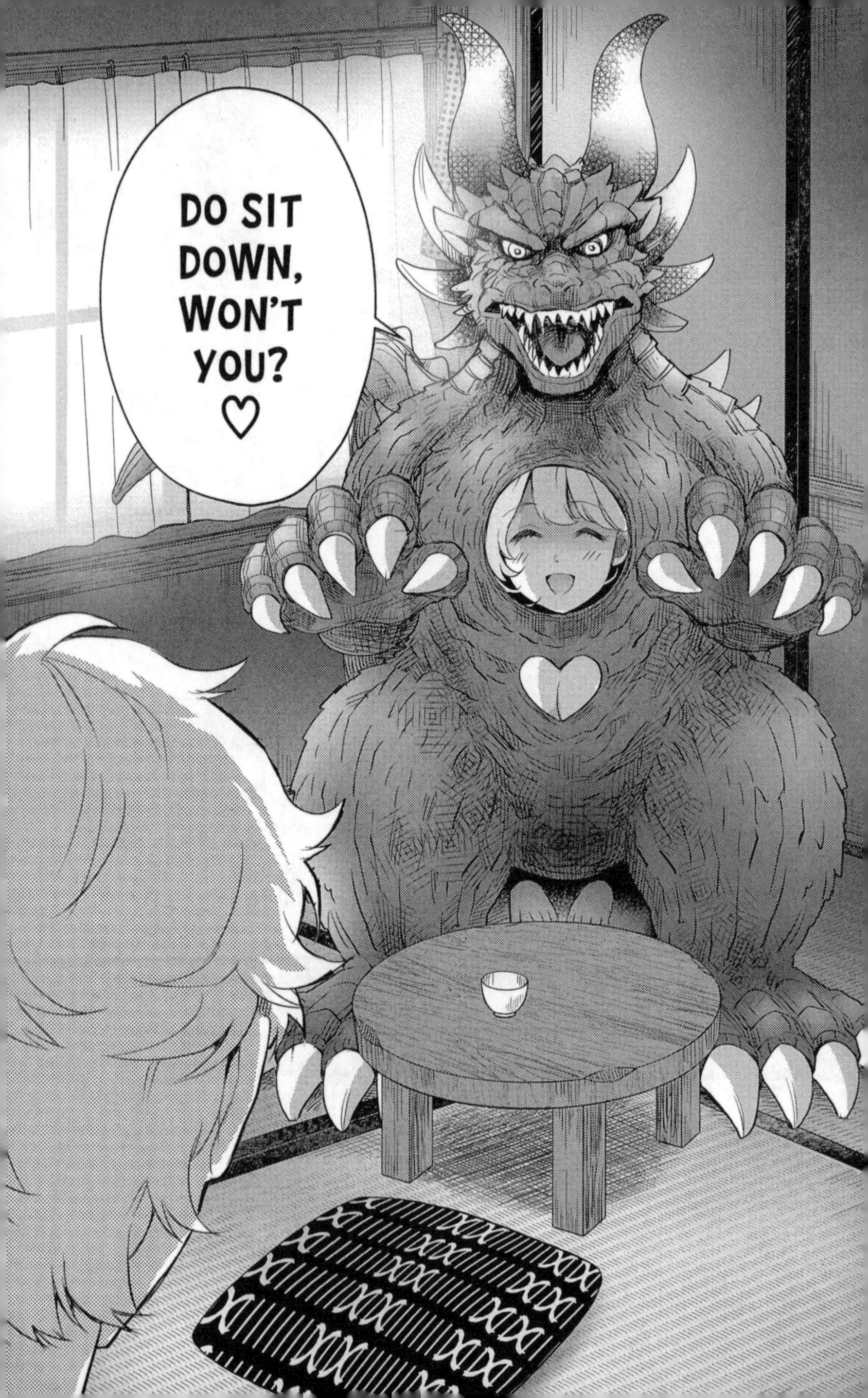
DO SIT DOWN, WON'T YOU? ♡

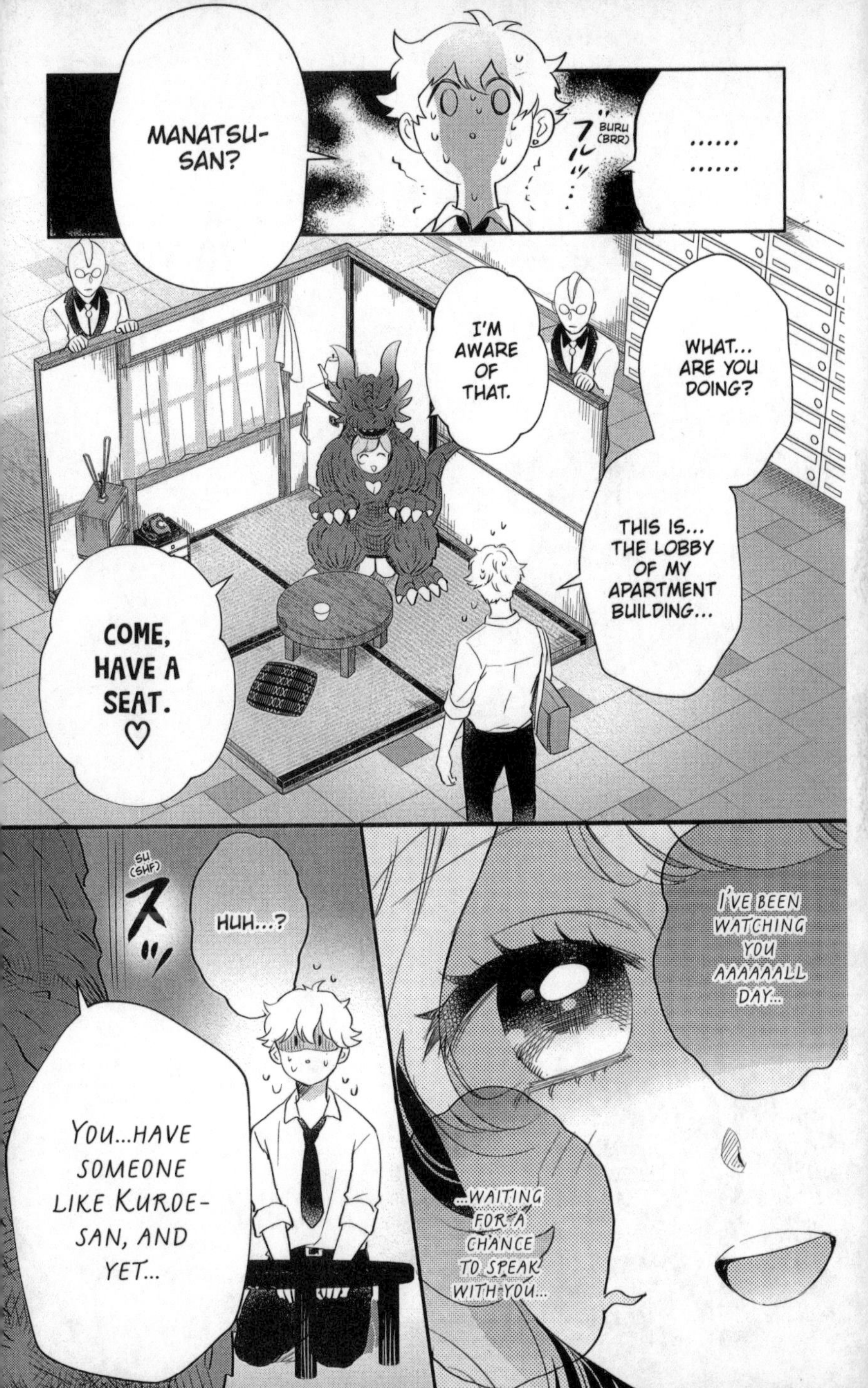

......
......
BURU (BRR)
MANATSU-SAN?
WHAT... ARE YOU DOING?
THIS IS... THE LOBBY OF MY APARTMENT BUILDING...
I'M AWARE OF THAT.
COME, HAVE A SEAT. ♡
I'VE BEEN WATCHING YOU AAAAAALL DAY...
...WAITING FOR A CHANCE TO SPEAK WITH YOU...
SU (SHF)
HUH...?
YOU...HAVE SOMEONE LIKE KUROE-SAN, AND YET...

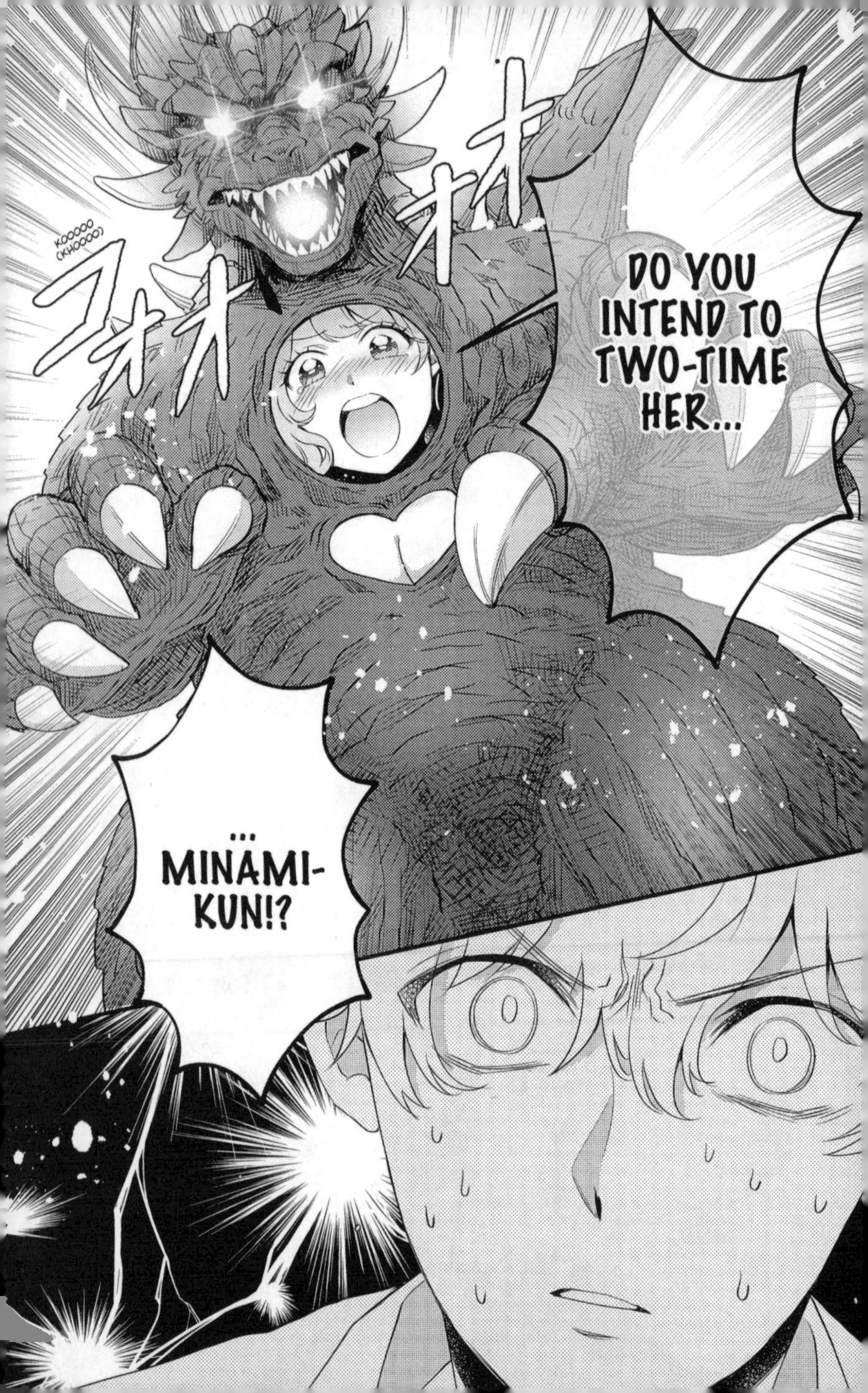
DO YOU INTEND TO TWO-TIME HER...
KOOOOO (KHOOOO)
... MINÄMI-KUN!?

KAIJU♥GIRL
CARAMELISE

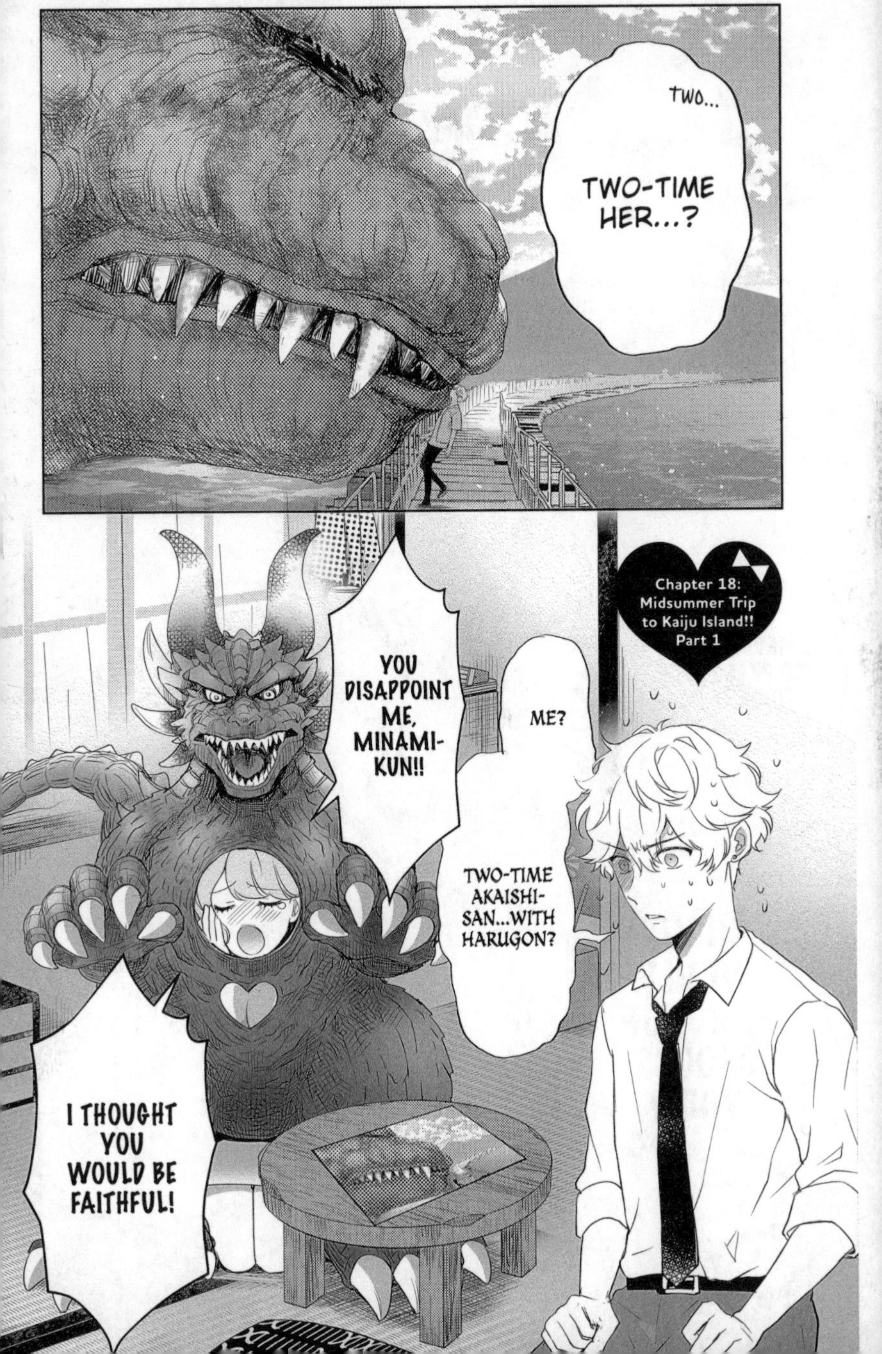
TWO...
TWO-TIME HER...?
Chapter 18: Midsummer Trip to Kaiju Island!! Part 1
ME?
TWO-TIME AKAISHI-SAN...WITH HARUGON?
YOU DISAPPOINT ME, MINAMI-KUN!!
I THOUGHT YOU WOULD BE FAITHFUL!

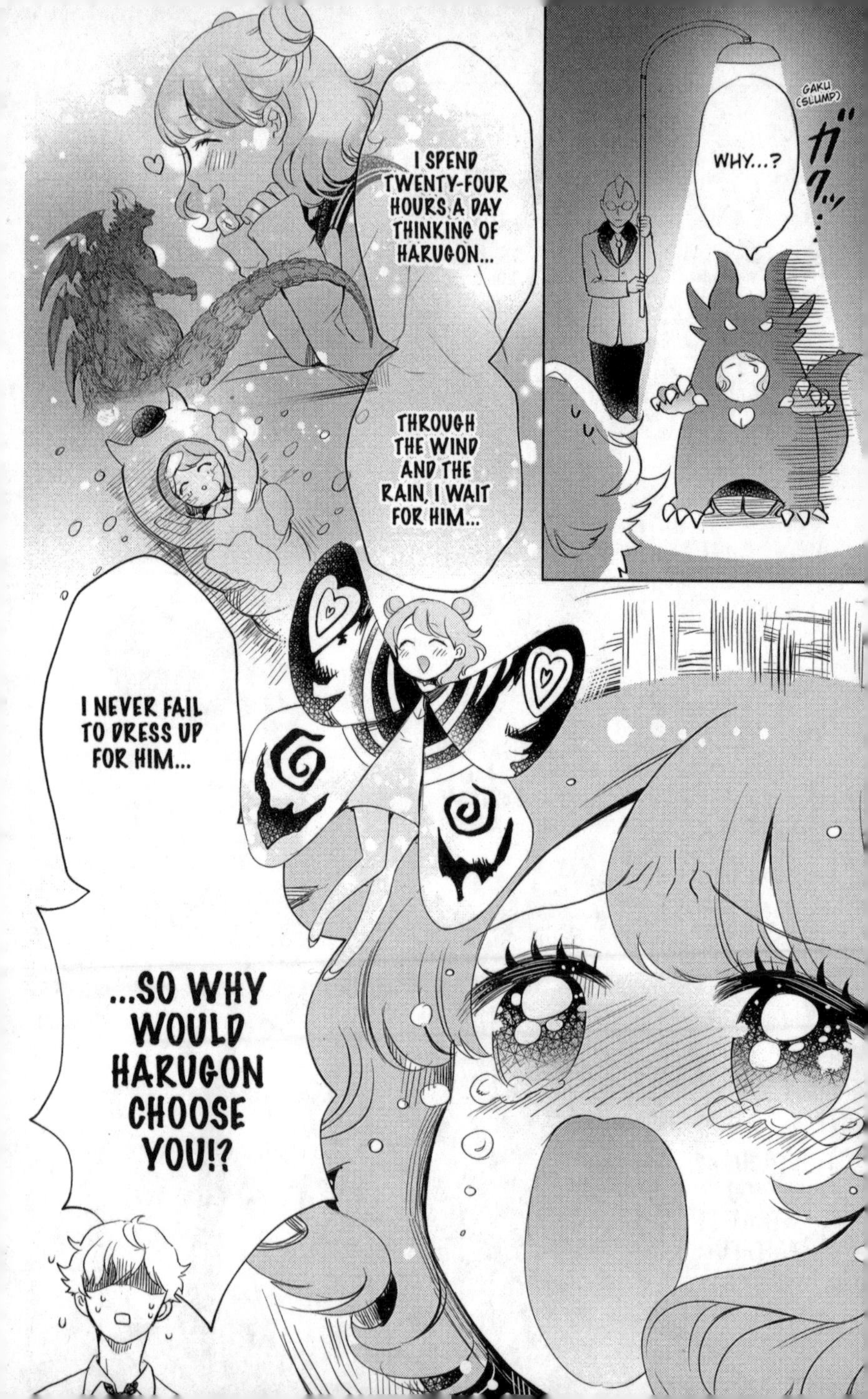
GAKU (SLUMP)
ガクッ
WHY...?
I SPEND TWENTY-FOUR HOURS A DAY THINKING OF HARUGON...
THROUGH THE WIND AND THE RAIN, I WAIT FOR HIM...
I NEVER FAIL TO DRESS UP FOR HIM...
...SO WHY WOULD HARUGON CHOOSE YOU!?

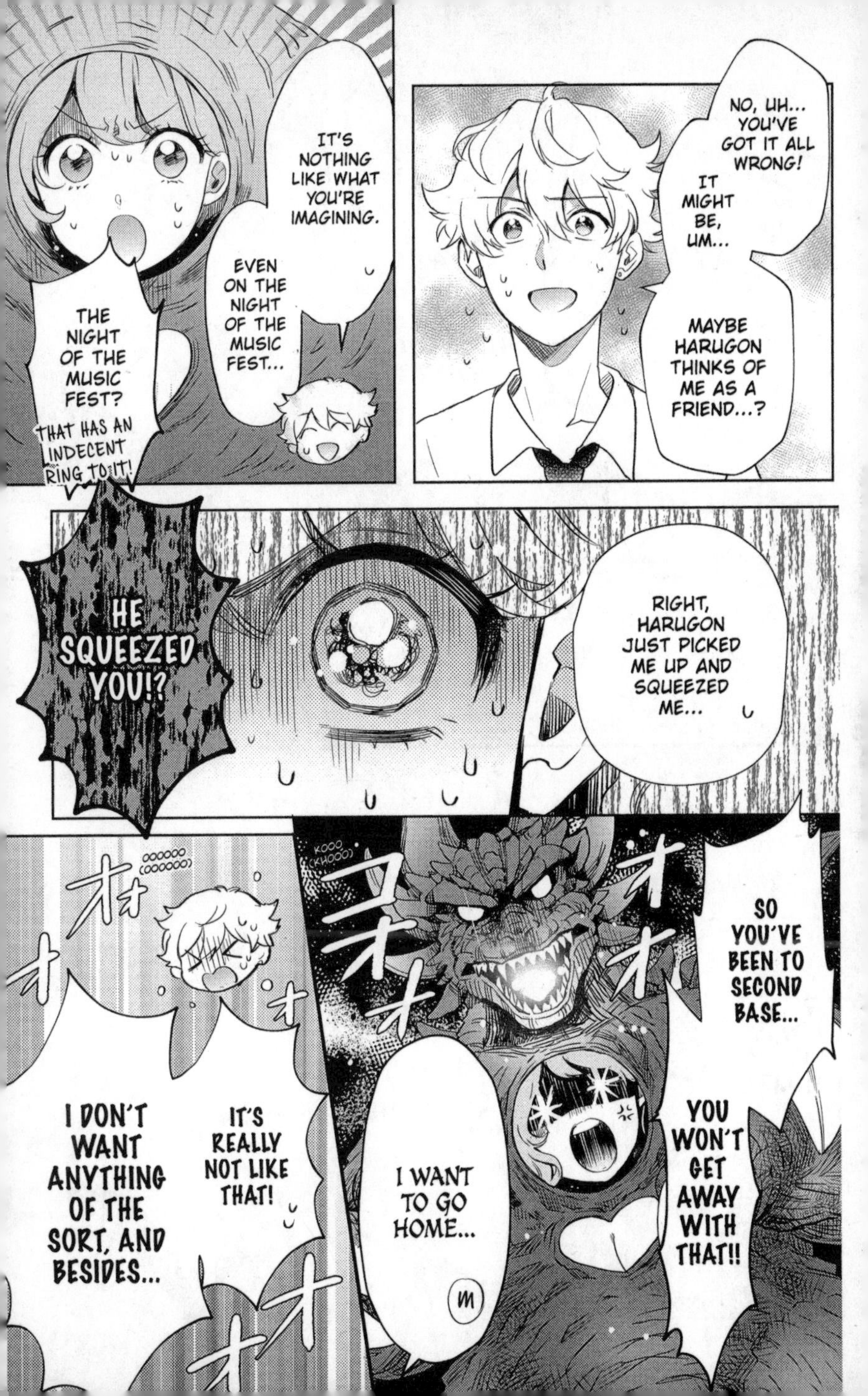
NO, UH... YOU'VE GOT IT ALL WRONG!
IT MIGHT BE, UM...
MAYBE HARUGON THINKS OF ME AS A FRIEND...?
IT'S NOTHING LIKE WHAT YOU'RE IMAGINING.
EVEN ON THE NIGHT OF THE MUSIC FEST...
THE NIGHT OF THE MUSIC FEST?
THAT HAS AN INDECENT RING TO IT!
RIGHT, HARUGON JUST PICKED ME UP AND SQUEEZED ME...
HE SQUEEZED YOU!?
KOOO (KHOOO)
SO YOU'VE BEEN TO SECOND BASE...
YOU WON'T GET AWAY WITH THAT!!
I WANT TO GO HOME...
OOOOOO (OOOOOO)
IT'S REALLY NOT LIKE THAT!
I DON'T WANT ANYTHING OF THE SORT, AND BESIDES...

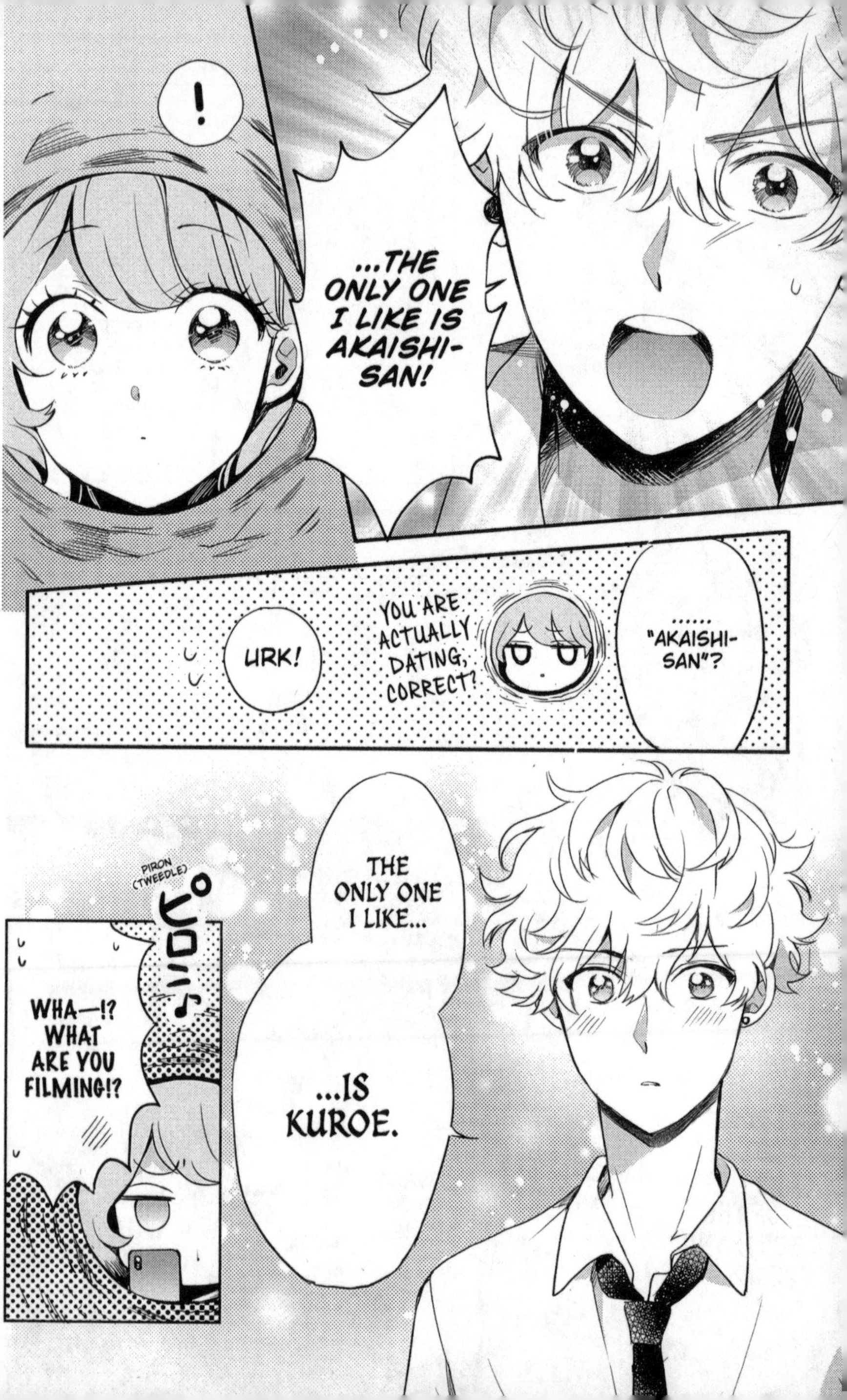
...THE ONLY ONE I LIKE IS AKAISHI-SAN!
!
...... "AKAISHI-SAN"?
YOU ARE ACTUALLY DATING, CORRECT?
URK!
THE ONLY ONE I LIKE...
...IS KUROE.
PIRON (TWEEDLE)
WHA—!? WHAT ARE YOU FILMING!?

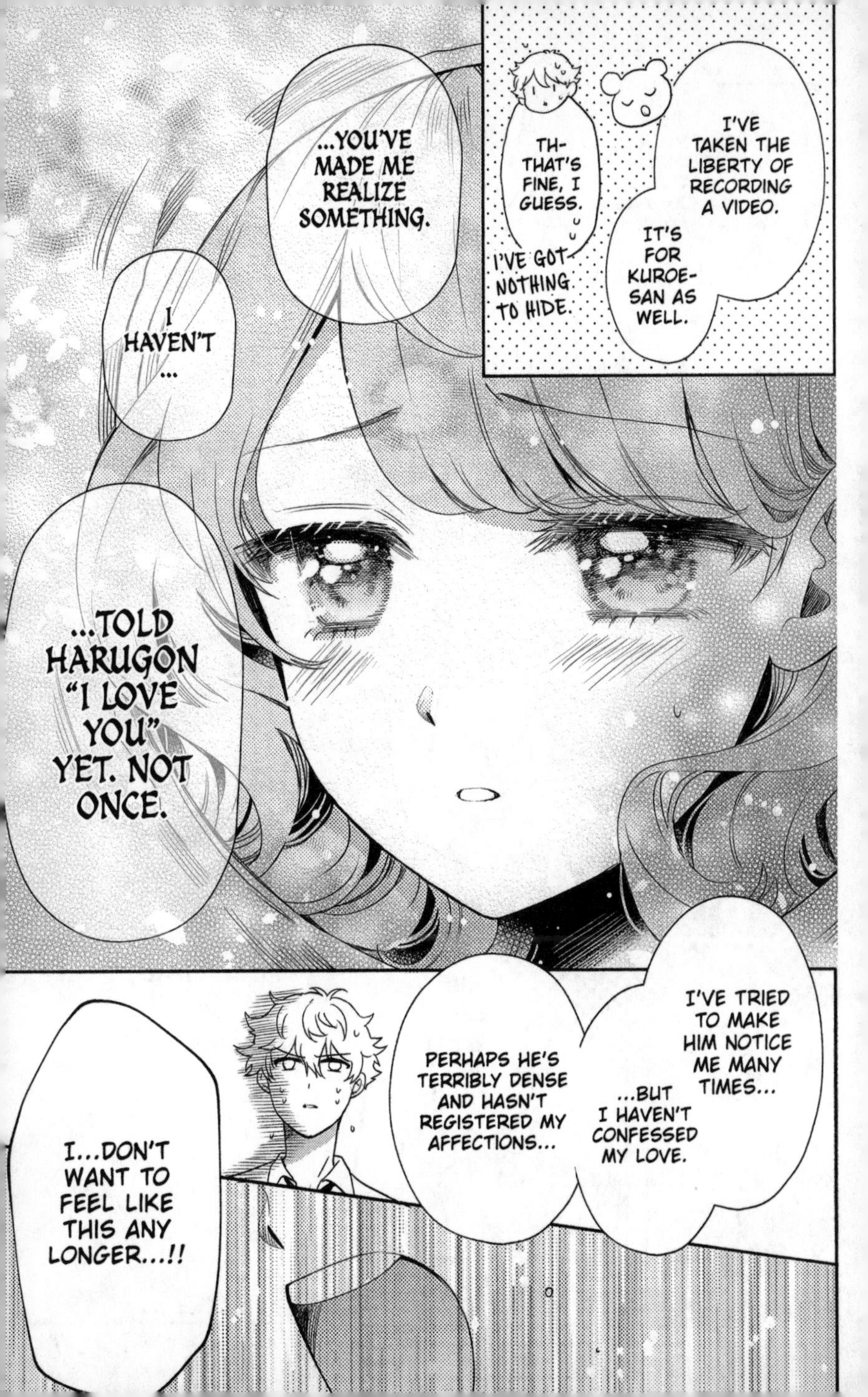
I'VE TAKEN THE LIBERTY OF RECORDING A VIDEO.
IT'S FOR KUROE-SAN AS WELL.
TH-THAT'S FINE, I GUESS.
I'VE GOT NOTHING TO HIDE.
...YOU'VE MADE ME REALIZE SOMETHING.
I HAVEN'T ...
...TOLD HARUGON "I LOVE YOU" YET. NOT ONCE.
I'VE TRIED TO MAKE HIM NOTICE ME MANY TIMES...
...BUT I HAVEN'T CONFESSED MY LOVE.
PERHAPS HE'S TERRIBLY DENSE AND HASN'T REGISTERED MY AFFECTIONS...
I...DON'T WANT TO FEEL LIKE THIS ANY LONGER...!!

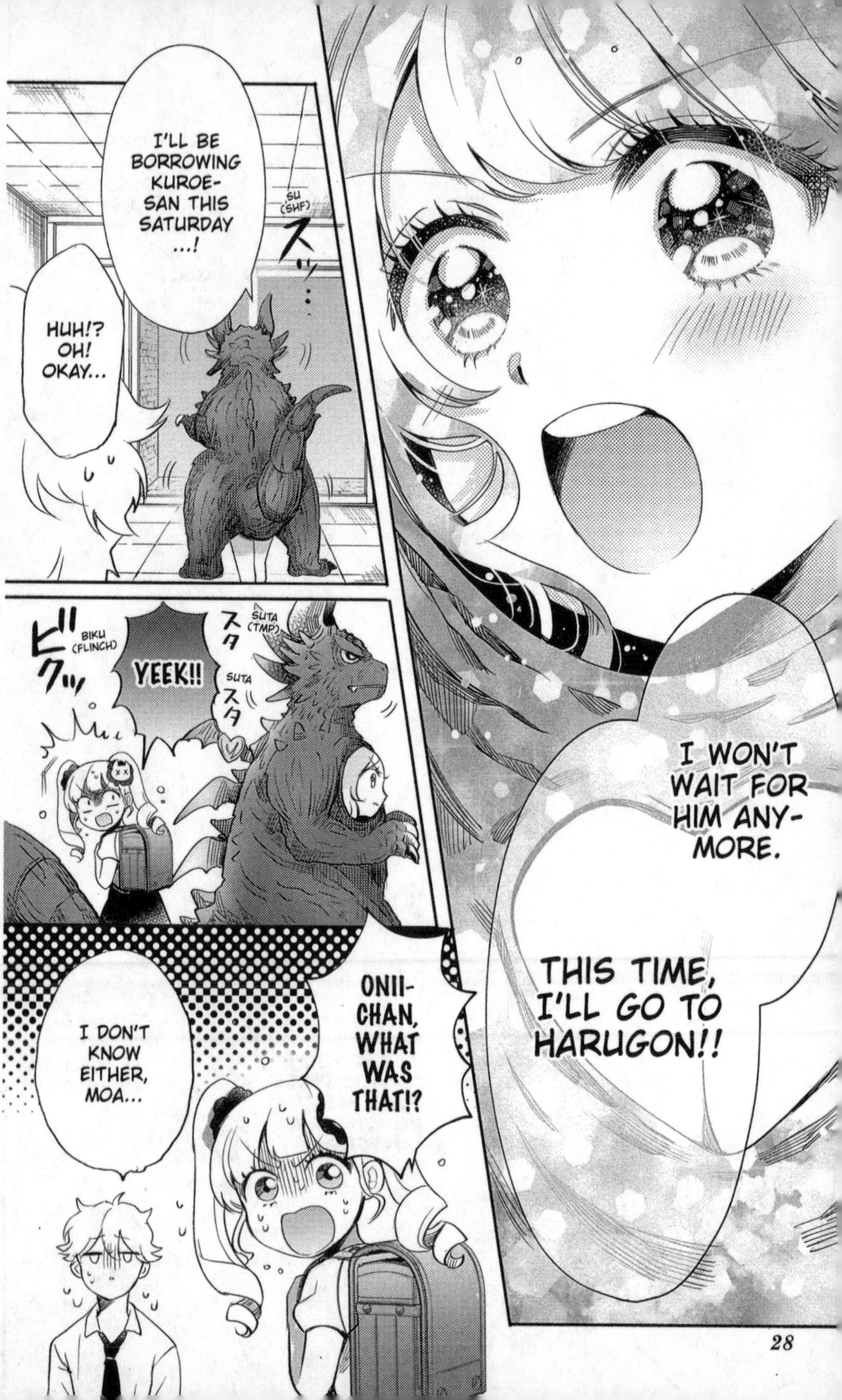

I WON'T WAIT FOR HIM ANY-MORE.
THIS TIME, I'LL GO TO HARUGON!!
I'LL BE BORROWING KUROE-SAN THIS SATURDAY ...!
SU (SHF)
スッ
HUH!? OH! OKAY...
SUTA (TMP)
スタ
SUTA
スタ
YEEK!!
BIKU (FLINCH)
ビクッ
ONII-CHAN, WHAT WAS THAT!?
I DON'T KNOW EITHER, MOA...

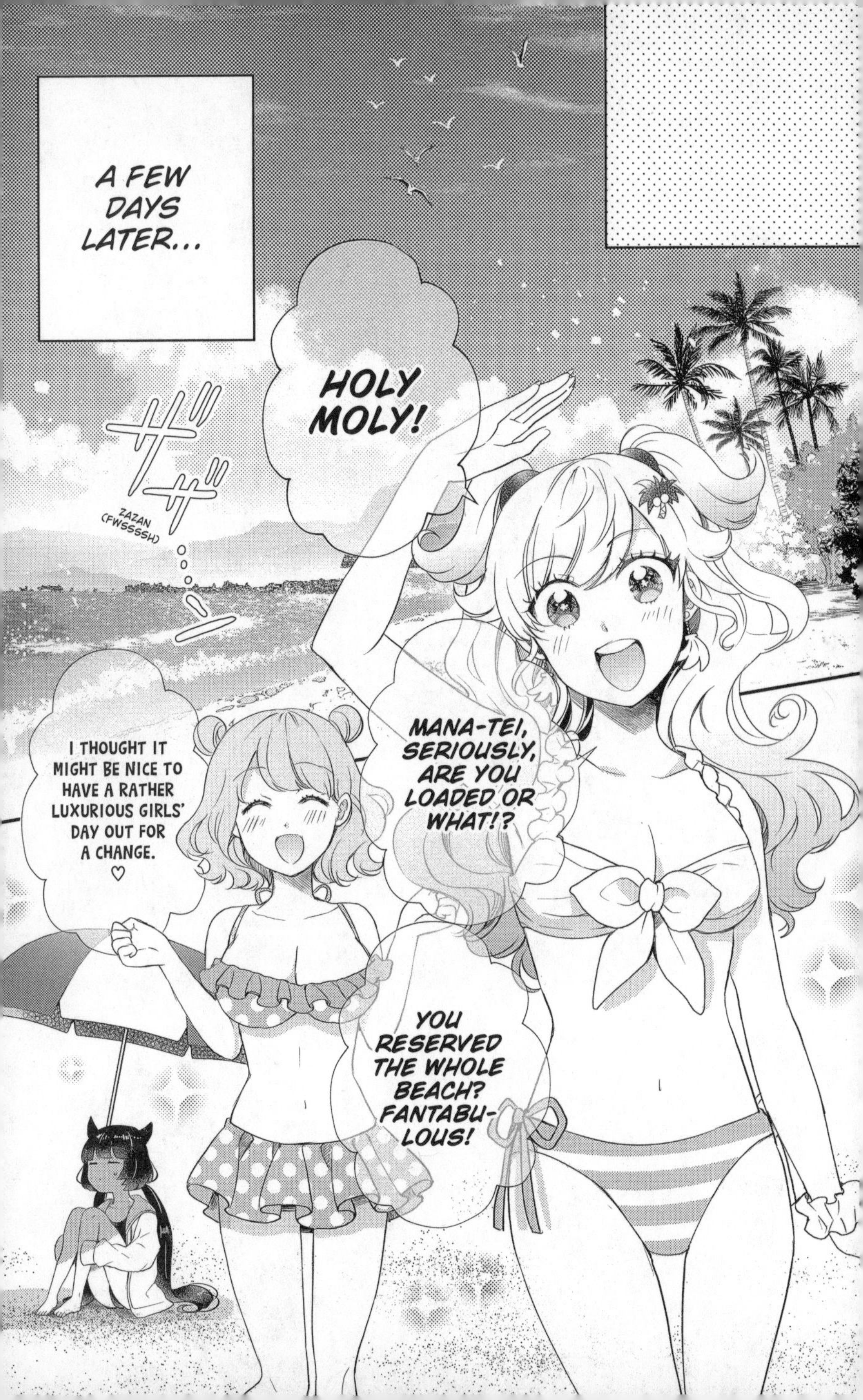
A FEW DAYS LATER...
HOLY MOLY!
MANA-TEI, SERIOUSLY, ARE YOU LOADED OR WHAT!?
YOU RESERVED THE WHOLE BEACH? FANTABU-LOUS!
ZAZAN (FWSSSSH)
I THOUGHT IT MIGHT BE NICE TO HAVE A RATHER LUXURIOUS GIRLS' DAY OUT FOR A CHANGE. ♡

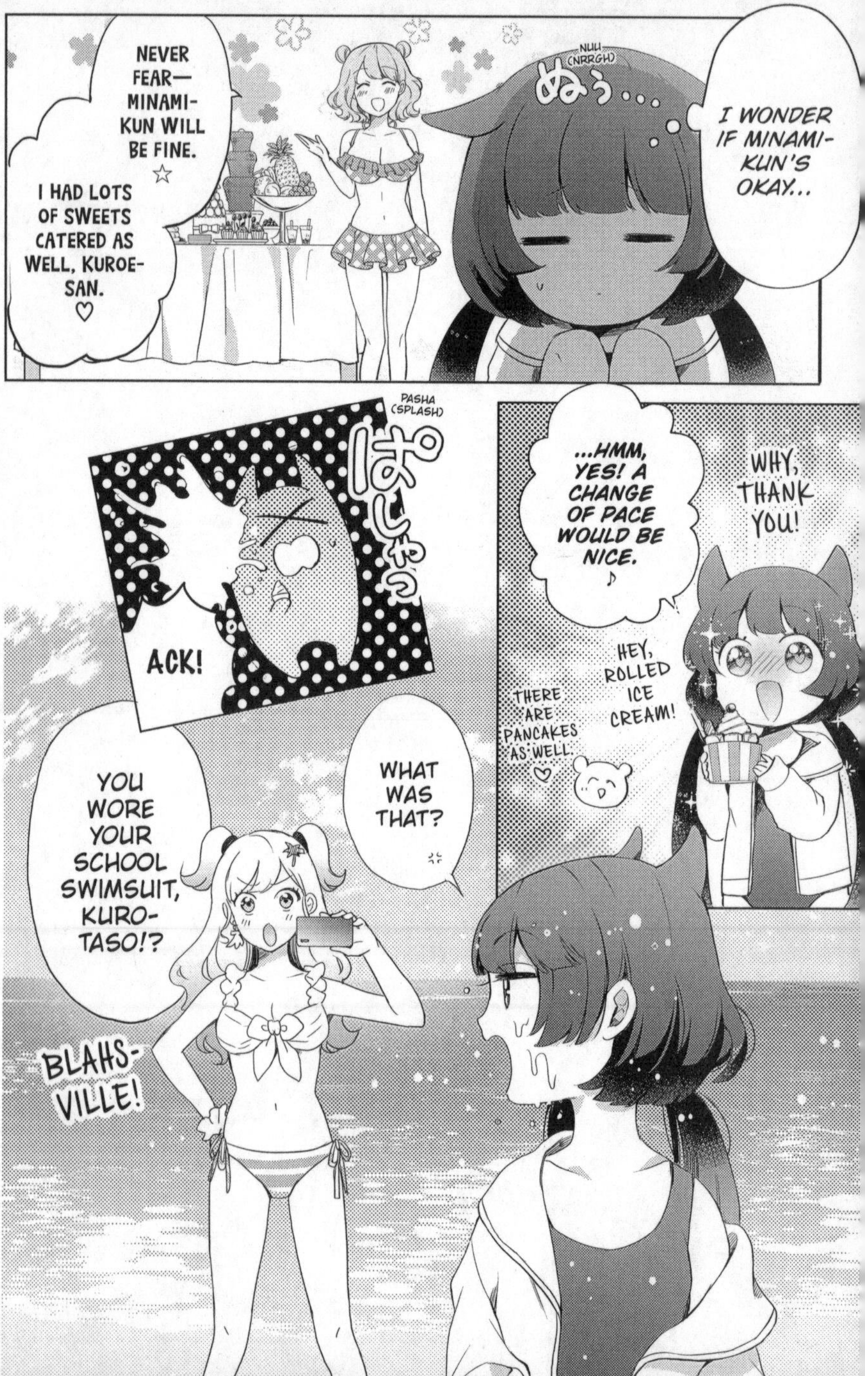
NUU (NRRGH)
ぬぅ…
I WONDER IF MINAMI-KUN'S OKAY...
NEVER FEAR—MINAMI-KUN WILL BE FINE. ☆
I HAD LOTS OF SWEETS CATERED AS WELL, KUROE-SAN. ♡
WHY, THANK YOU!
...HMM, YES! A CHANGE OF PACE WOULD BE NICE. ♪
HEY, ROLLED ICE CREAM!
THERE ARE PANCAKES AS WELL. ♡
PASHA (SPLASH)
ぱしゃっ
ACK!
WHAT WAS THAT?
YOU WORE YOUR SCHOOL SWIMSUIT, KURO-TASO!?
BLAHS-VILLE!

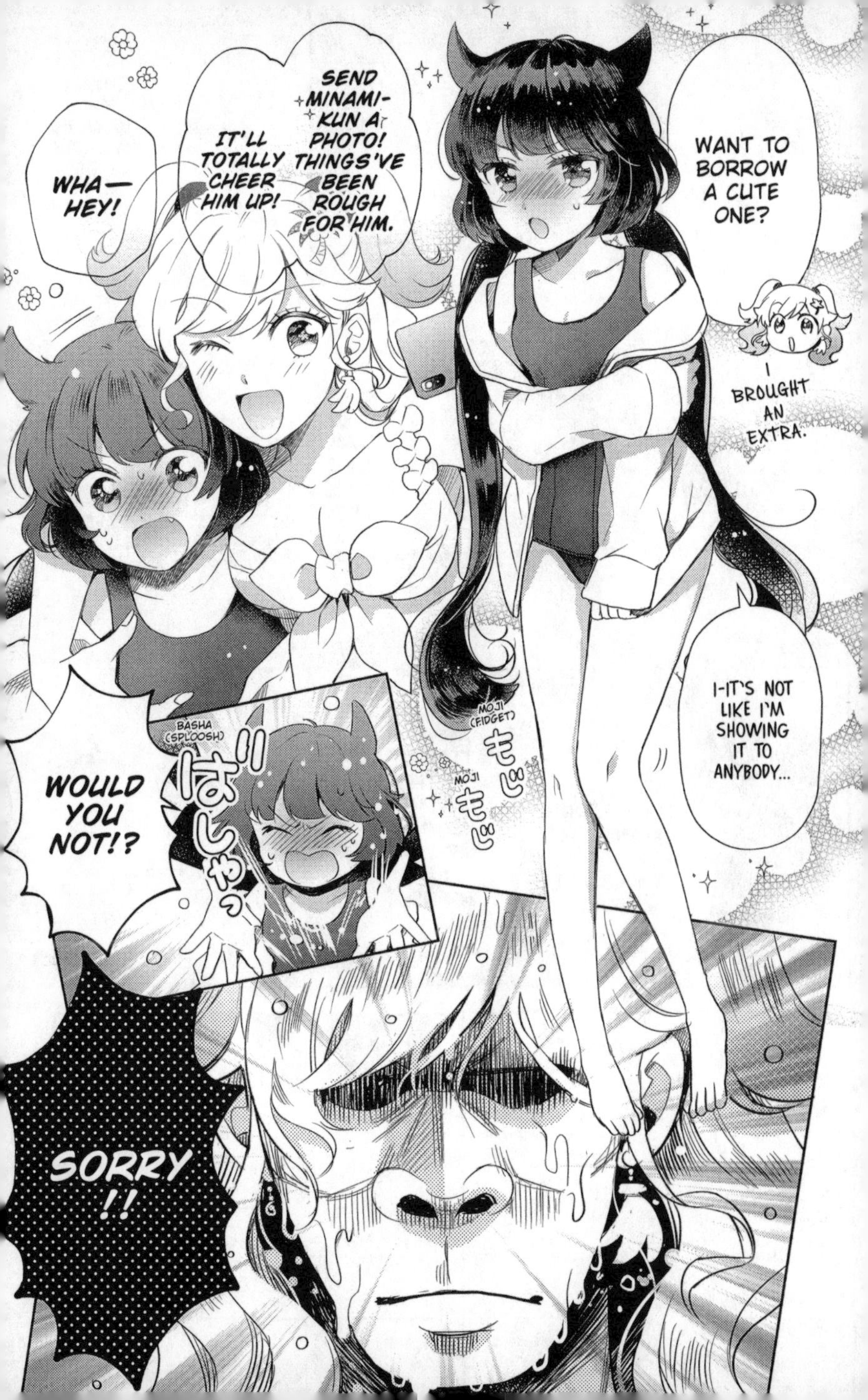
WANT TO BORROW A CUTE ONE?
I BROUGHT AN EXTRA.
SEND MINAMI-KUN A PHOTO! THINGS'VE BEEN ROUGH FOR HIM.
IT'LL TOTALLY CHEER HIM UP!
WHA—HEY!
I-IT'S NOT LIKE I'M SHOWING IT TO ANYBODY...
MOJI (FIDGET)
もじ
MOJI
もじ
BASHA (SPLOOSH)
ばしゃっ
WOULD YOU NOT!?
SORRY!!

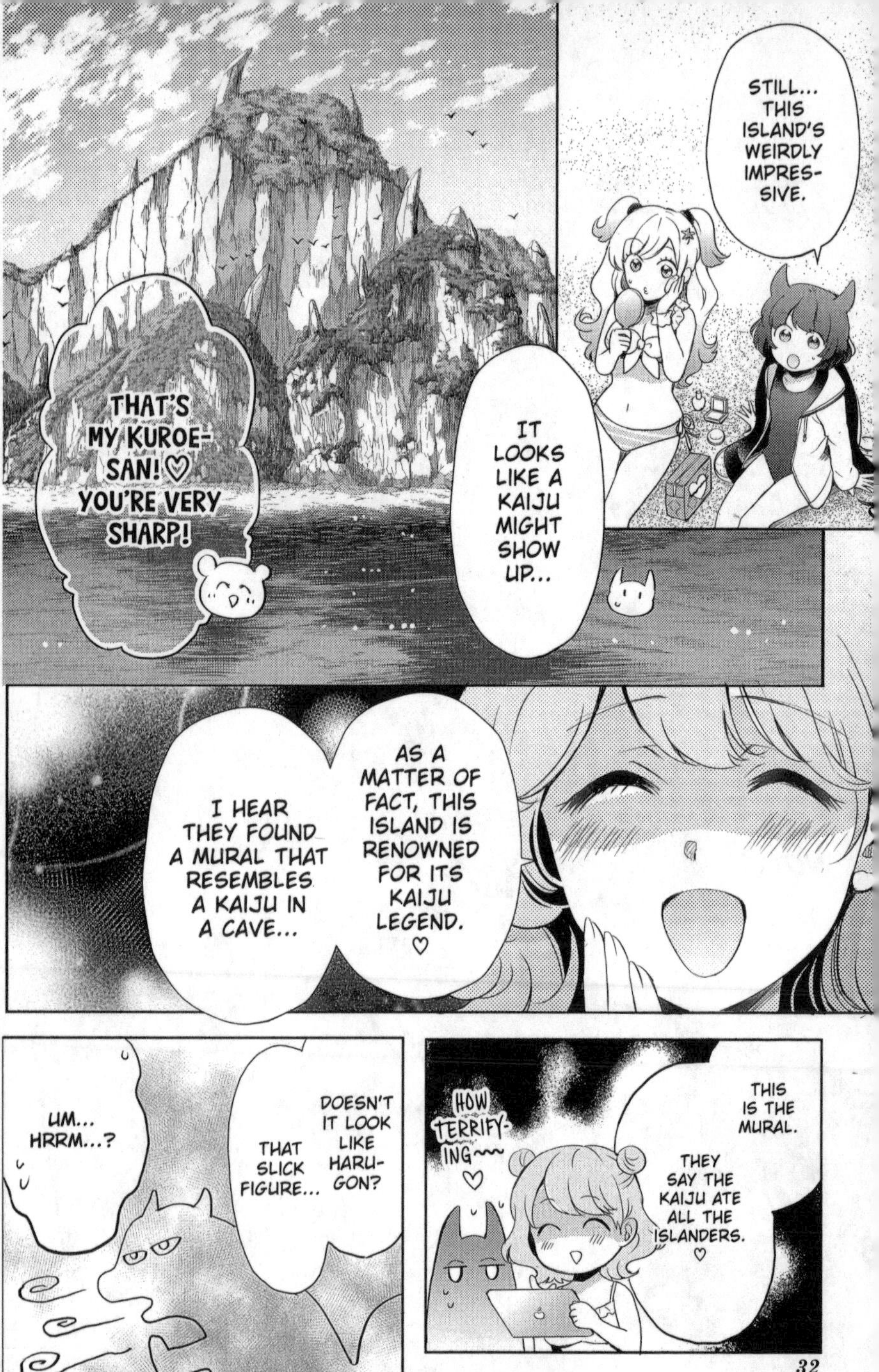
STILL... THIS ISLAND'S WEIRDLY IMPRES-SIVE.
IT LOOKS LIKE A KAIJU MIGHT SHOW UP...
THAT'S MY KUROE-SAN! ♡ YOU'RE VERY SHARP!
AS A MATTER OF FACT, THIS ISLAND IS RENOWNED FOR ITS KAIJU LEGEND. ♡
I HEAR THEY FOUND A MURAL THAT RESEMBLES A KAIJU IN A CAVE...
THIS IS THE MURAL.
THEY SAY THE KAIJU ATE ALL THE ISLANDERS. ♡
HOW TERRIFY-ING~~~ ♡
DOESN'T IT LOOK LIKE HARU-GON?
THAT SLICK FIGURE...
UM... HRRM...?

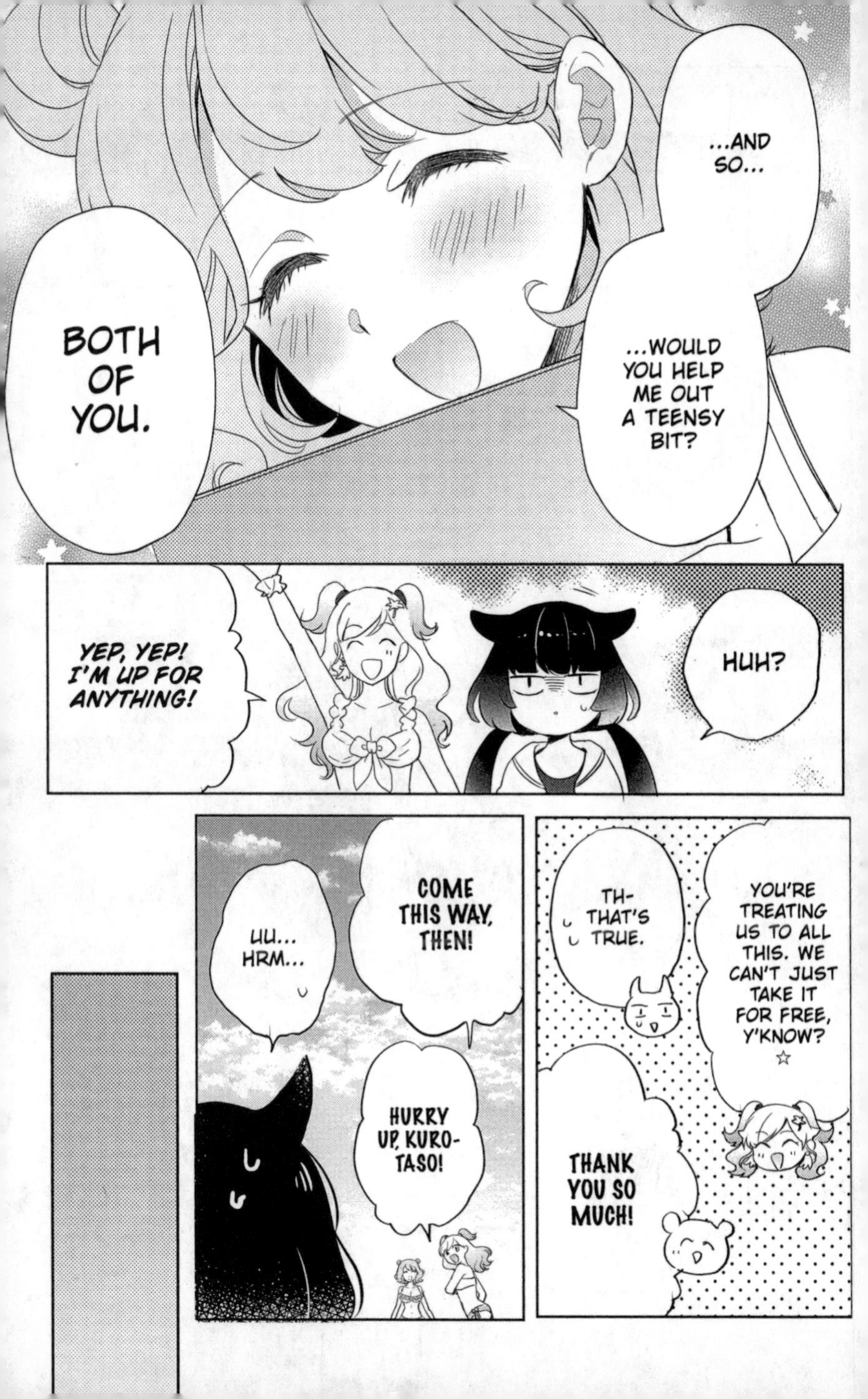
...AND SO...
...WOULD YOU HELP ME OUT A TEENSY BIT?
BOTH OF YOU.
HUH?
YEP, YEP! I'M UP FOR ANYTHING!
YOU'RE TREATING US TO ALL THIS. WE CAN'T JUST TAKE IT FOR FREE, Y'KNOW? ☆
TH- THAT'S TRUE.
THANK YOU SO MUCH!
COME THIS WAY, THEN!
UU... HRM...
HURRY UP, KURO-TASO!

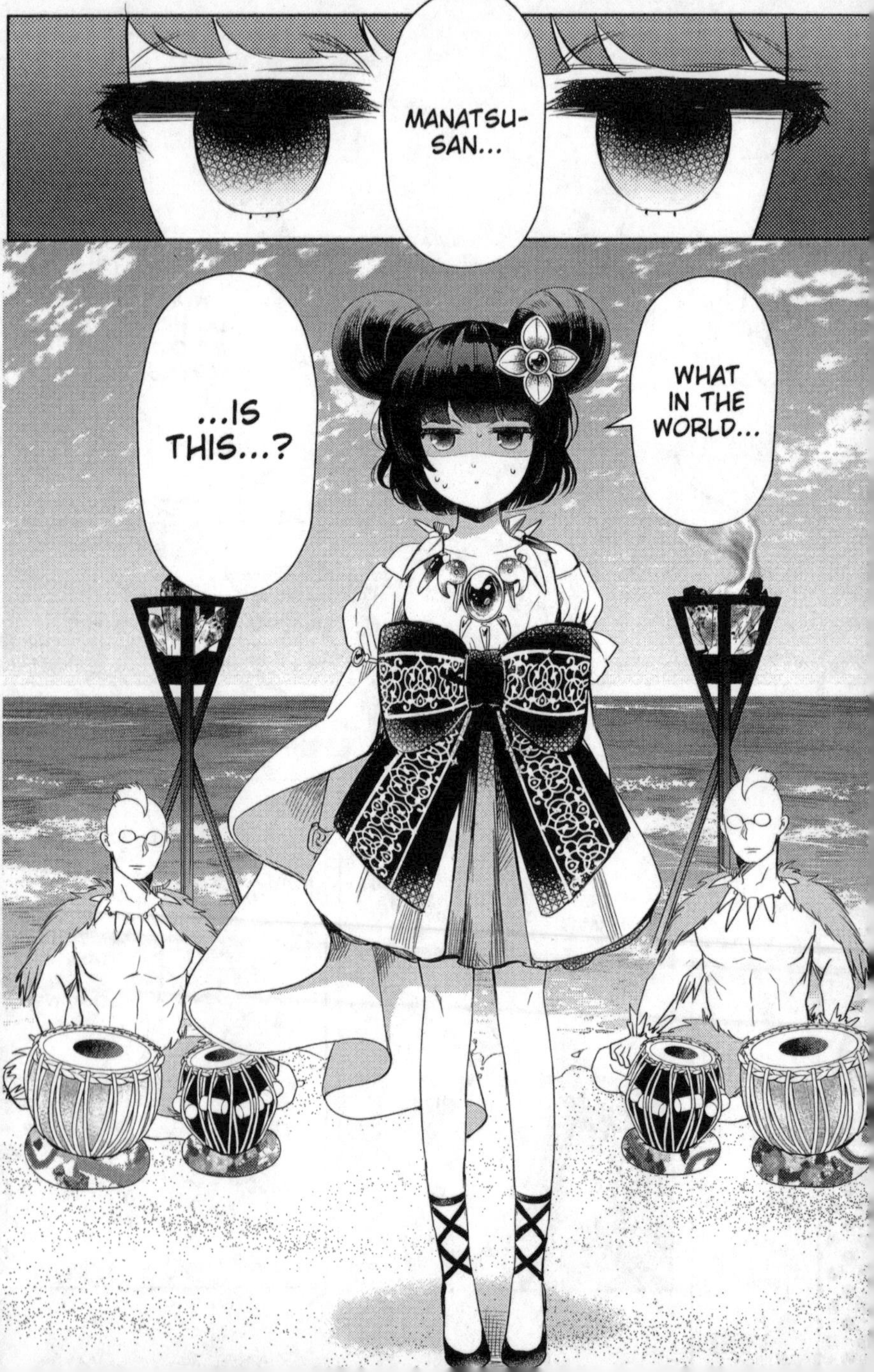
MANATSU-SAN...
WHAT IN THE WORLD...
...IS THIS...?

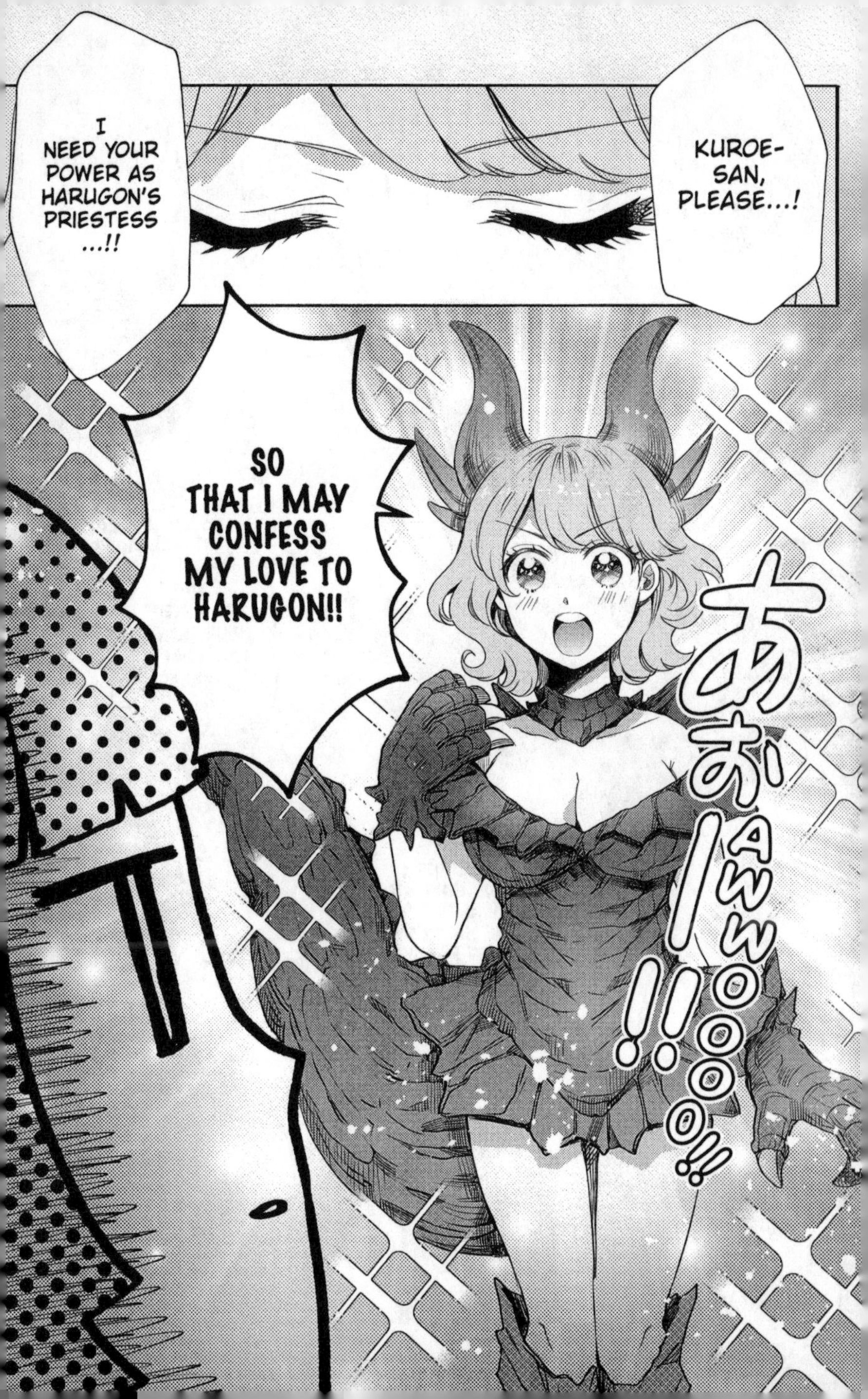
KUROE-SAN, PLEASE...!
I NEED YOUR POWER AS HARUGON'S PRIESTESS ...!!
SO THAT I MAY CONFESS MY LOVE TO HARUGON!!
あおー!!
AWWOOOOOO!!

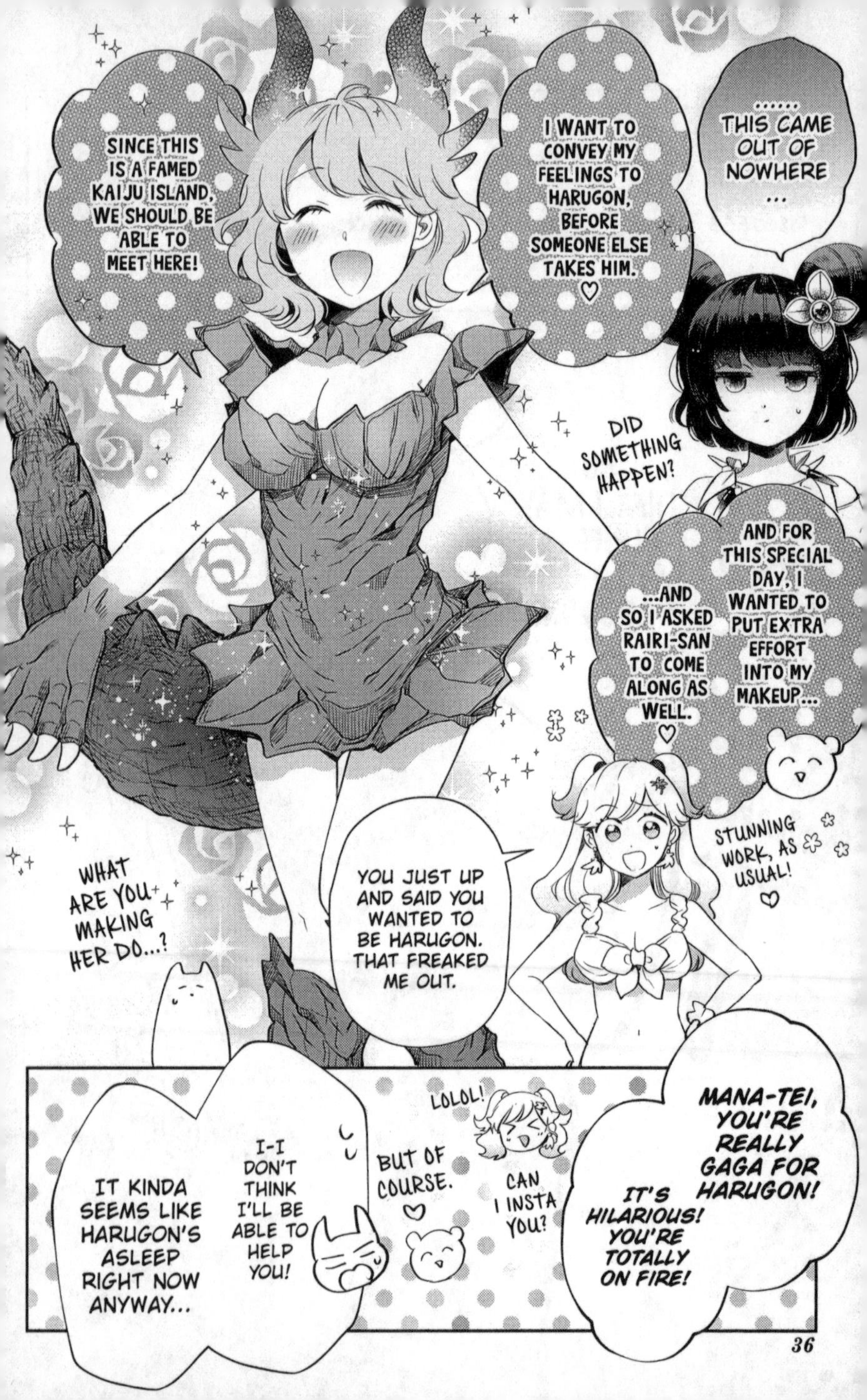
...... THIS CAME OUT OF NOWHERE ...
I WANT TO CONVEY MY FEELINGS TO HARUGON, BEFORE SOMEONE ELSE TAKES HIM. ♡
SINCE THIS IS A FAMED KAIJU ISLAND, WE SHOULD BE ABLE TO MEET HERE!
DID SOMETHING HAPPEN?
AND FOR THIS SPECIAL DAY, I WANTED TO PUT EXTRA EFFORT INTO MY MAKEUP...
...AND SO I ASKED RAIRI-SAN TO COME ALONG AS WELL. ♡
STUNNING WORK, AS USUAL! ♡
YOU JUST UP AND SAID YOU WANTED TO BE HARUGON. THAT FREAKED ME OUT.
WHAT ARE YOU MAKING HER DO...?
MANA-TEI, YOU'RE REALLY GAGA FOR HARUGON!
IT'S HILARIOUS! YOU'RE TOTALLY ON FIRE!
LOLOL!
CAN I INSTA YOU?
BUT OF COURSE. ♡
I-I DON'T THINK I'LL BE ABLE TO HELP YOU!
IT KINDA SEEMS LIKE HARUGON'S ASLEEP RIGHT NOW ANYWAY...

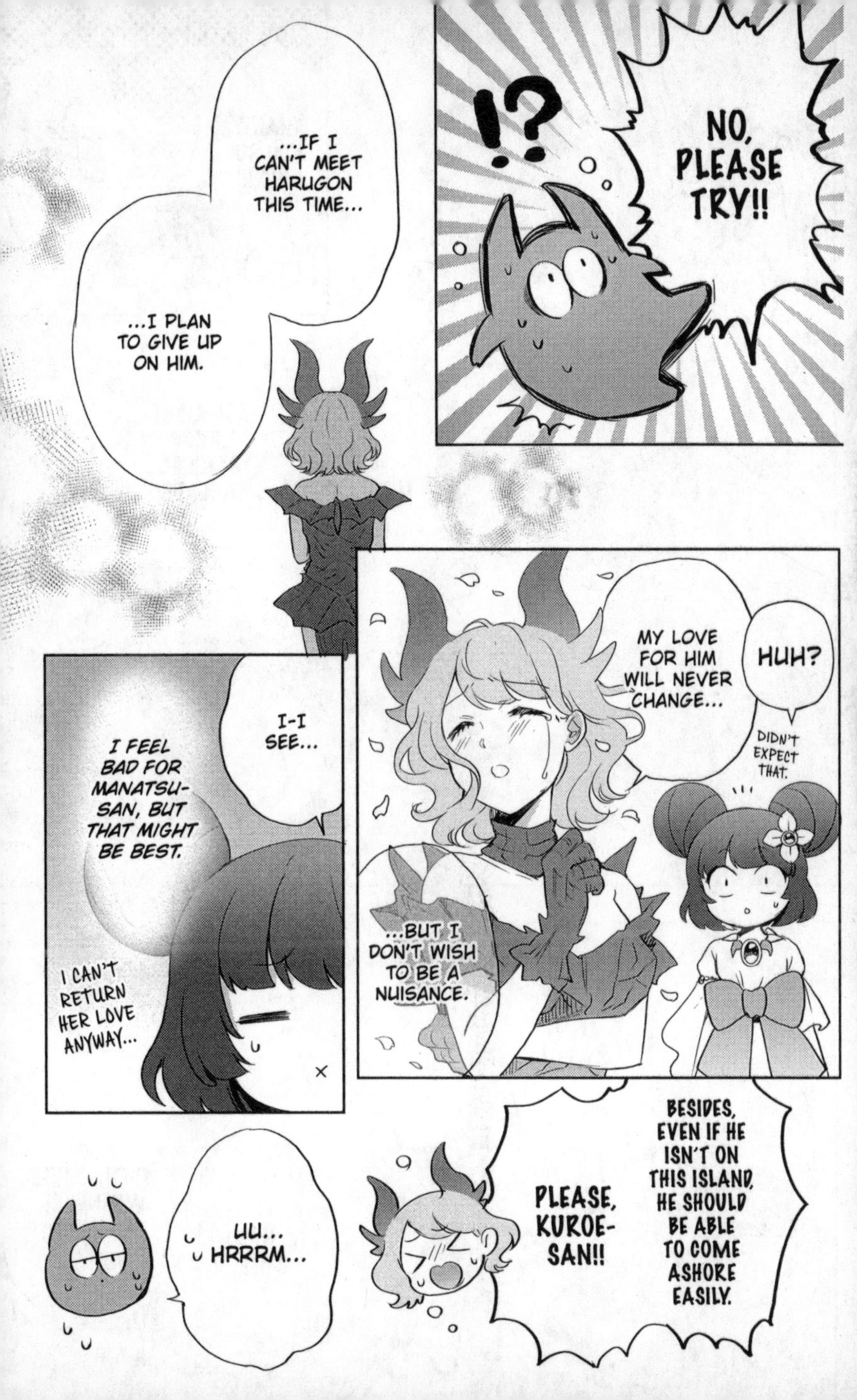
!?
NO, PLEASE TRY!!
...IF I CAN'T MEET HARUGON THIS TIME...
...I PLAN TO GIVE UP ON HIM.
MY LOVE FOR HIM WILL NEVER CHANGE...
...BUT I DON'T WISH TO BE A NUISANCE.
HUH?
DIDN'T EXPECT THAT.
I-I SEE...
I FEEL BAD FOR MANATSU-SAN, BUT THAT MIGHT BE BEST.
I CAN'T RETURN HER LOVE ANYWAY...
BESIDES, EVEN IF HE ISN'T ON THIS ISLAND, HE SHOULD BE ABLE TO COME ASHORE EASILY.
PLEASE, KUROE-SAN!!
UU... HRRRM...

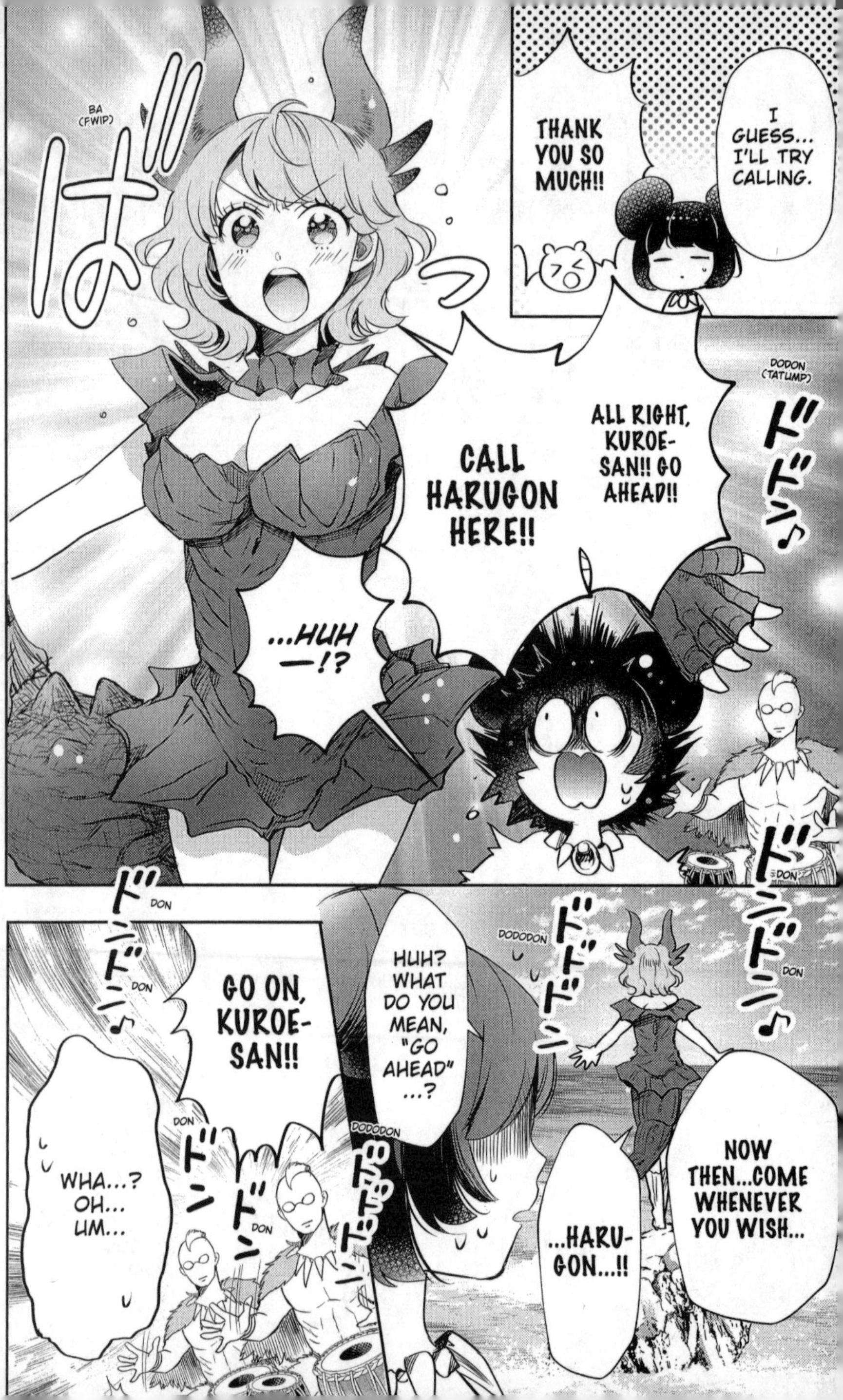
I GUESS... I'LL TRY CALLING.
THANK YOU SO MUCH!!
BA (FWIP)
DODON (TATUMP)
ALL RIGHT, KUROE-SAN!! GO AHEAD!!
CALL HARUGON HERE!!
...HUH—!?
DON
DON
DODODON
NOW THEN...COME WHENEVER YOU WISH...
...HARU-GON...!!
HUH? WHAT DO YOU MEAN, "GO AHEAD"...?
DODODON
DON
DON
GO ON, KUROE-SAN!!
DON
DON
WHA...? OH... UM...

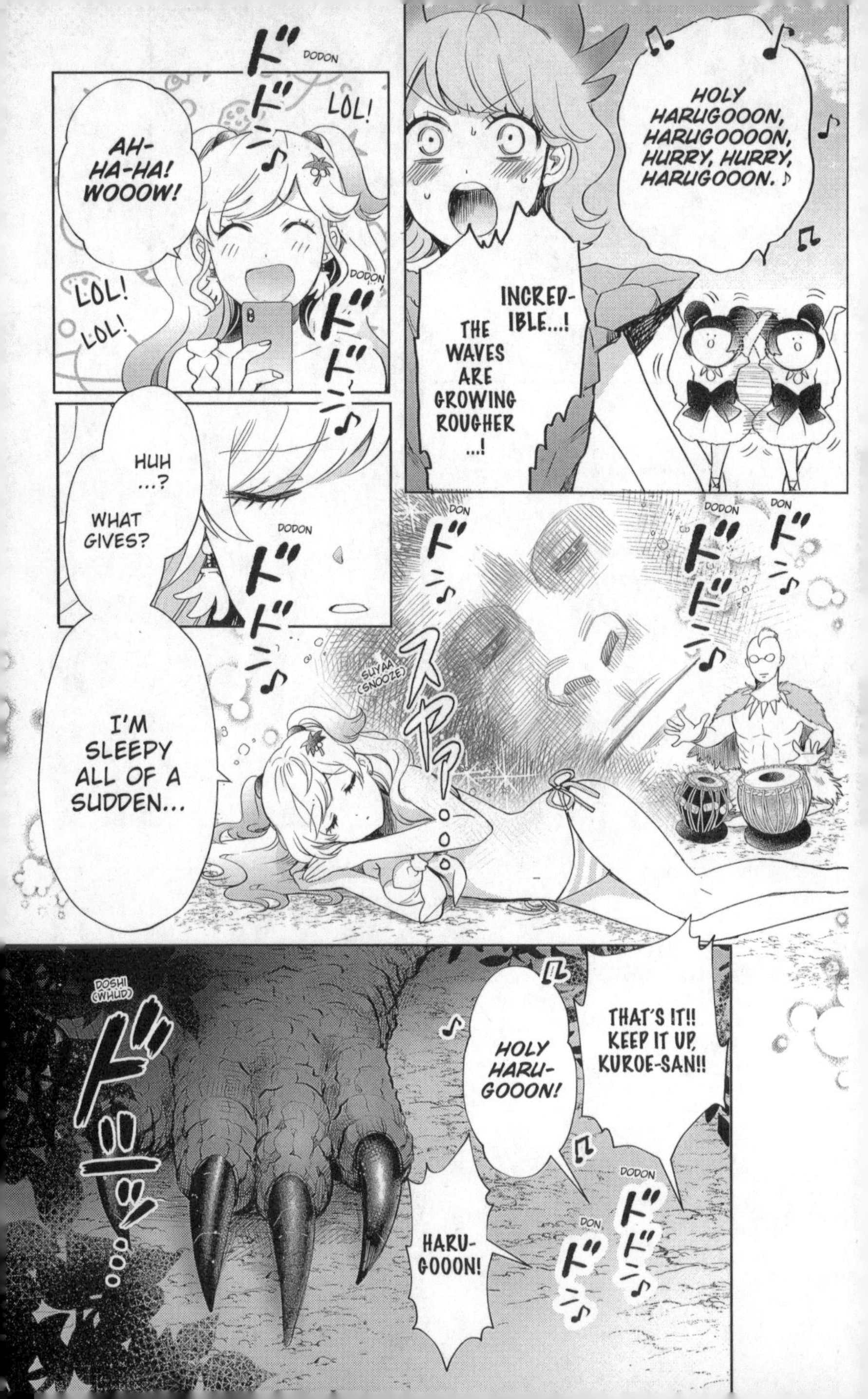
HOLY HARUGOOON, HARUGOOOON, HURRY, HURRY, HARUGOOON. ♪
INCRED-IBLE...!
THE WAVES ARE GROWING ROUGHER ...!
DODON
AH-HA-HA! WOOOW!
LOL!
LOL!
LOL!
DODON
HUH ...?
WHAT GIVES?
DODON
DON
DODON
DON
I'M SLEEPY ALL OF A SUDDEN...
SUYAA (SNOOZE)
THAT'S IT!! KEEP IT UP, KUROE-SAN!!
HOLY HARU-GOOON!
HARU-GOOON!
DODON
DON
DOSHI (WHUD)

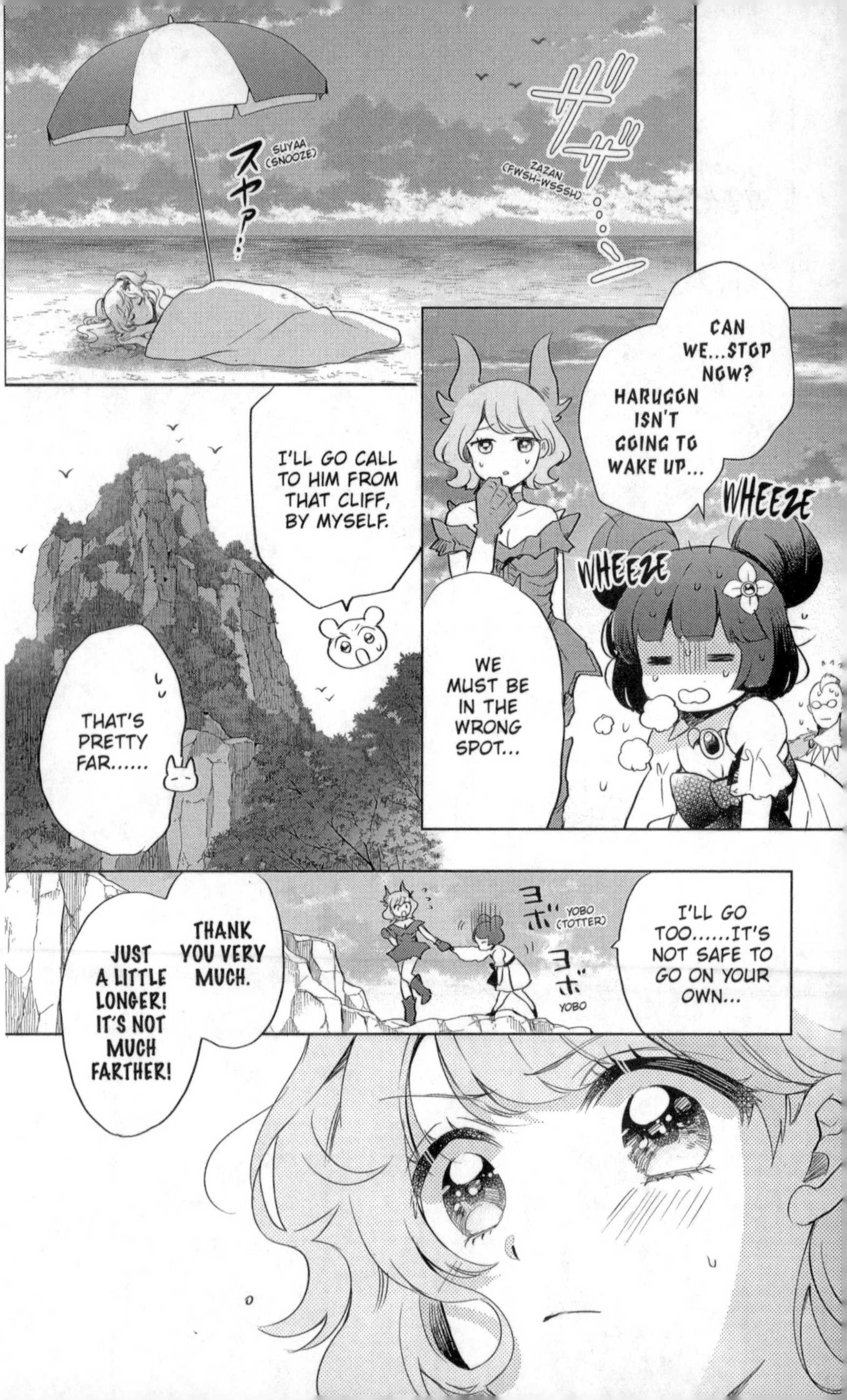
ザザ…ン
ZAZAN (FWSH-WSSSH)
スヤァ‥
SUYAA (SNOOZE)
CAN WE...STOP NOW? HARUGON ISN'T GOING TO WAKE UP...
WHEEZE
WHEEZE
WE MUST BE IN THE WRONG SPOT...
I'LL GO CALL TO HIM FROM THAT CLIFF, BY MYSELF.
THAT'S PRETTY FAR......
I'LL GO TOO......IT'S NOT SAFE TO GO ON YOUR OWN...
ヨボ
YOBO (TOTTER)
ヨボ
YOBO
THANK YOU VERY MUCH.
JUST A LITTLE LONGER! IT'S NOT MUCH FARTHER!

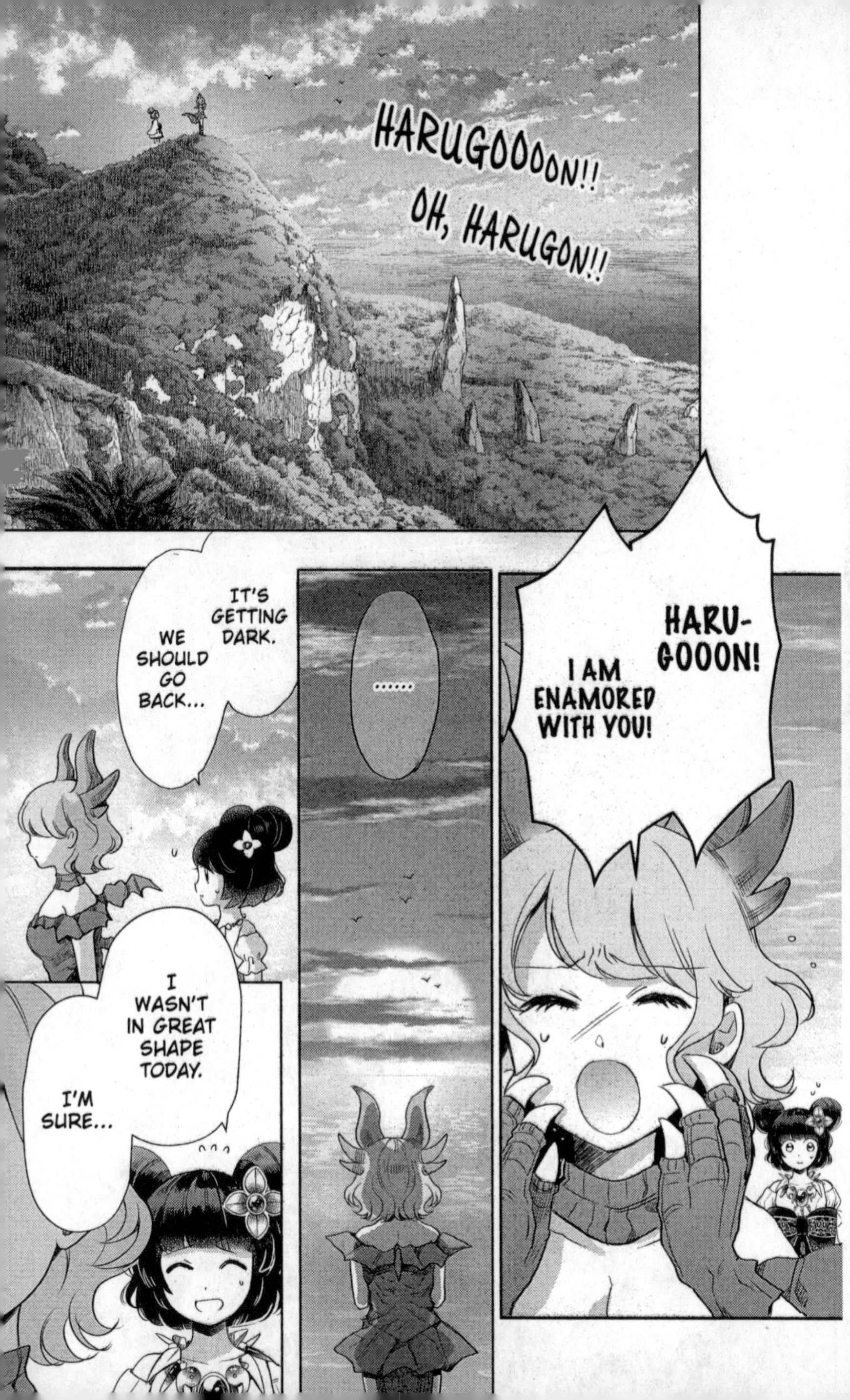
HARUGOOOOON!!
OH, HARUGON!!
HARU-GOOON!
I AM ENAMORED WITH YOU!
......
IT'S GETTING DARK.
WE SHOULD GO BACK...
I WASN'T IN GREAT SHAPE TODAY.
I'M SURE...

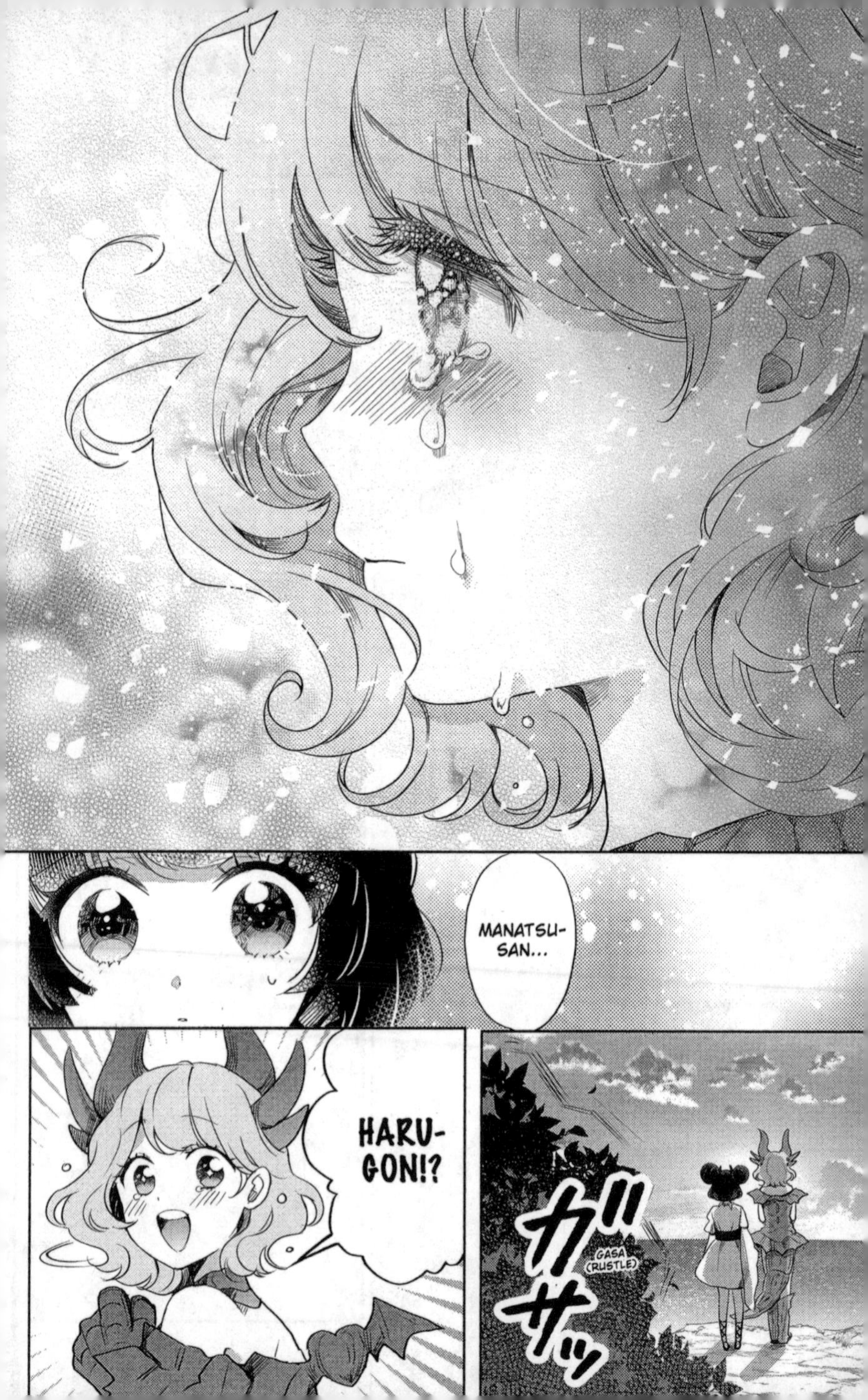
MANATSU-SAN...
ガサッ
GASA (RUSTLE)
HARU-GON!?

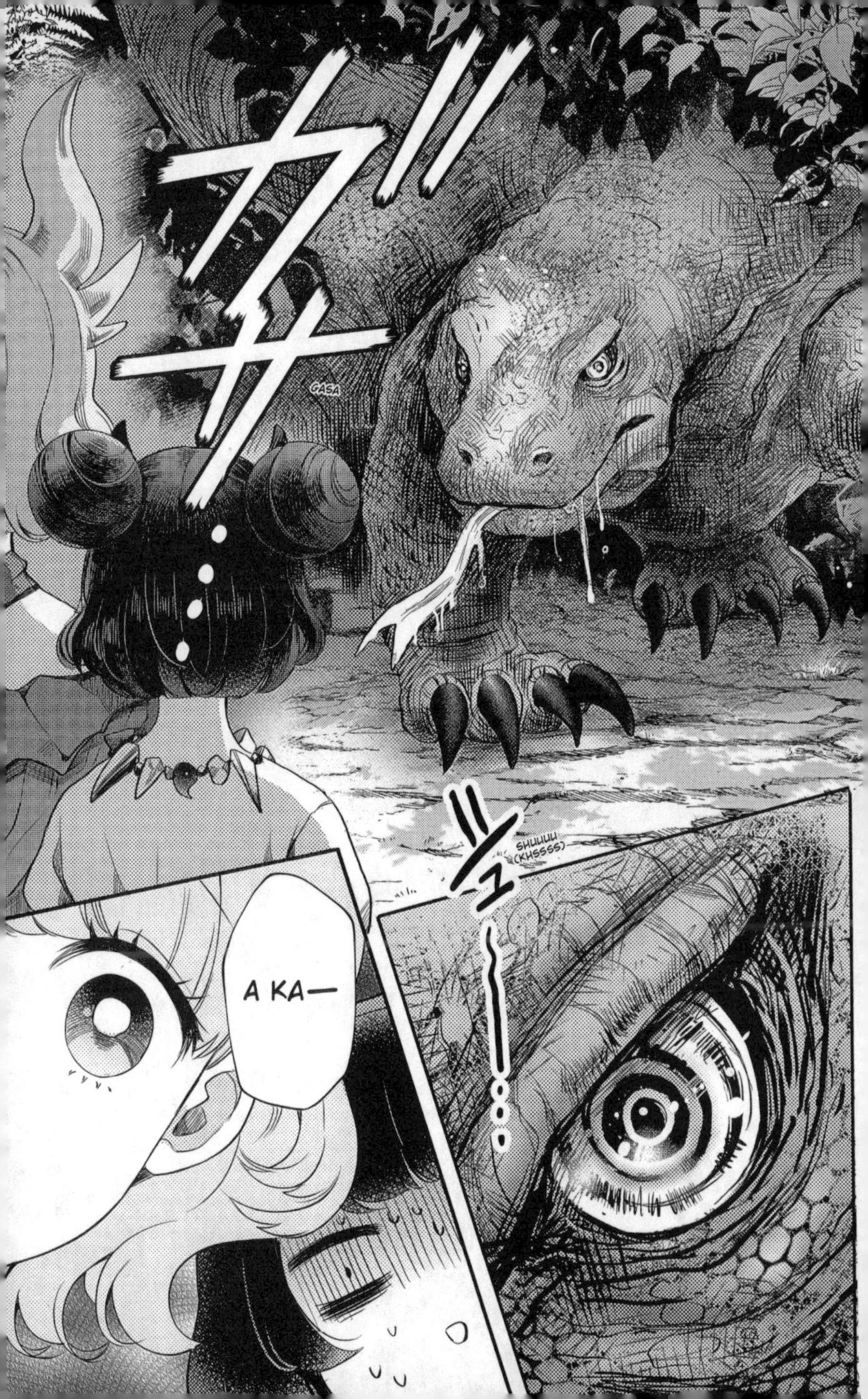
GASA
SHUUUU (KHSSSS)
A KA—

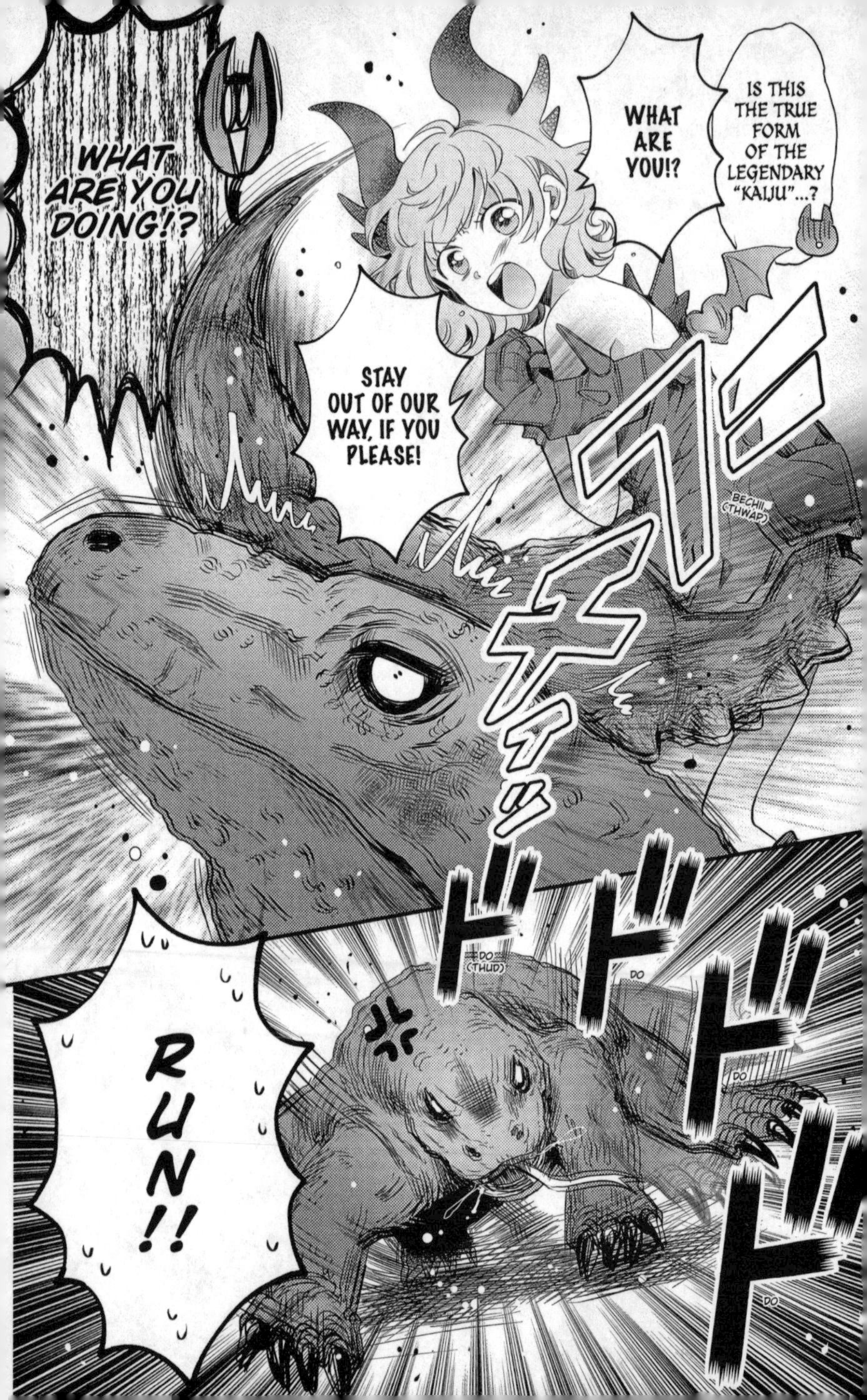
IS THIS THE TRUE FORM OF THE LEGENDARY "KAIJU"...?
WHAT ARE YOU!?
WHAT ARE YOU DOING!?
STAY OUT OF OUR WAY, IF YOU PLEASE!
BECHII (THWAP)
DO (THUD)
DO
DO
DO
RUN!!

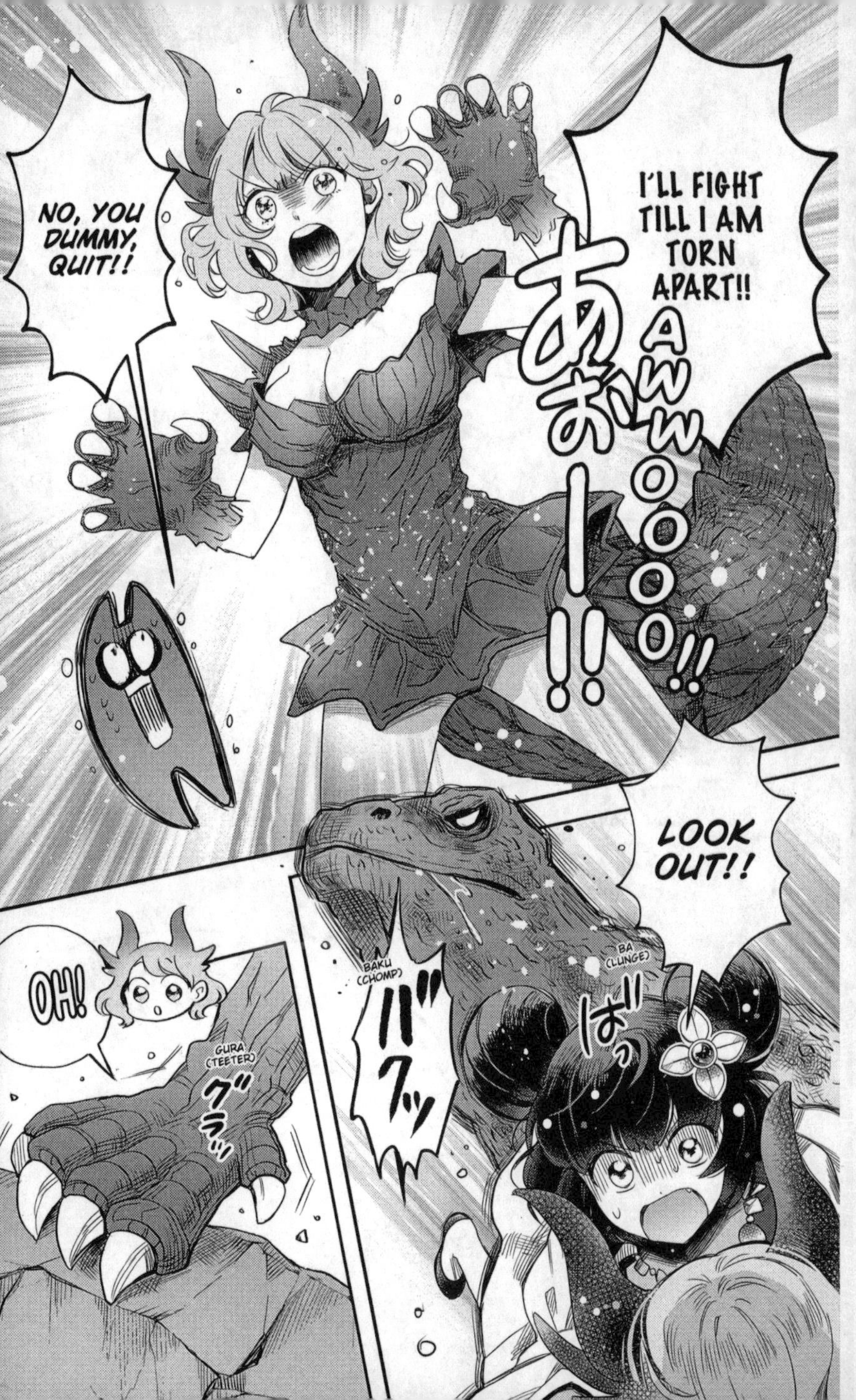
I'LL FIGHT TILL I AM TORN APART!!
あおー!!
AWWOOOOO!!
NO, YOU DUMMY, QUIT!!
LOOK OUT!!
BA (LUNGE)
ばっ
BAKU (CHOMP)
バクッ
OH!
GURA (TEETER)
グラッ

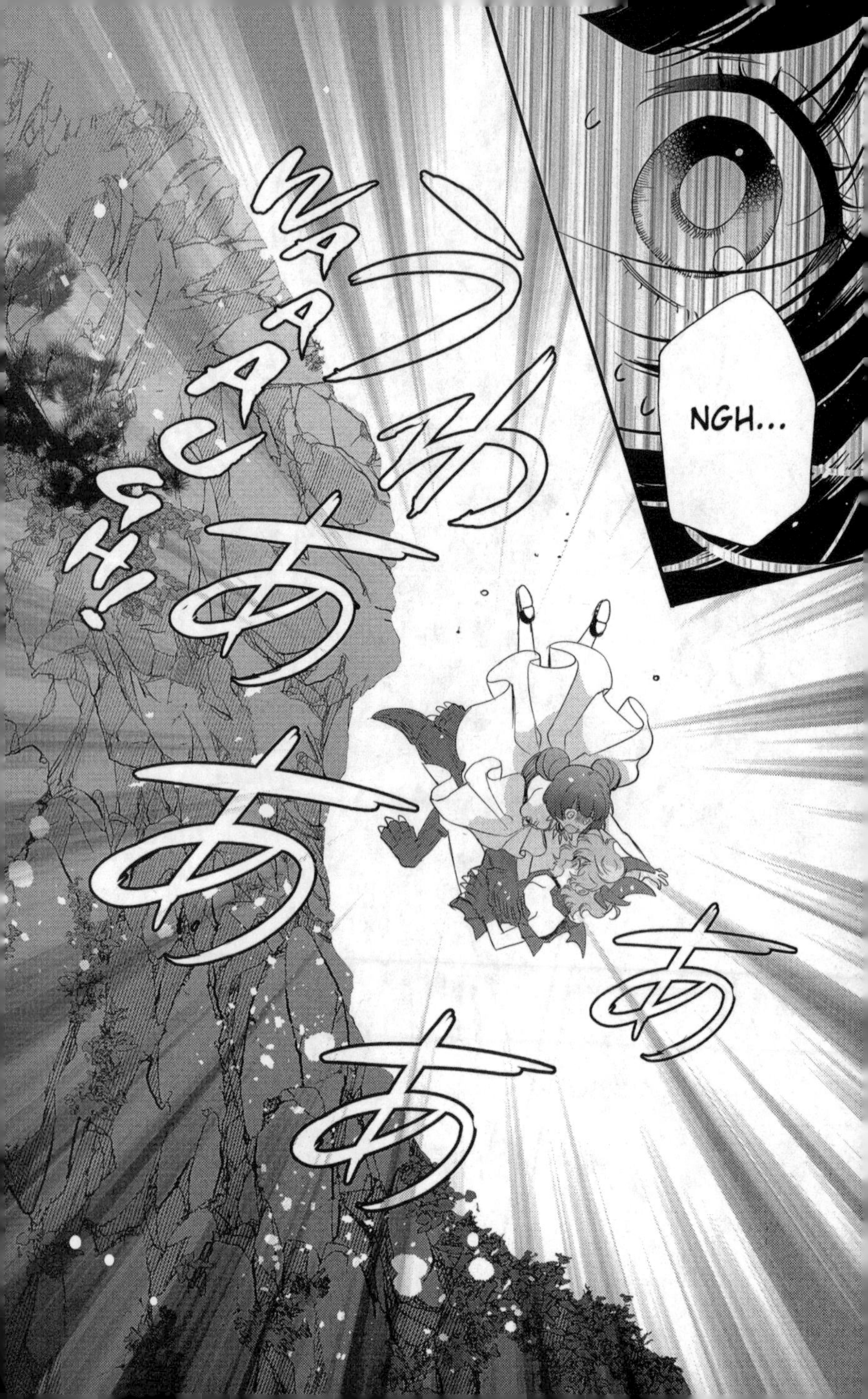
NGH...
NAAAUGH!!

KAIJU♥GIRL
CARAMELISE

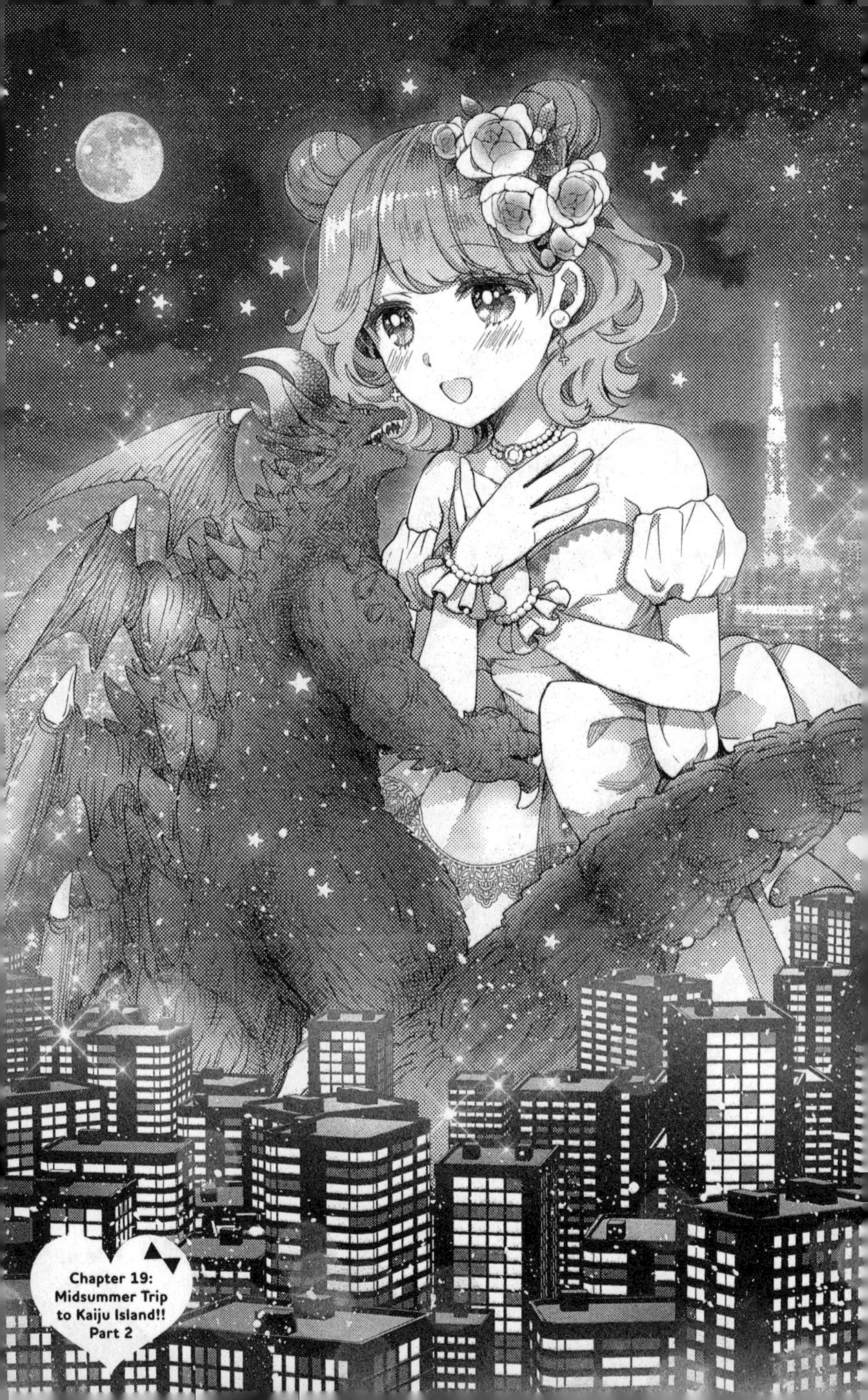
Chapter 19:
Midsummer Trip
to Kaiju Island!!
Part 2

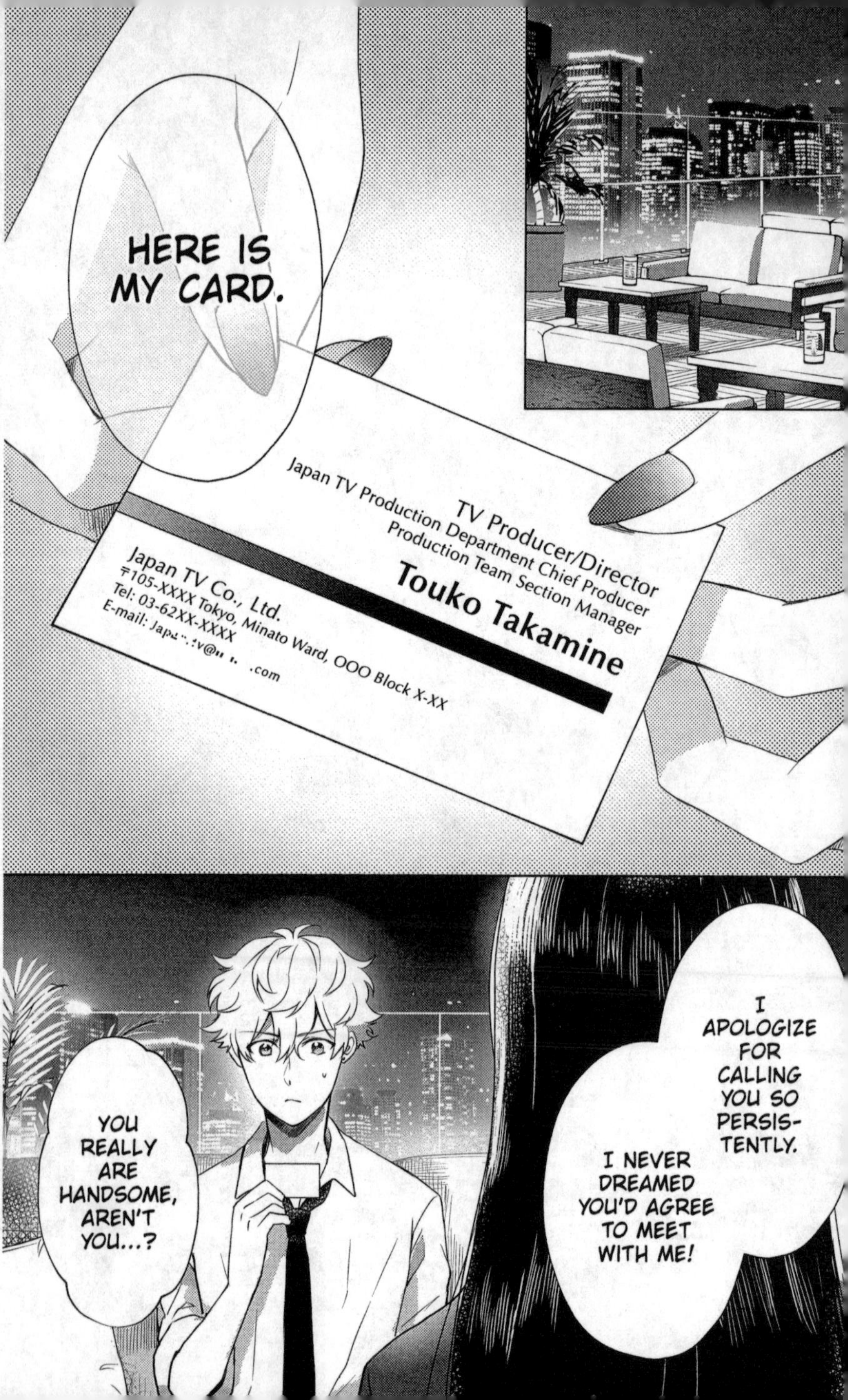
HERE IS MY CARD.
TV Producer/Director
Japan TV Production Department Chief Producer
Production Team Section Manager
Touko Takamine
Japan TV Co., Ltd.
〒105-XXXX Tokyo, Minato Ward, OOO Block X-XX
Tel: 03-62XX-XXXX
I APOLOGIZE FOR CALLING YOU SO PERSIS-TENTLY.
I NEVER DREAMED YOU'D AGREE TO MEET WITH ME!
YOU REALLY ARE HANDSOME, AREN'T YOU...?

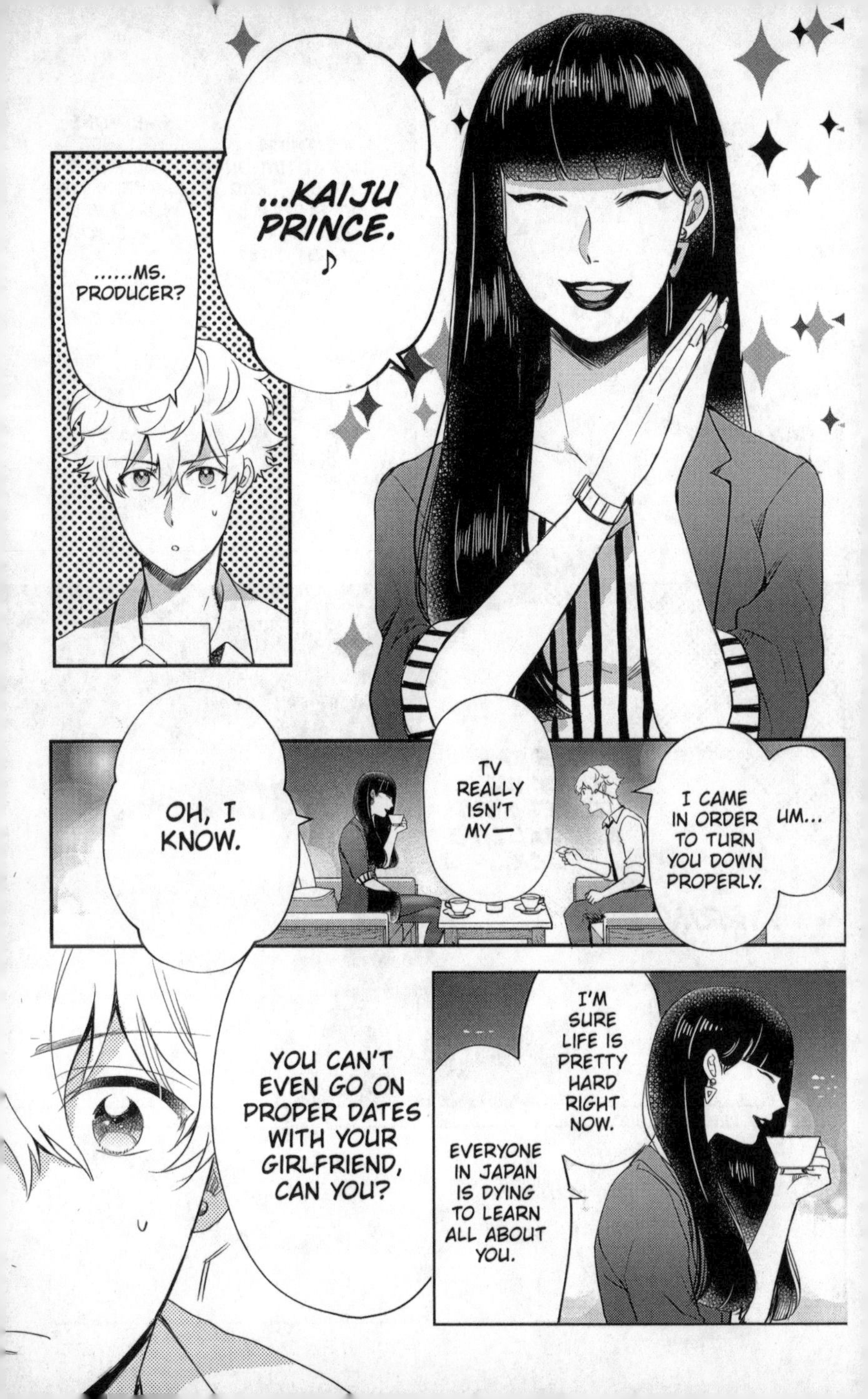
...KAIJU PRINCE. ♪
......MS. PRODUCER?
UM...
I CAME IN ORDER TO TURN YOU DOWN PROPERLY.
TV REALLY ISN'T MY—
OH, I KNOW.
I'M SURE LIFE IS PRETTY HARD RIGHT NOW.
EVERYONE IN JAPAN IS DYING TO LEARN ALL ABOUT YOU.
YOU CAN'T EVEN GO ON PROPER DATES WITH YOUR GIRLFRIEND, CAN YOU?

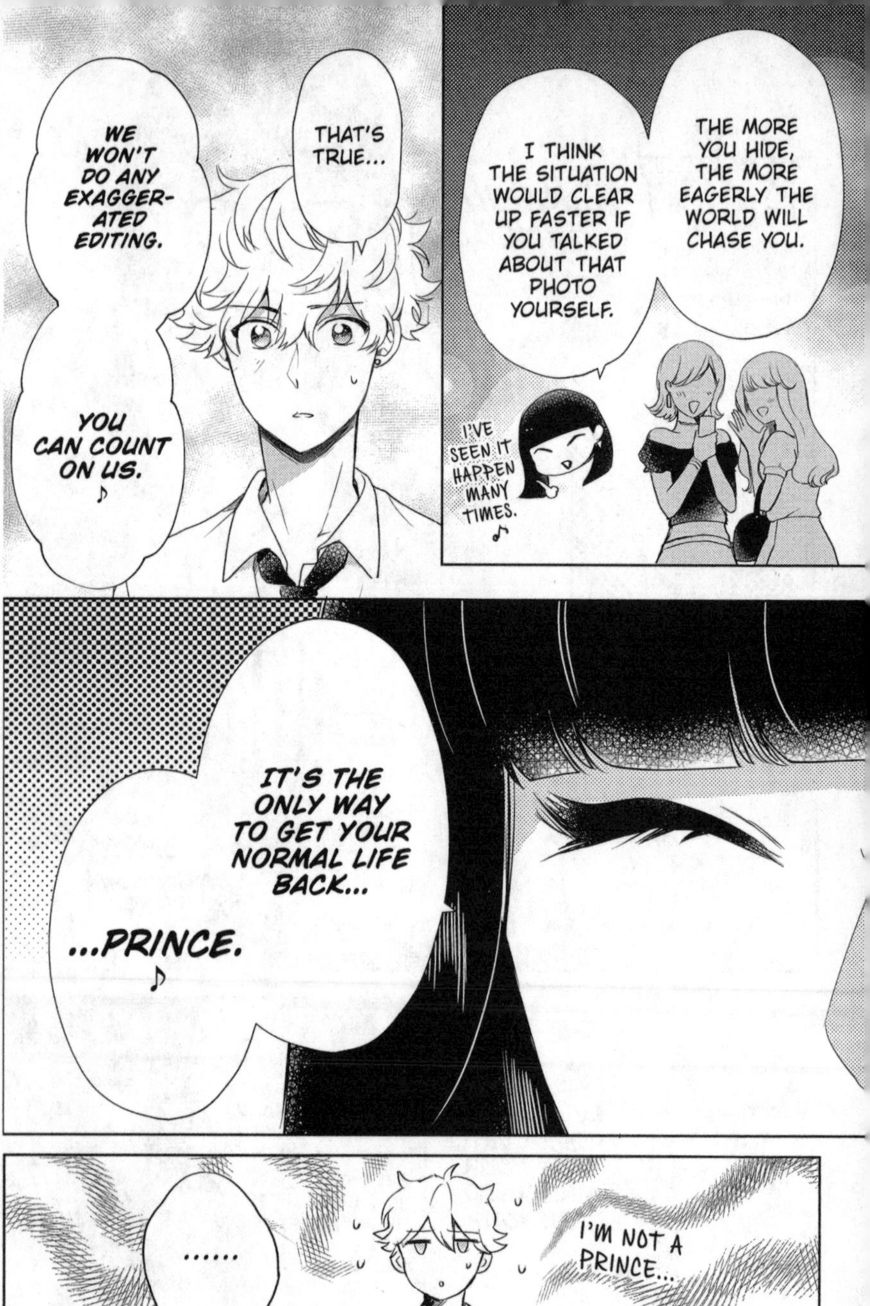
THE MORE YOU HIDE, THE MORE EAGERLY THE WORLD WILL CHASE YOU.
I THINK THE SITUATION WOULD CLEAR UP FASTER IF YOU TALKED ABOUT THAT PHOTO YOURSELF.
I'VE SEEN IT HAPPEN MANY TIMES. ♪
THAT'S TRUE...
WE WON'T DO ANY EXAGGER-ATED EDITING.
YOU CAN COUNT ON US. ♪
IT'S THE ONLY WAY TO GET YOUR NORMAL LIFE BACK...
...PRINCE. ♪
I'M NOT A PRINCE...
......

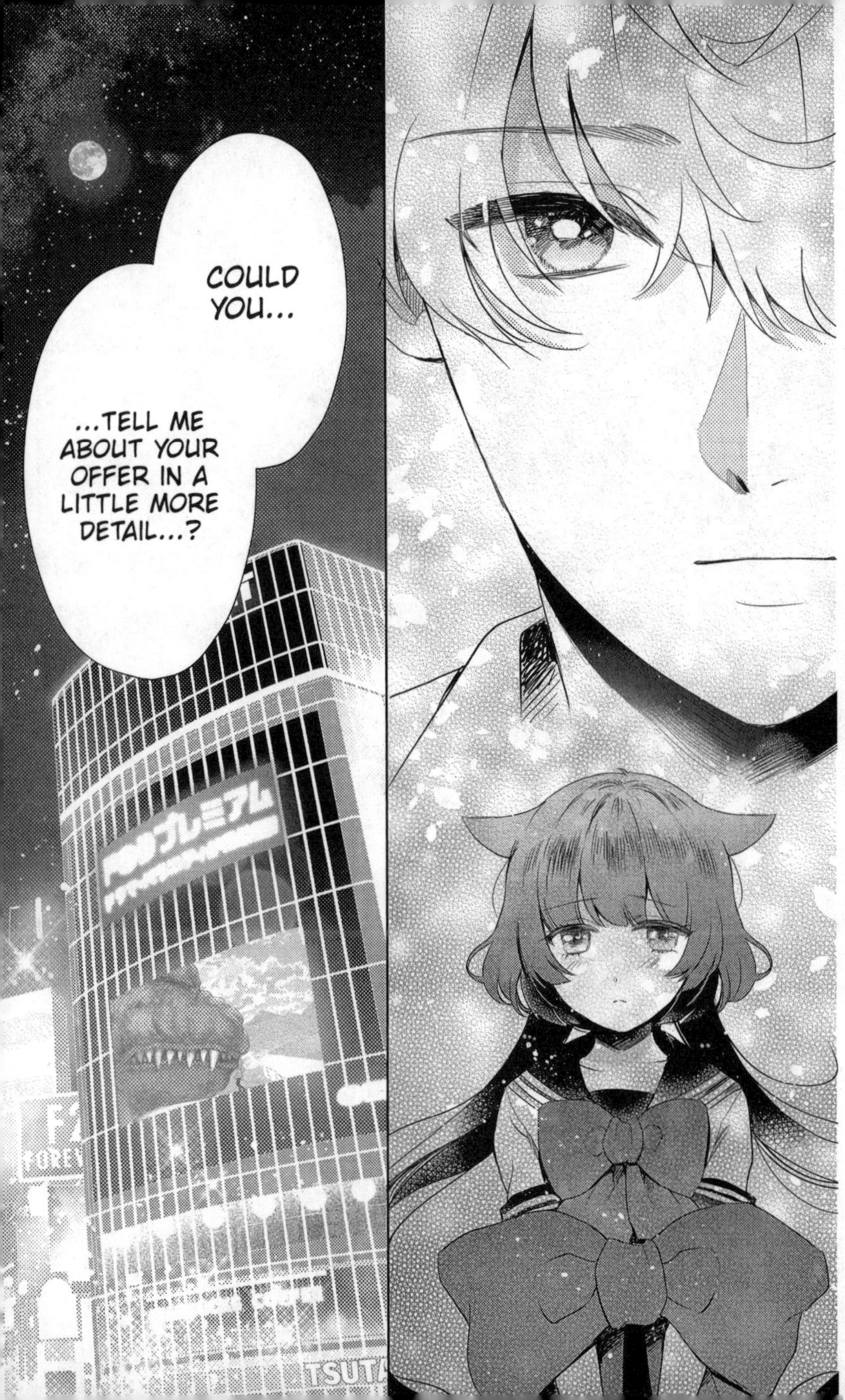
COULD YOU...
...TELL ME ABOUT YOUR OFFER IN A LITTLE MORE DETAIL...?

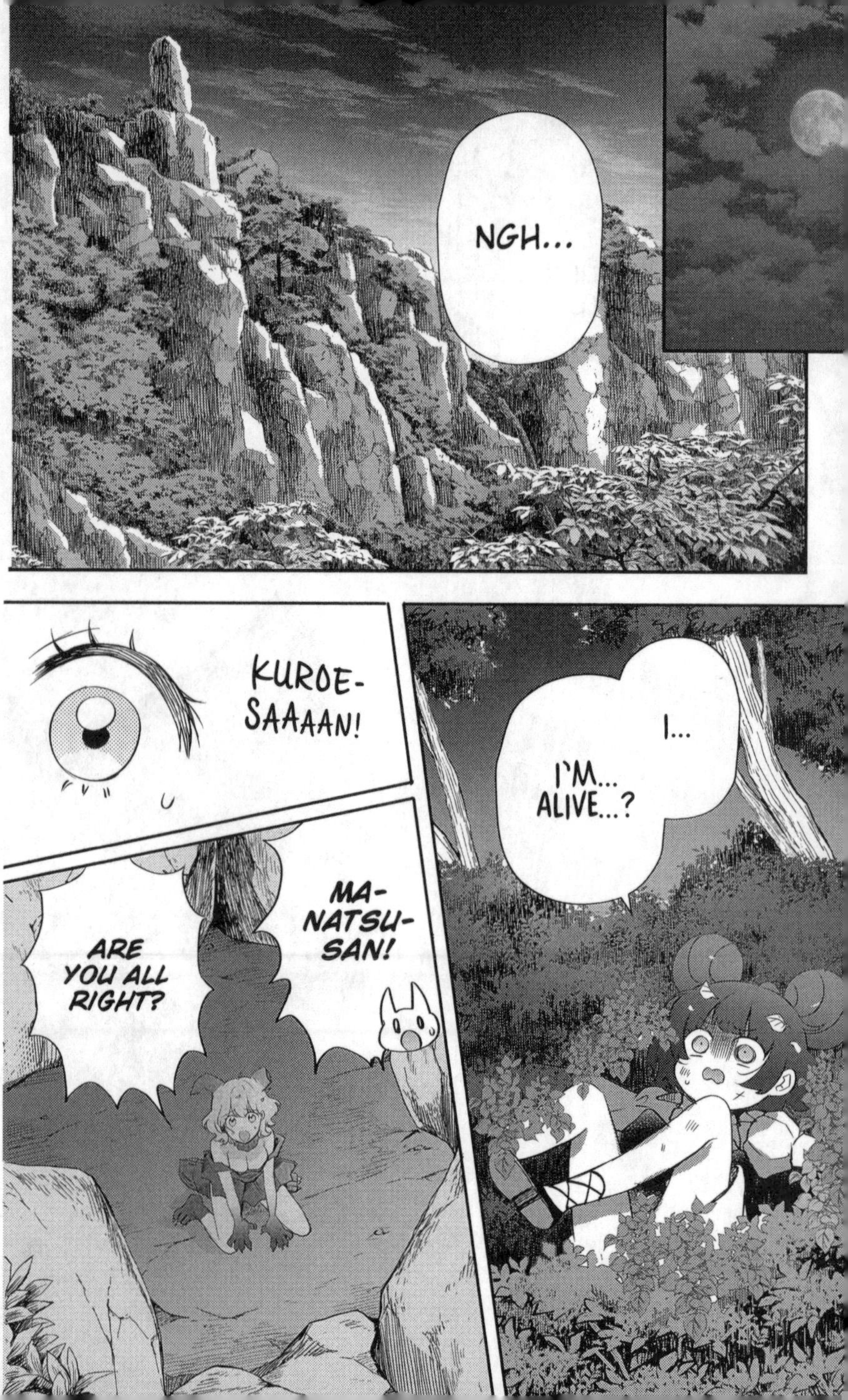
NGH...
I...
I'M... ALIVE...?
KUROE-SAAAAN!
MA-NATSU-SAN!
ARE YOU ALL RIGHT?

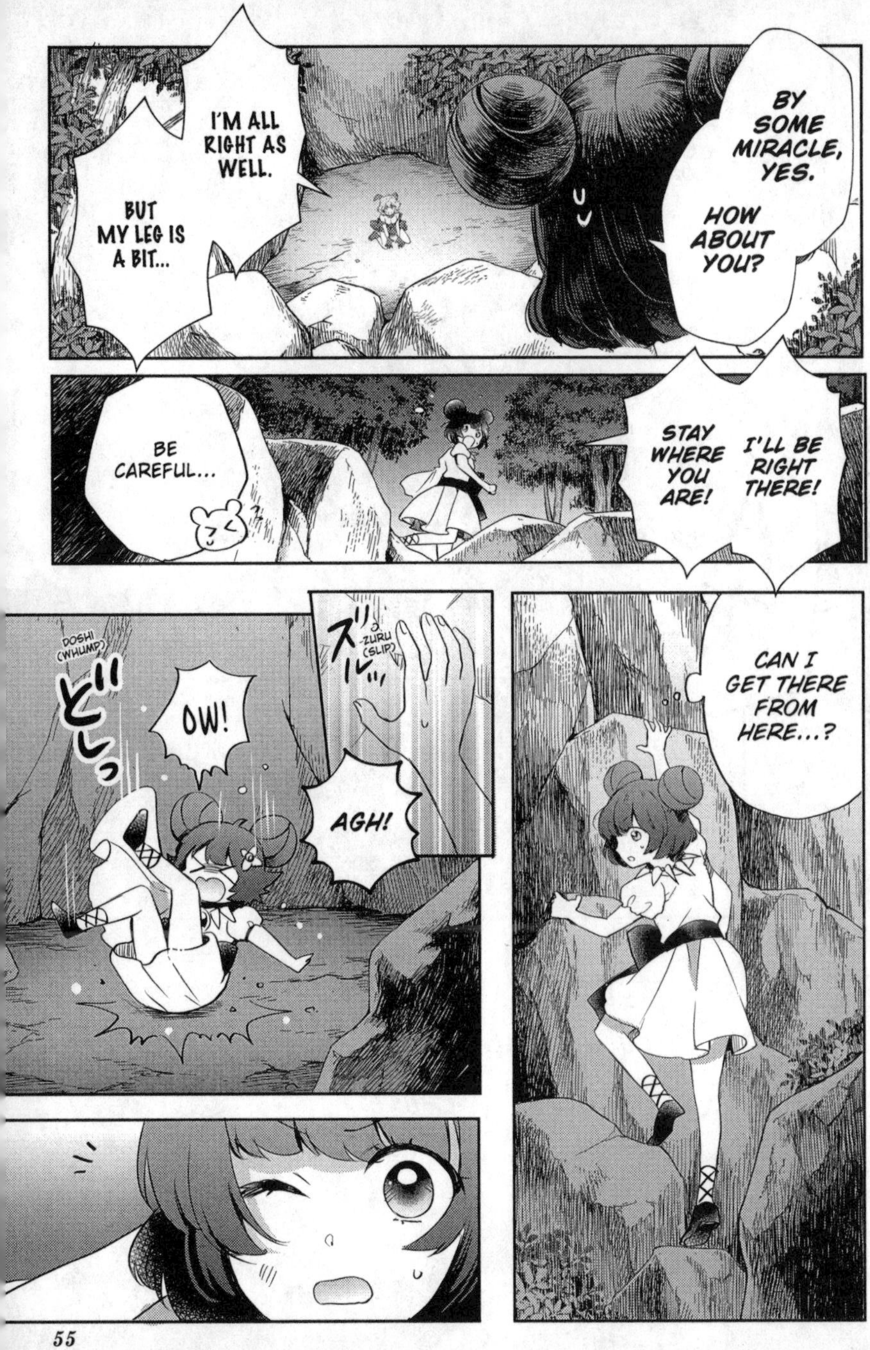
BY SOME MIRACLE, YES.
HOW ABOUT YOU?
I'M ALL RIGHT AS WELL.
BUT MY LEG IS A BIT...
STAY WHERE YOU ARE!
I'LL BE RIGHT THERE!
BE CAREFUL...
CAN I GET THERE FROM HERE...?
ZURU (SLIP)
AGH!
DOSHI (WHUMP)
OW!

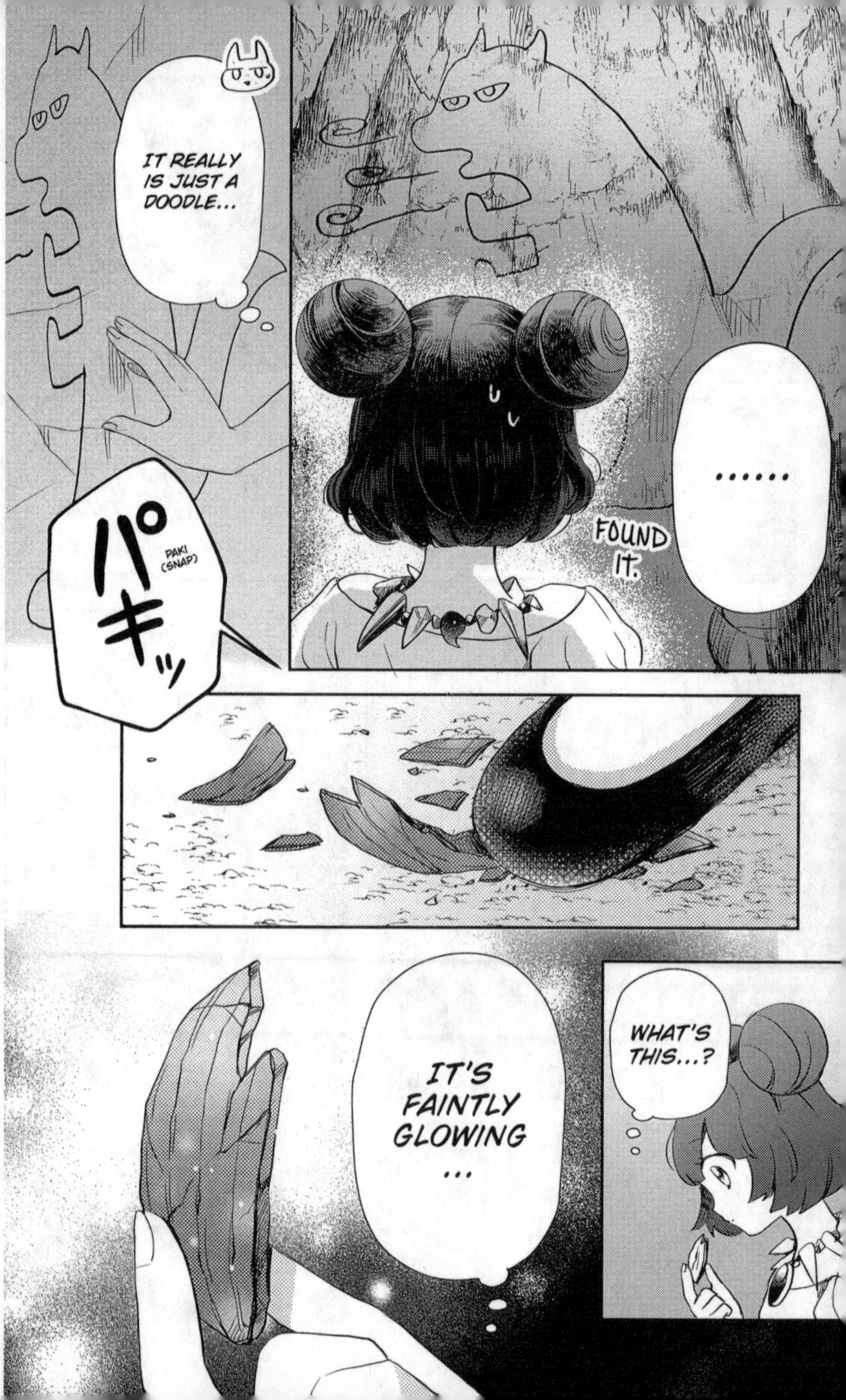

......
FOUND IT.
IT REALLY IS JUST A DOODLE...
パキッ
PAKI (SNAP)
WHAT'S THIS...?
IT'S FAINTLY GLOWING...

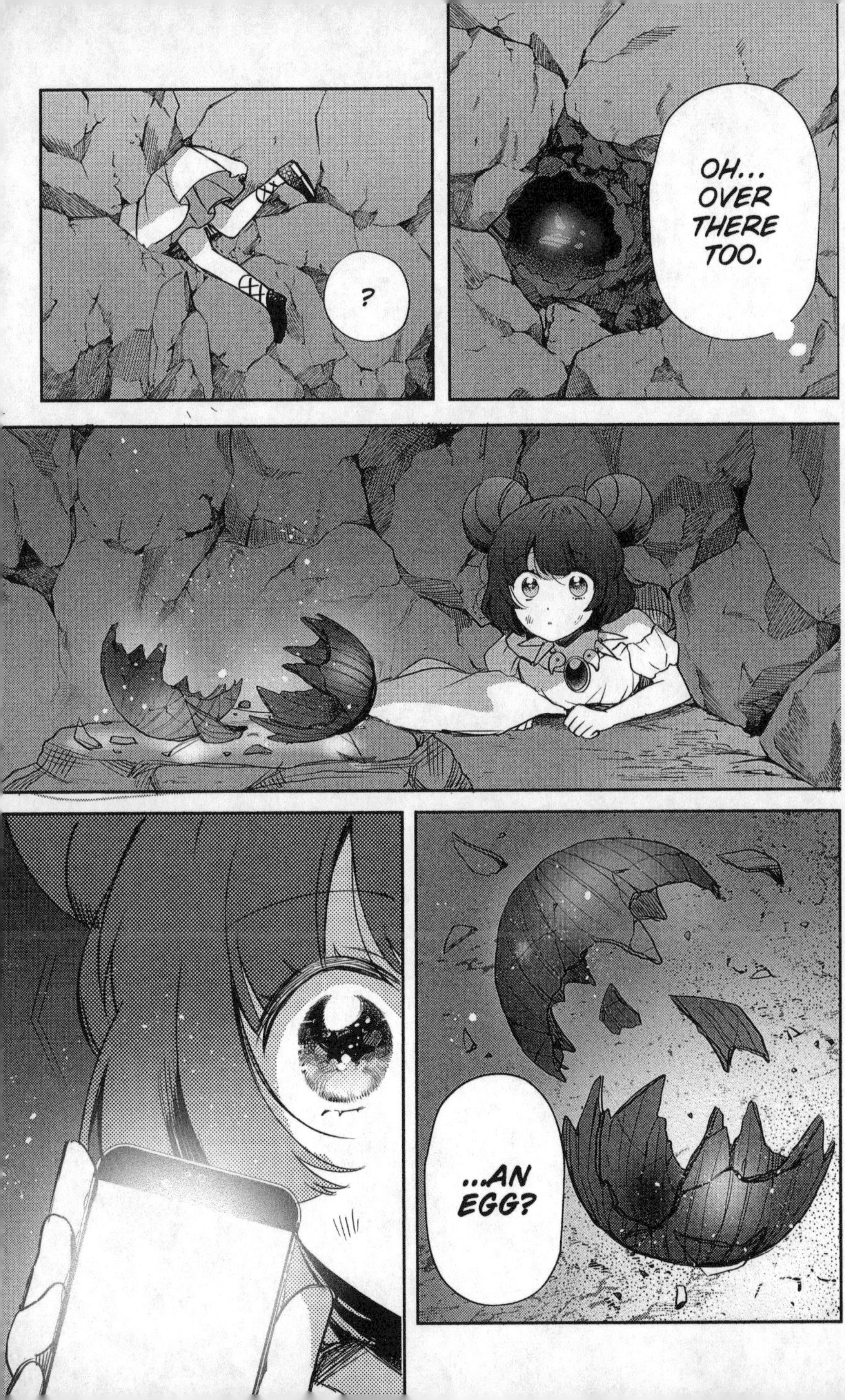
OH... OVER THERE TOO.
?
...AN EGG?

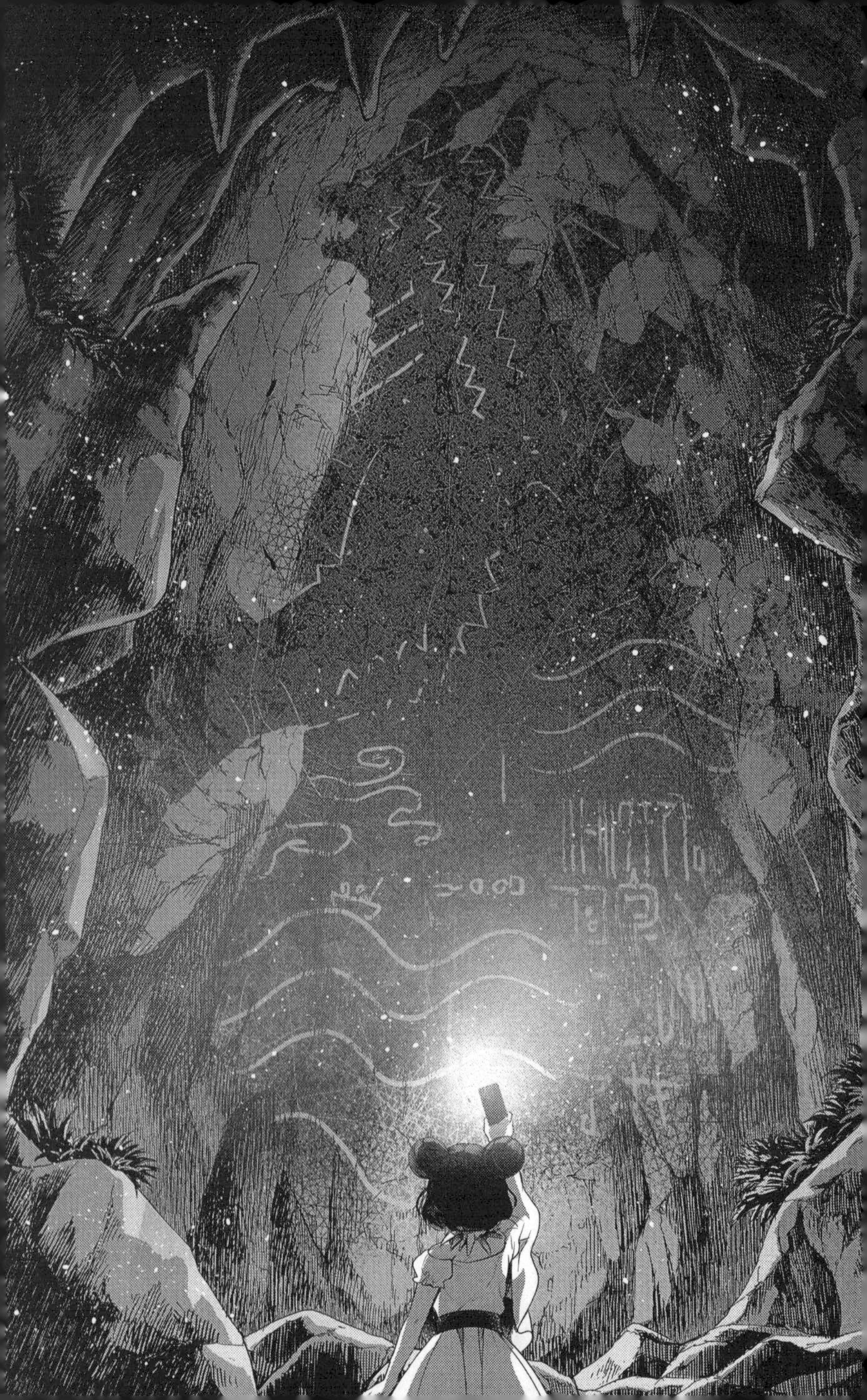

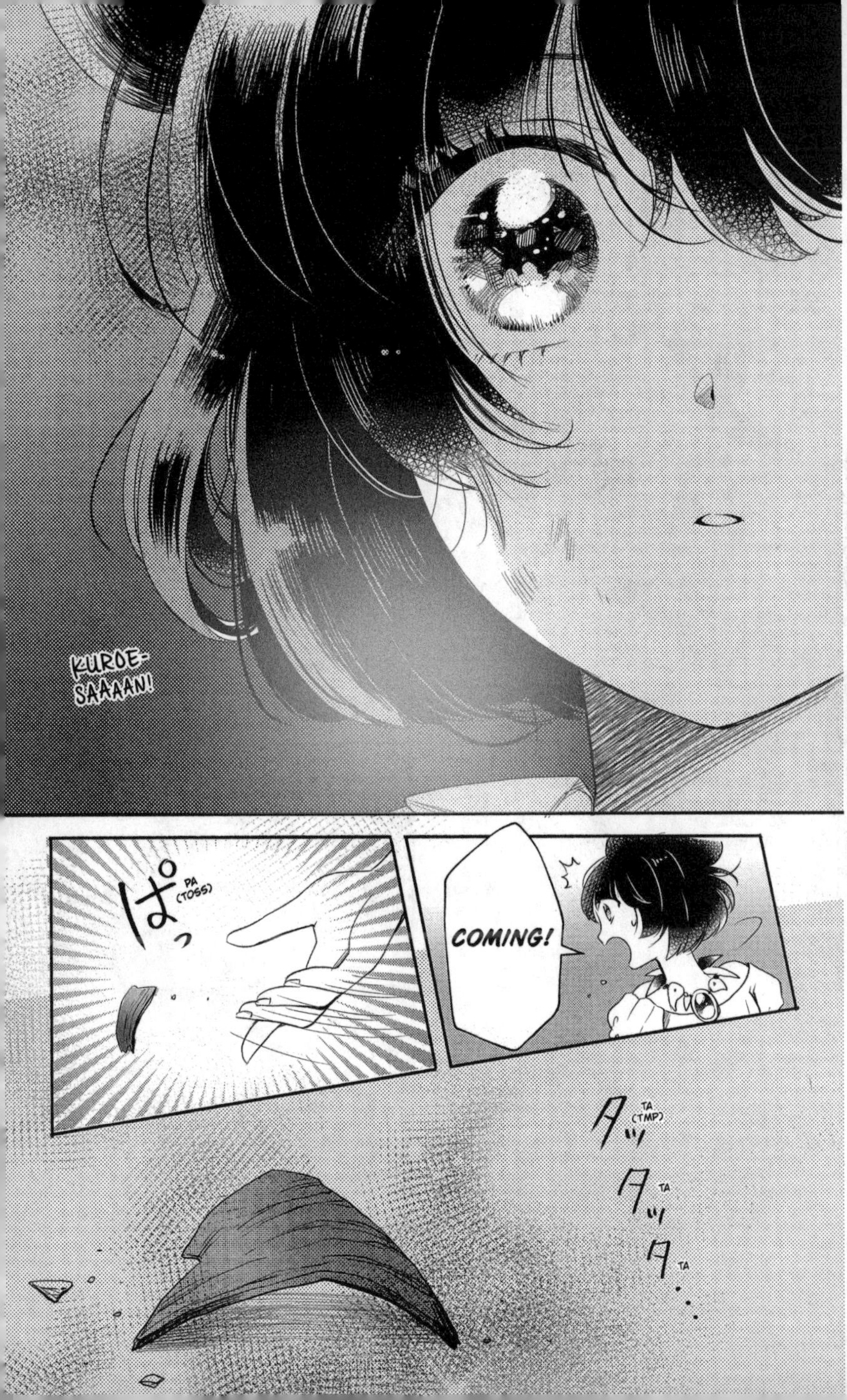
KUROE-SAAAAN!
COMING!
ぱっ
PA (TOSS)
タッ
TA (TMP)
タッ
TA
タ
TA

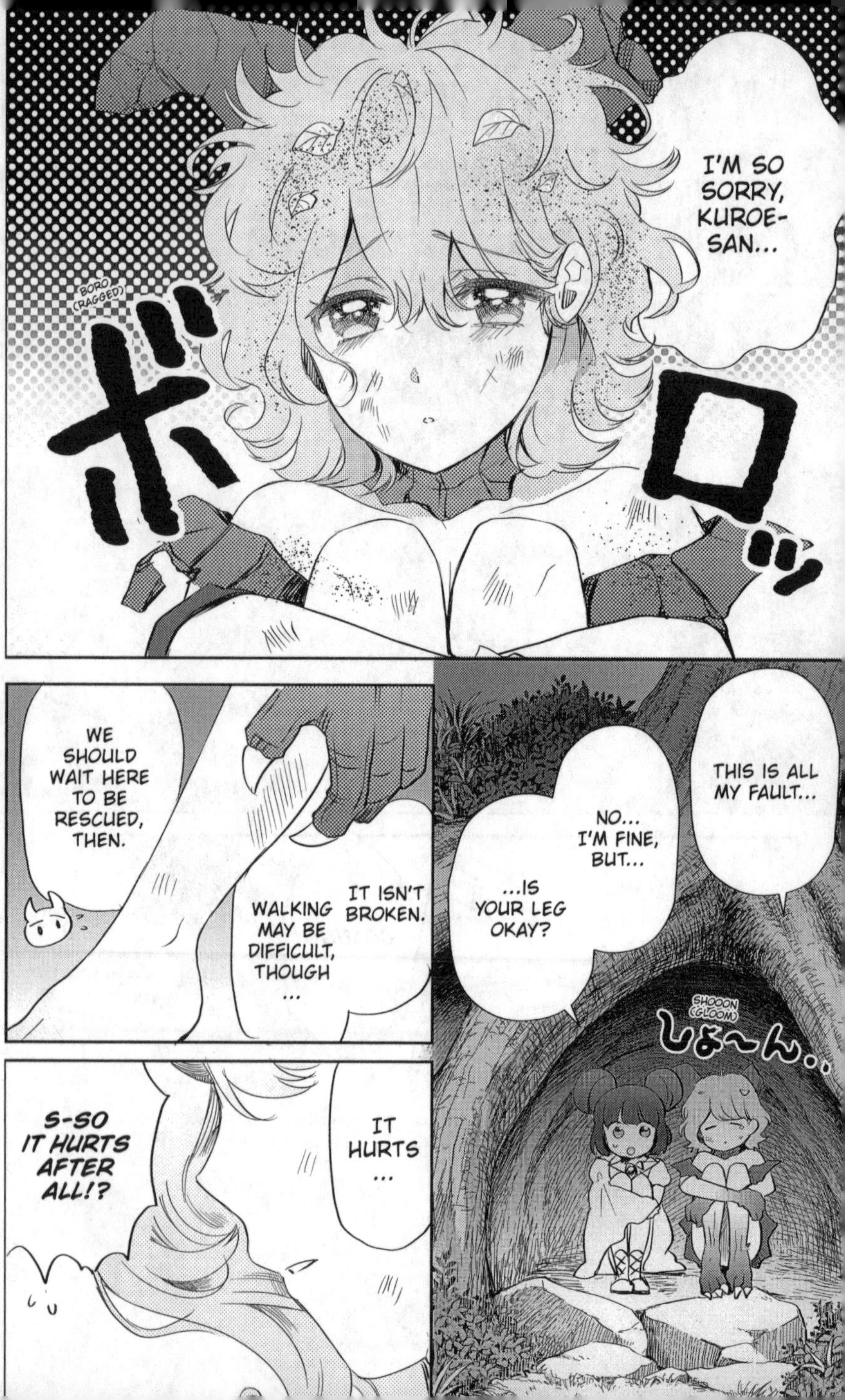
I'M SO SORRY, KUROE-SAN...
BORO (RAGGED)
ボロッ
THIS IS ALL MY FAULT...
NO... I'M FINE, BUT...
...IS YOUR LEG OKAY?
SHOOON (GLOOM)
しょ～ん。。
IT ISN'T BROKEN.
WALKING MAY BE DIFFICULT, THOUGH...
WE SHOULD WAIT HERE TO BE RESCUED, THEN.
IT HURTS...
S-SO IT HURTS AFTER ALL!?

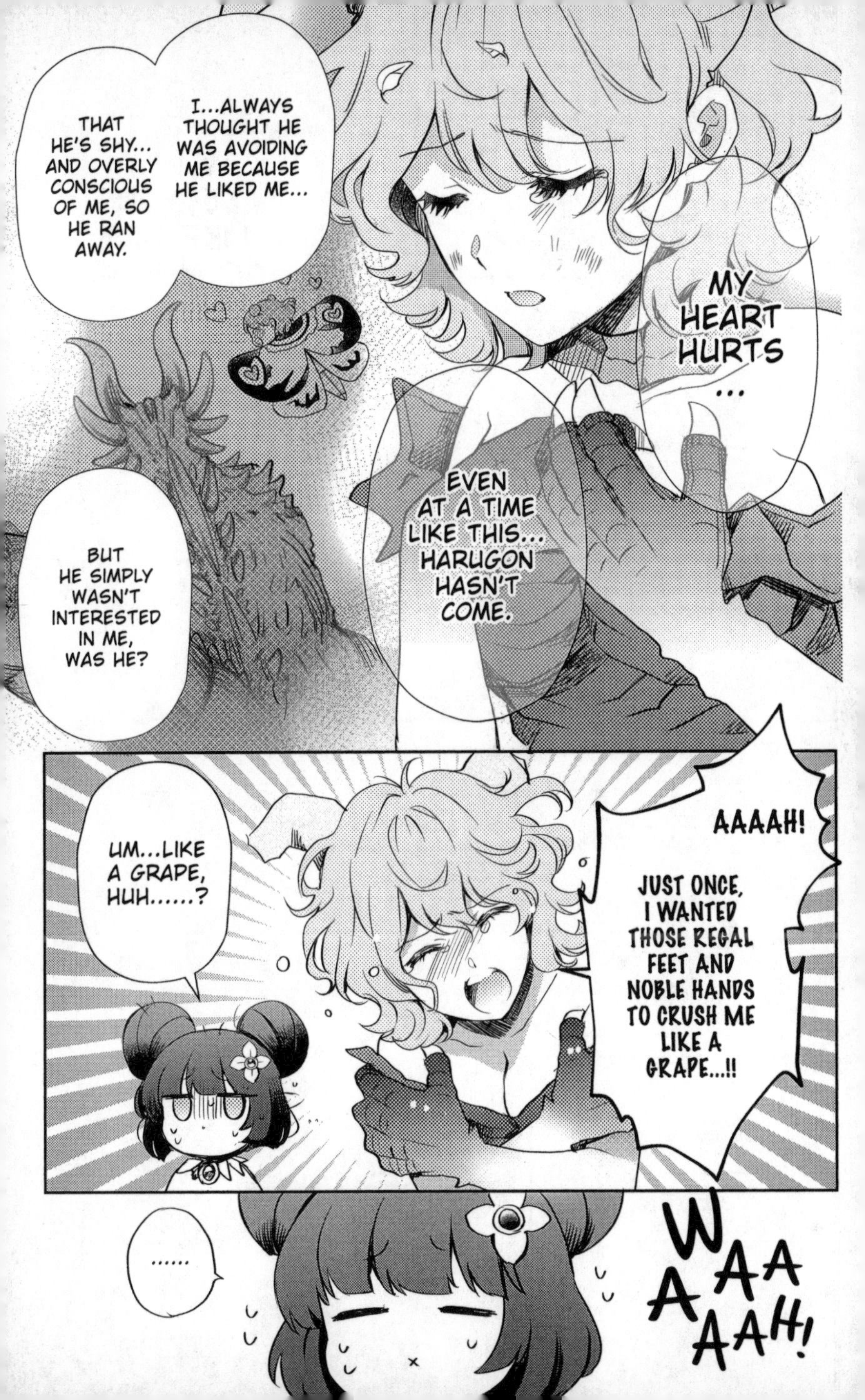
MY HEART HURTS ...
EVEN AT A TIME LIKE THIS... HARUGON HASN'T COME.
I...ALWAYS THOUGHT HE WAS AVOIDING ME BECAUSE HE LIKED ME...
THAT HE'S SHY... AND OVERLY CONSCIOUS OF ME, SO HE RAN AWAY.
BUT HE SIMPLY WASN'T INTERESTED IN ME, WAS HE?
AAAAH!
JUST ONCE, I WANTED THOSE REGAL FEET AND NOBLE HANDS TO CRUSH ME LIKE A GRAPE...!!
UM...LIKE A GRAPE, HUH......?
WAAAAAAH!
......

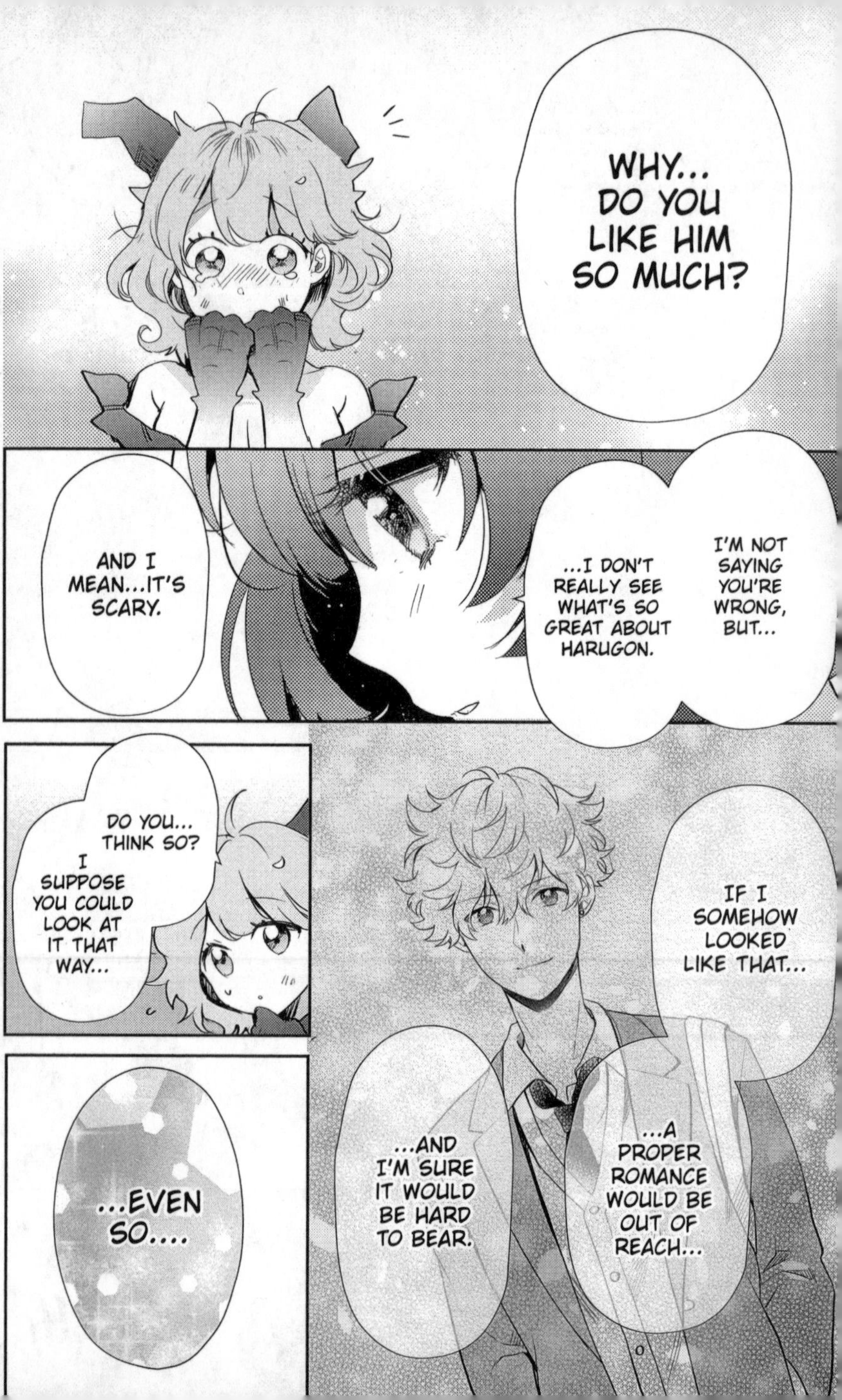
WHY... DO YOU LIKE HIM SO MUCH?
I'M NOT SAYING YOU'RE WRONG, BUT...
...I DON'T REALLY SEE WHAT'S SO GREAT ABOUT HARUGON.
AND I MEAN...IT'S SCARY.
IF I SOMEHOW LOOKED LIKE THAT...
...A PROPER ROMANCE WOULD BE OUT OF REACH...
...AND I'M SURE IT WOULD BE HARD TO BEAR.
DO YOU... THINK SO?
I SUPPOSE YOU COULD LOOK AT IT THAT WAY...
...EVEN SO....

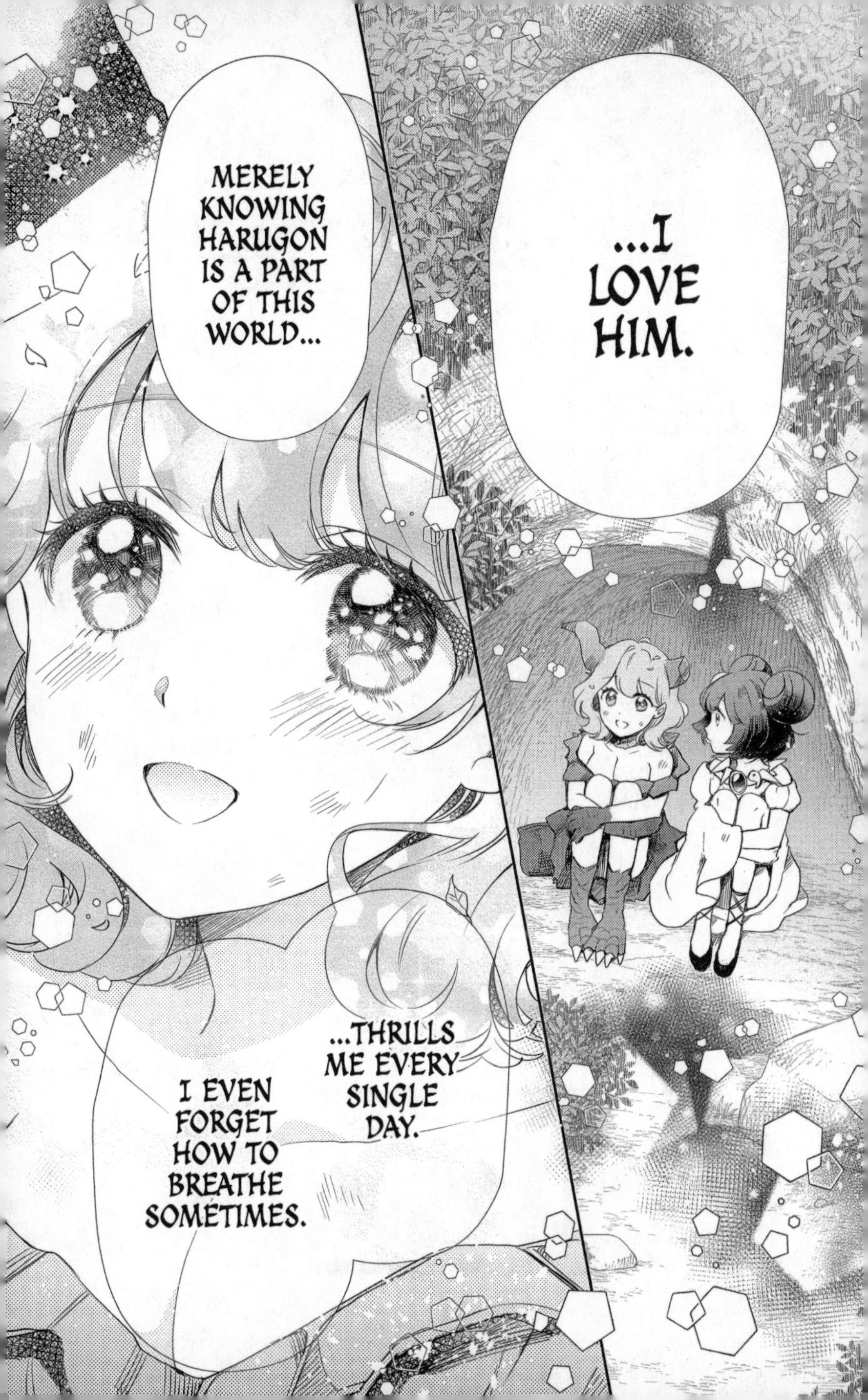
...I LOVE HIM.
MERELY KNOWING HARUGON IS A PART OF THIS WORLD...
...THRILLS ME EVERY SINGLE DAY.
I EVEN FORGET HOW TO BREATHE SOMETIMES.

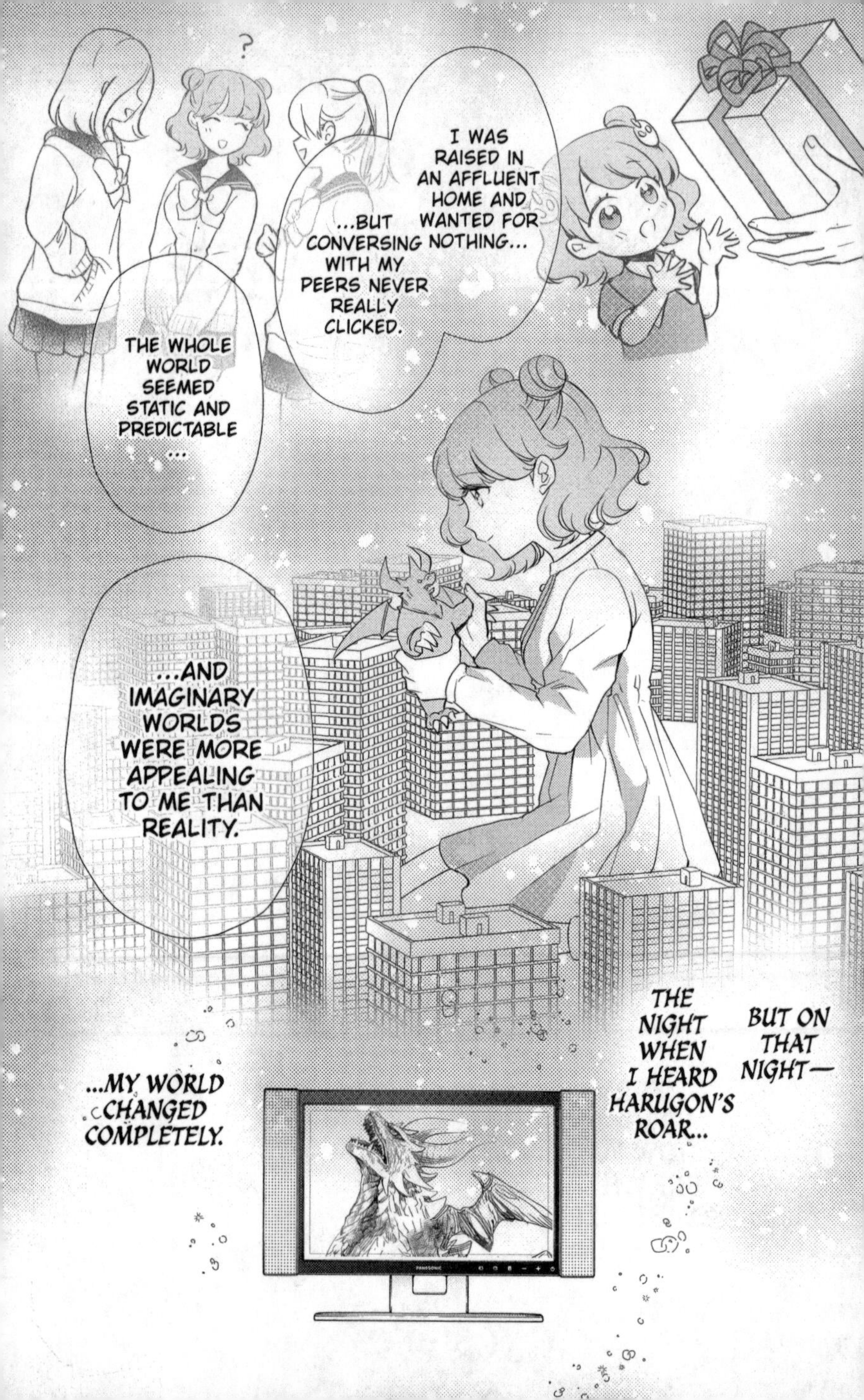
I WAS RAISED IN AN AFFLUENT HOME AND WANTED FOR NOTHING...
...BUT CONVERSING WITH MY PEERS NEVER REALLY CLICKED.
?
THE WHOLE WORLD SEEMED STATIC AND PREDICTABLE...
...AND IMAGINARY WORLDS WERE MORE APPEALING TO ME THAN REALITY.
BUT ON THAT NIGHT—
THE NIGHT WHEN I HEARD HARUGON'S ROAR...
...MY WORLD CHANGED COMPLETELY.

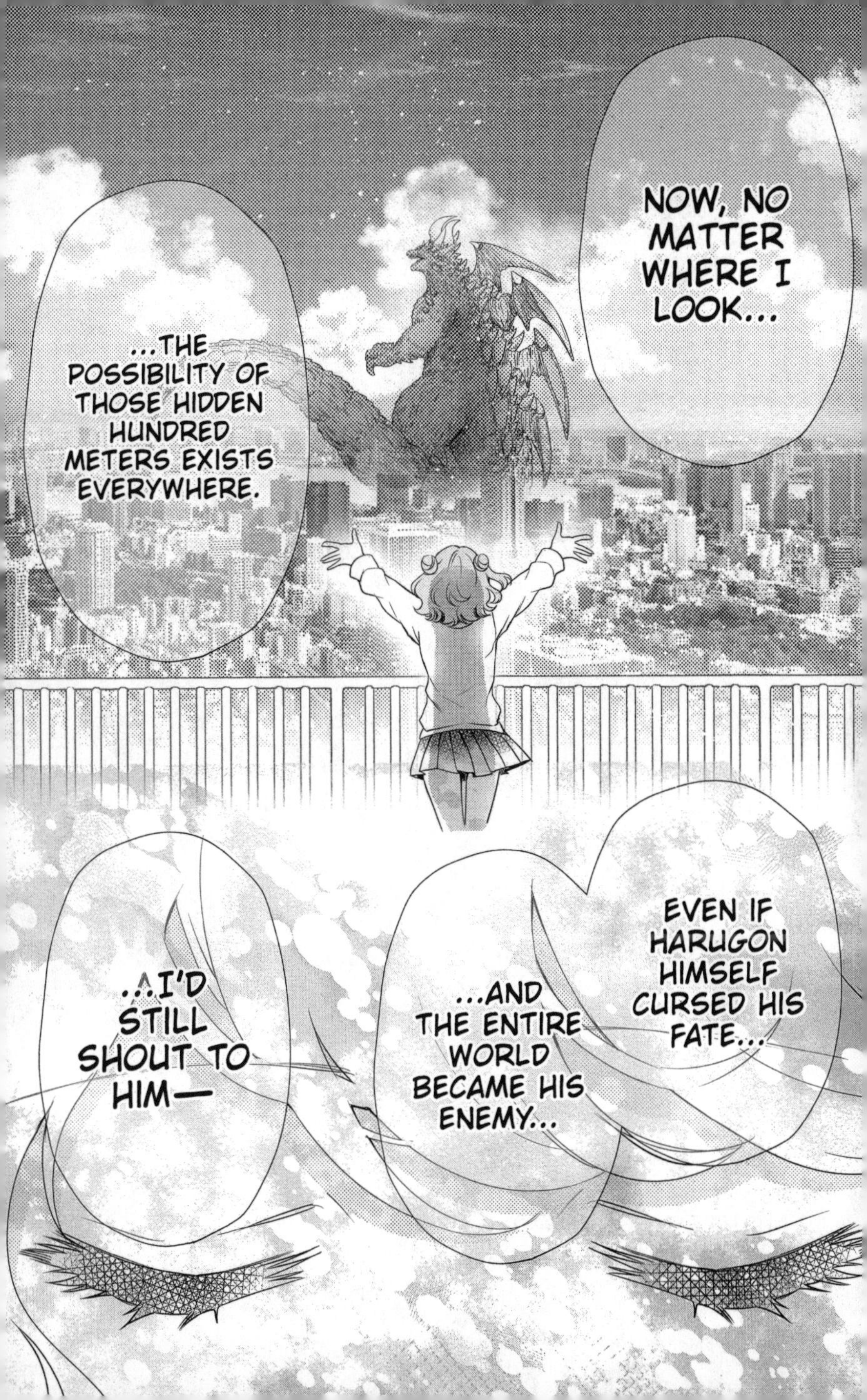
NOW, NO MATTER WHERE I LOOK...
...THE POSSIBILITY OF THOSE HIDDEN HUNDRED METERS EXISTS EVERYWHERE.
EVEN IF HARUGON HIMSELF CURSED HIS FATE...
...AND THE ENTIRE WORLD BECAME HIS ENEMY...
...I'D STILL SHOUT TO HIM—

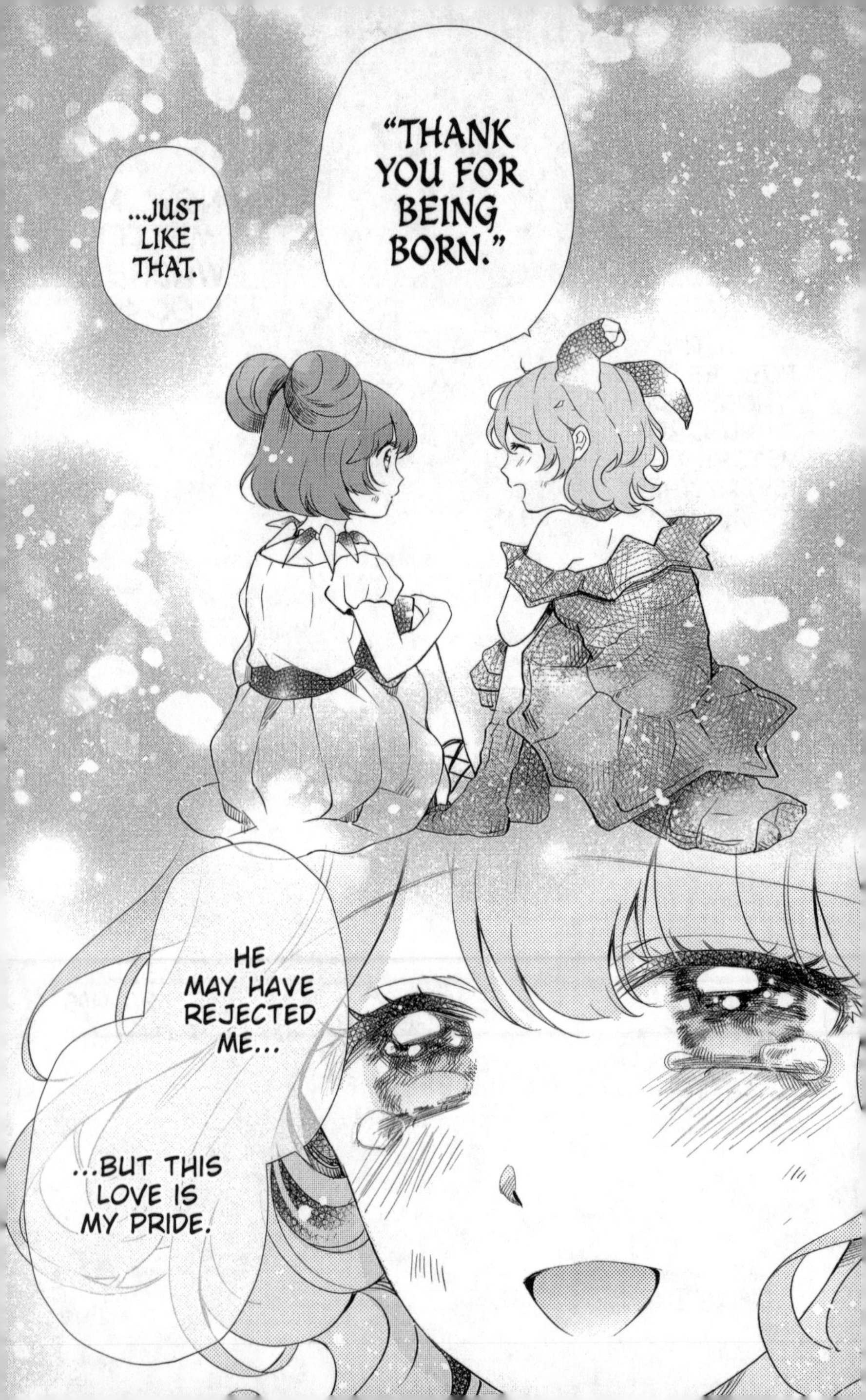
"THANK YOU FOR BEING BORN."
...JUST LIKE THAT.
HE MAY HAVE REJECTED ME...
...BUT THIS LOVE IS MY PRIDE.

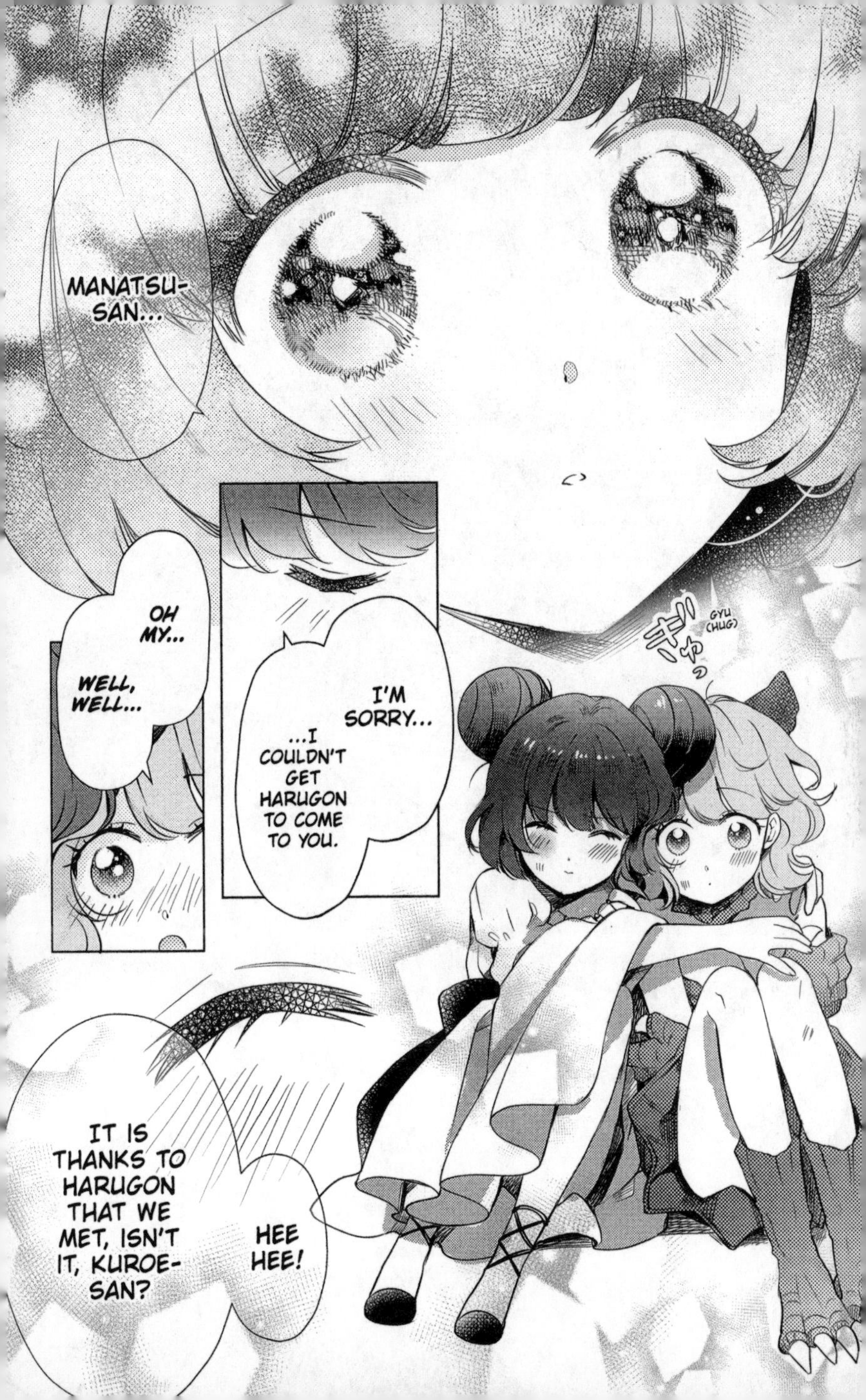
MANATSU-SAN...
ぎゅっ
GYU (HUG)
I'M SORRY... ...I COULDN'T GET HARUGON TO COME TO YOU.
OH MY... WELL, WELL...
IT IS THANKS TO HARUGON THAT WE MET, ISN'T IT, KUROE-SAN?
HEE HEE!

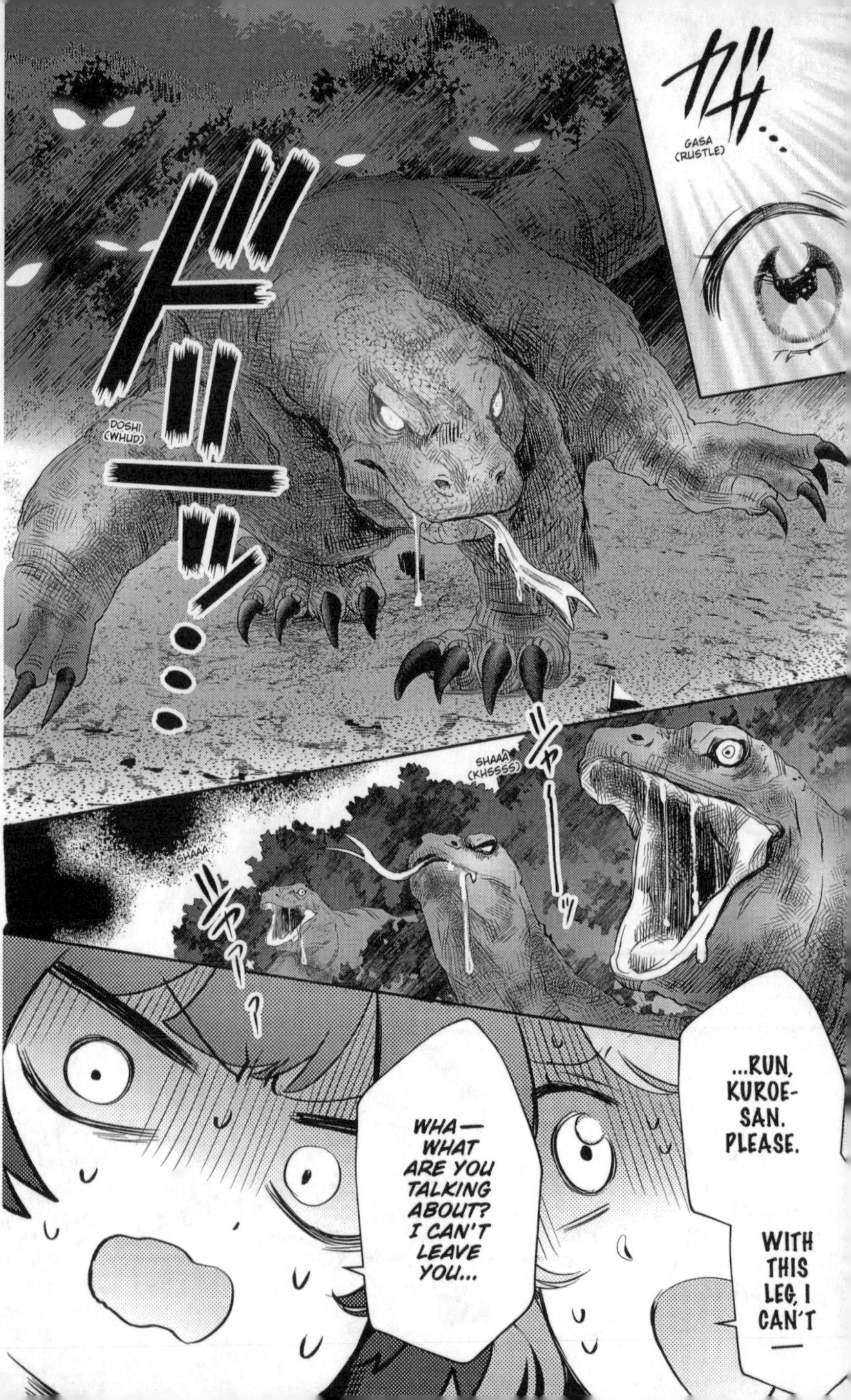
GASA (RUSTLE)
DOSHI (WHUD)
SHAAA (KHSSSS)
SHAAA
...RUN, KUROE-SAN. PLEASE.
WITH THIS LEG, I CAN'T—
WHA— WHAT ARE YOU TALKING ABOUT? I CAN'T LEAVE YOU...

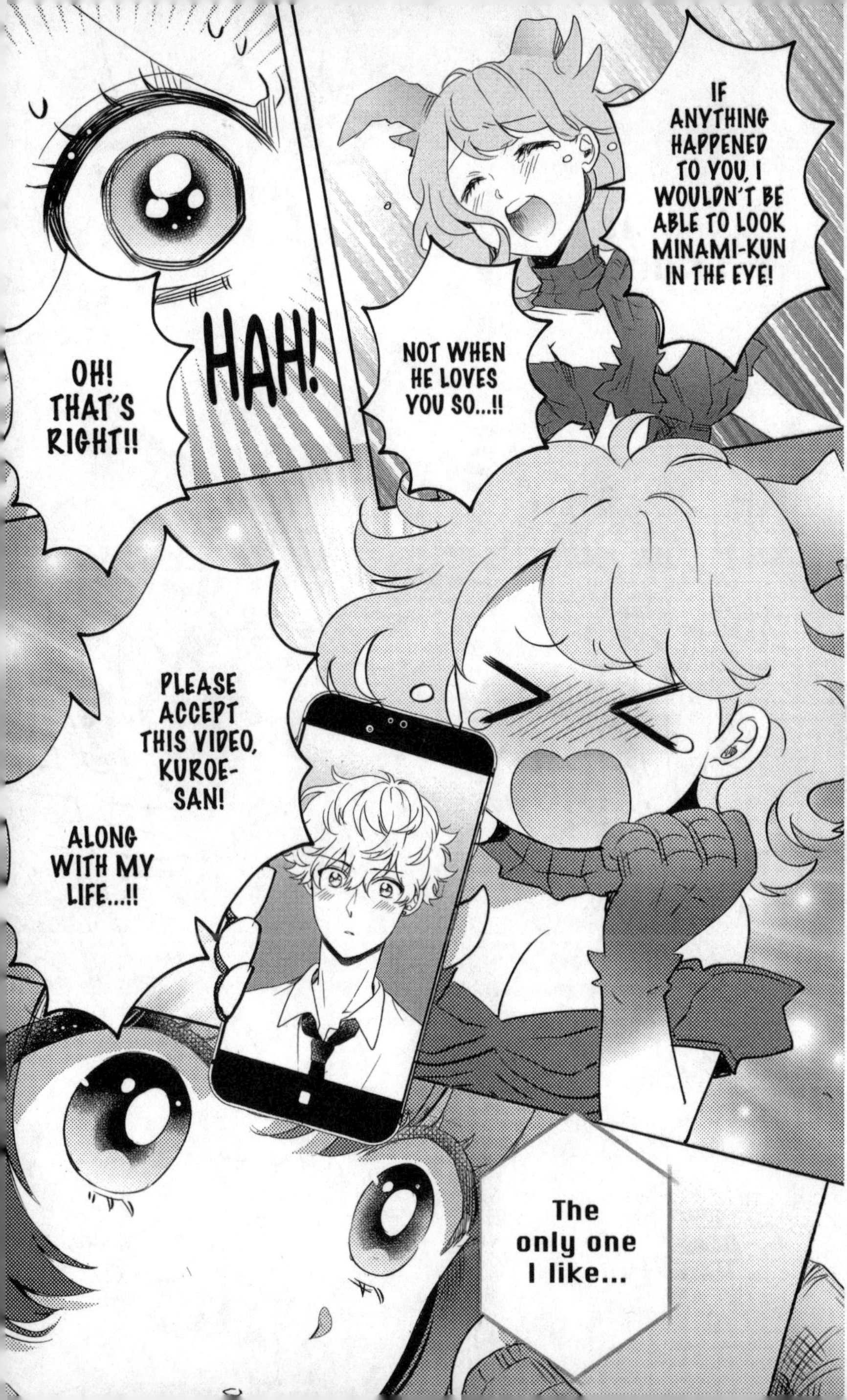
IF ANYTHING HAPPENED TO YOU, I WOULDN'T BE ABLE TO LOOK MINAMI-KUN IN THE EYE!
NOT WHEN HE LOVES YOU SO...!!
HAH!
OH! THAT'S RIGHT!!
PLEASE ACCEPT THIS VIDEO, KUROE-SAN!
ALONG WITH MY LIFE...!!
The only one I like...

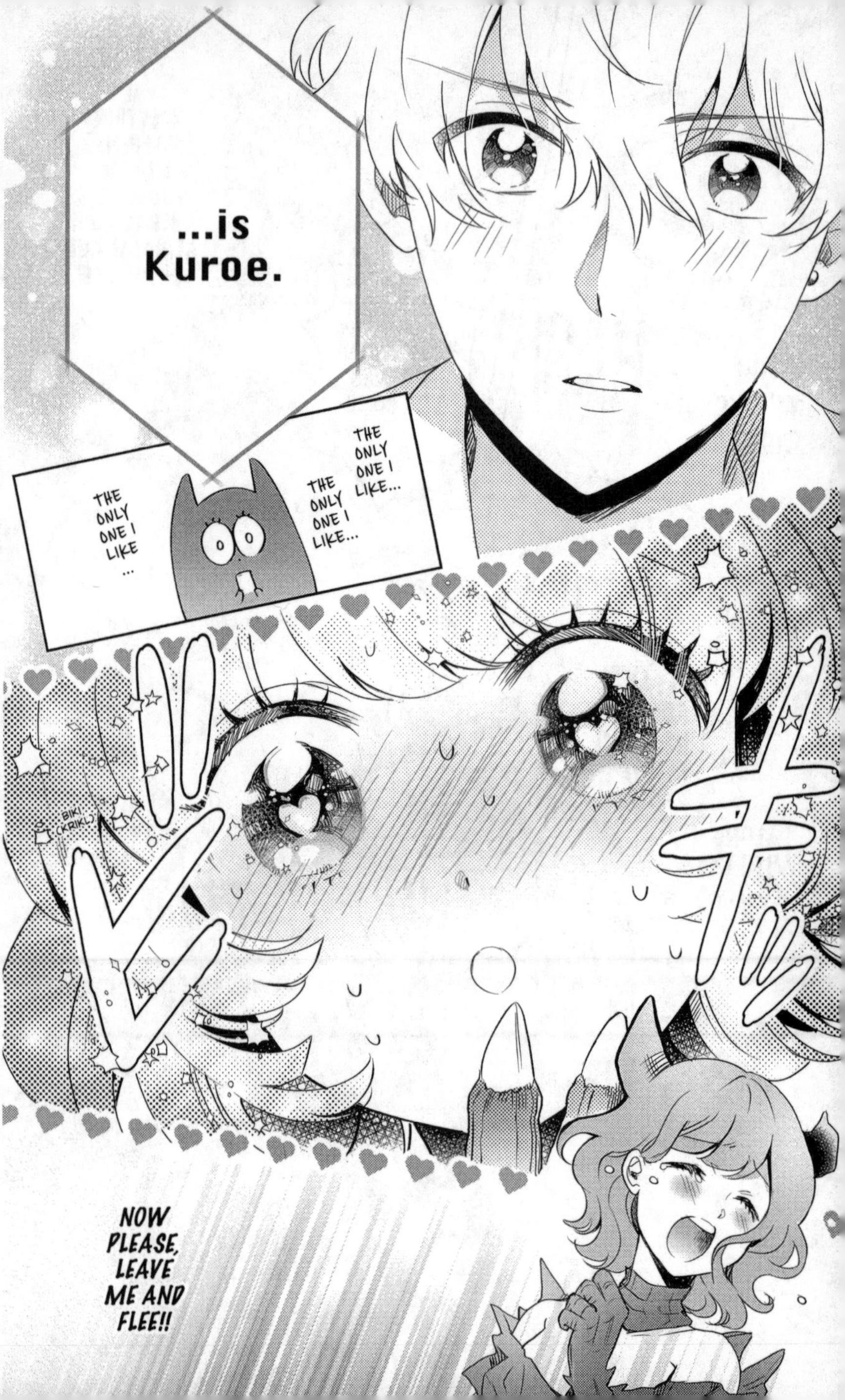
...is Kuroe.
THE ONLY ONE I LIKE...
THE ONLY ONE I LIKE...
THE ONLY ONE I LIKE...
BIKI (KRIK)
NOW PLEASE, LEAVE ME AND FLEE!!

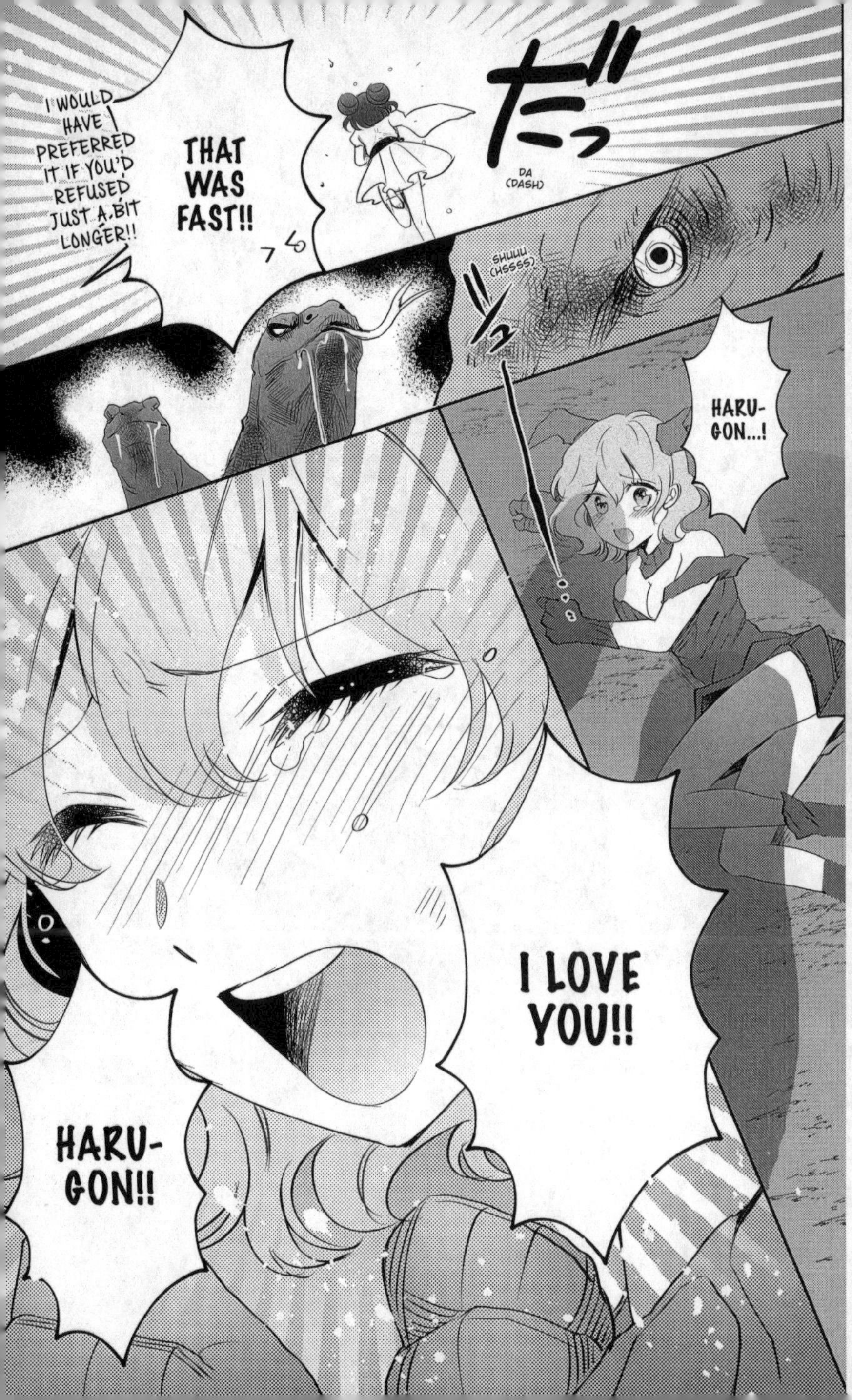
だっ
DA (DASH)
THAT WAS FAST!!
I WOULD HAVE PREFERRED IT IF YOU'D REFUSED JUST A BIT LONGER!!
SHUUU (HSSSS)
HARU-GON...!
I LOVE YOU!!
HARU-GON!!

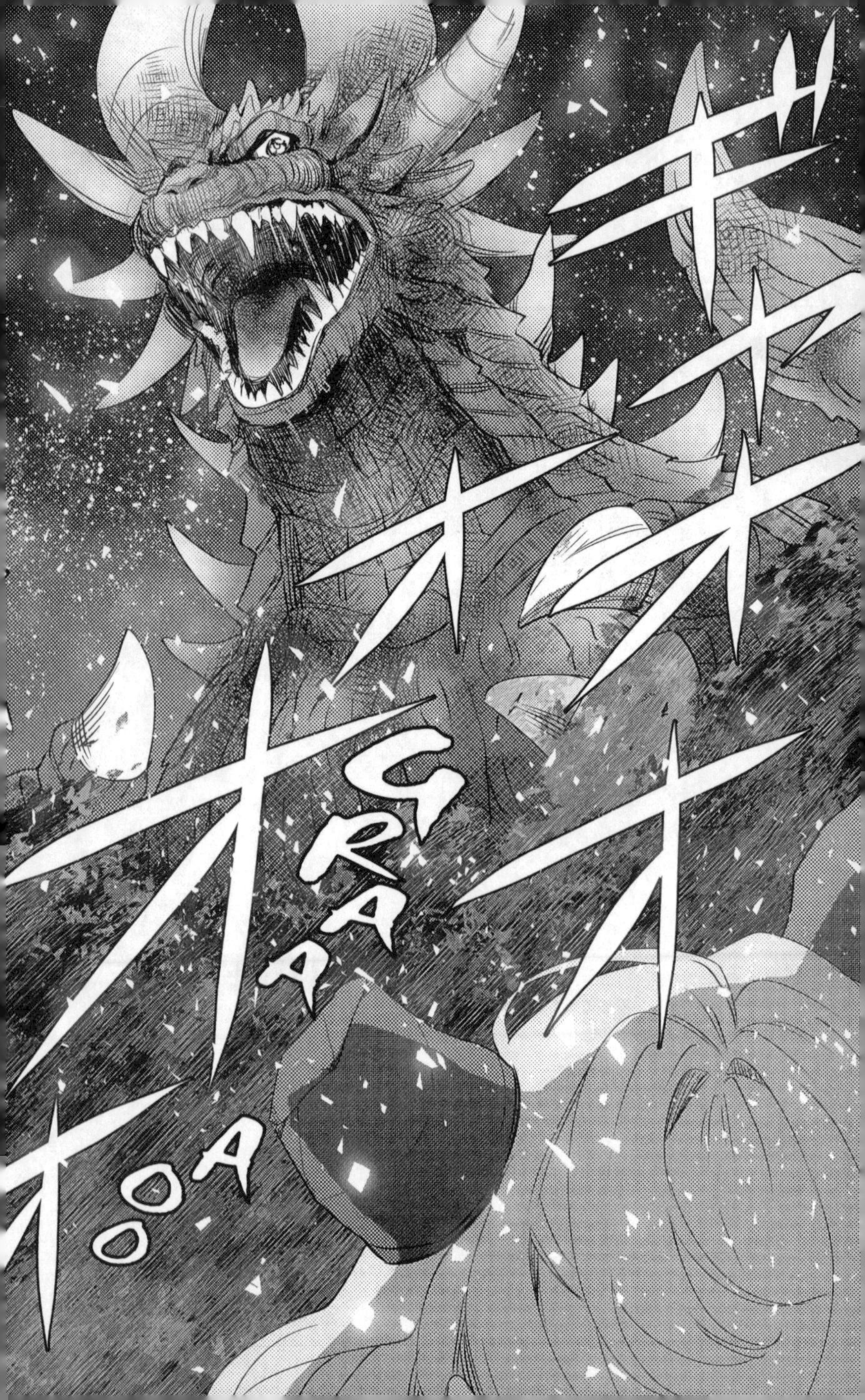
GRAAAOO

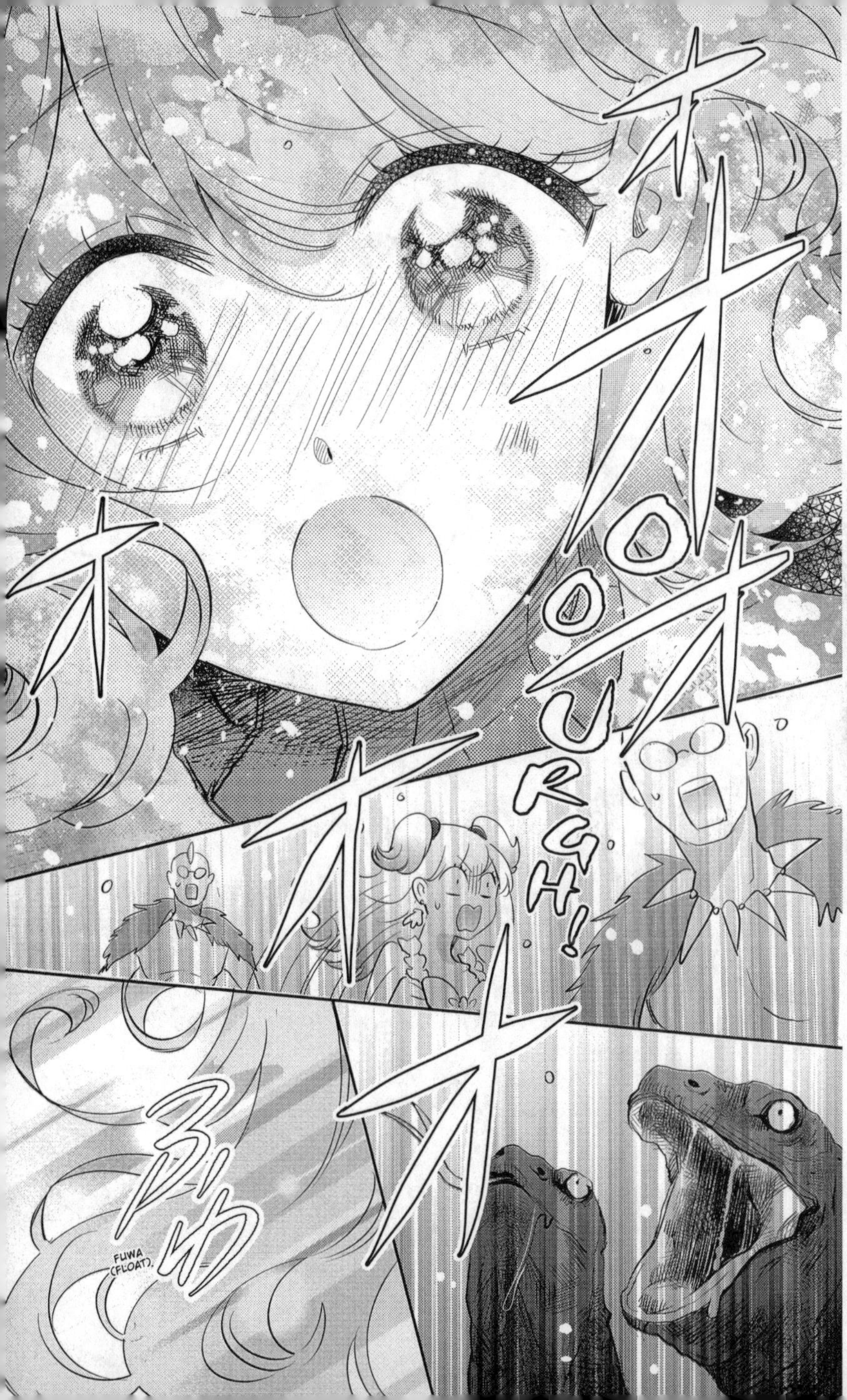

オオオオオ
OOURGH!
ふわ
FUWA (FLOAT)

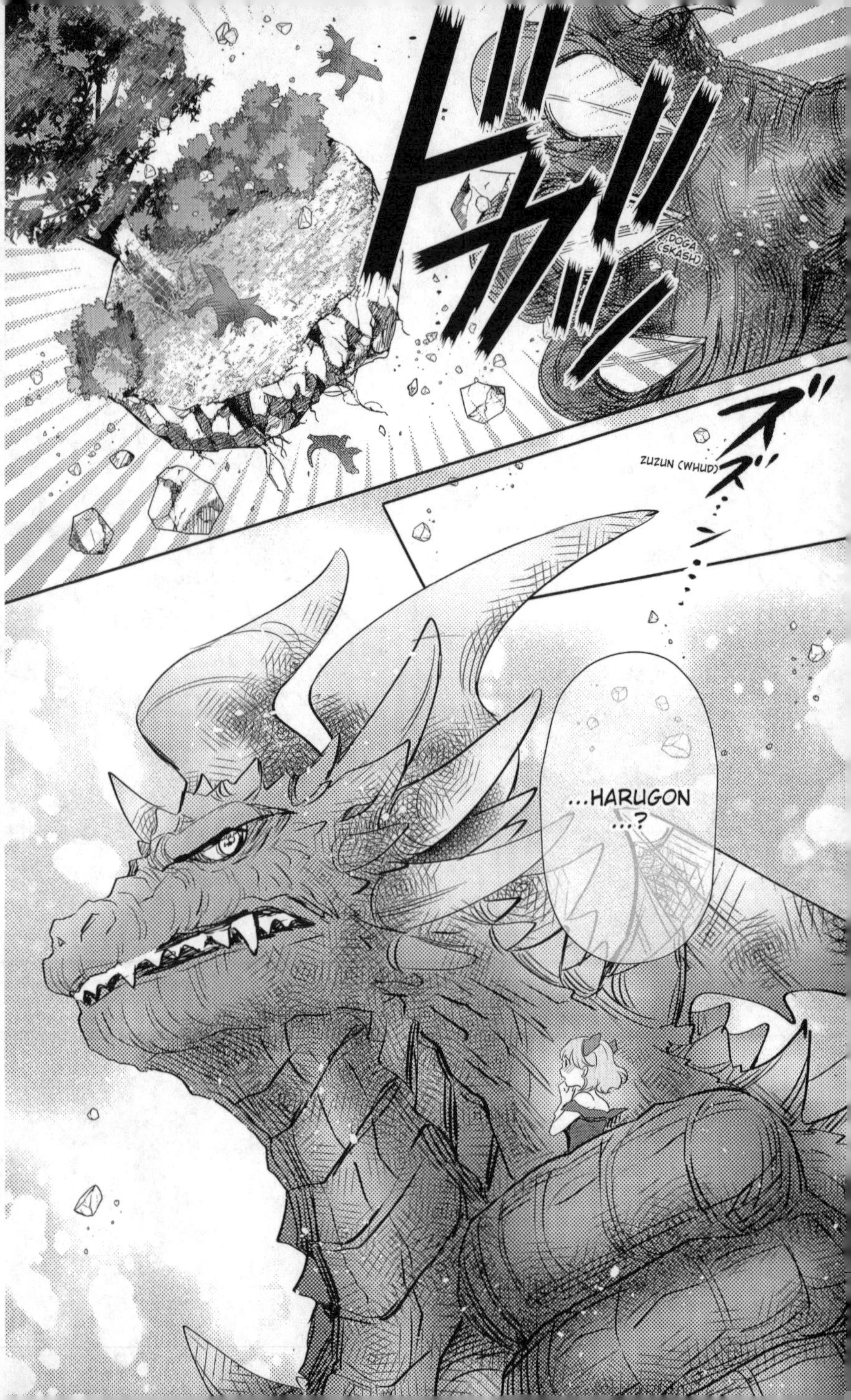
DOGA (SKASH)
ZUZUN (WHUD)
...HARUGON ...?

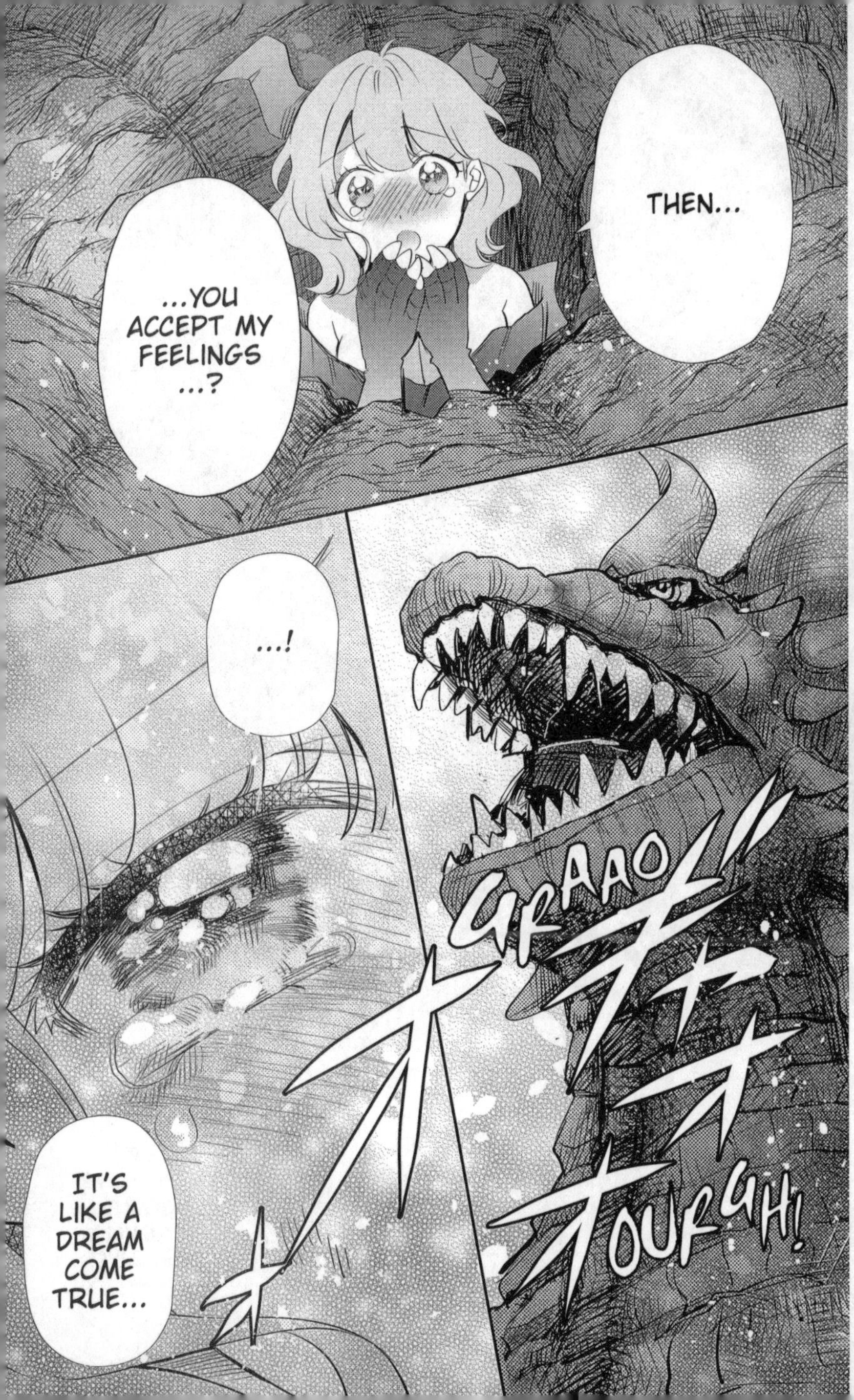
THEN...
...YOU ACCEPT MY FEELINGS ...?
GRAAOOOURGH!
...!
IT'S LIKE A DREAM COME TRUE...

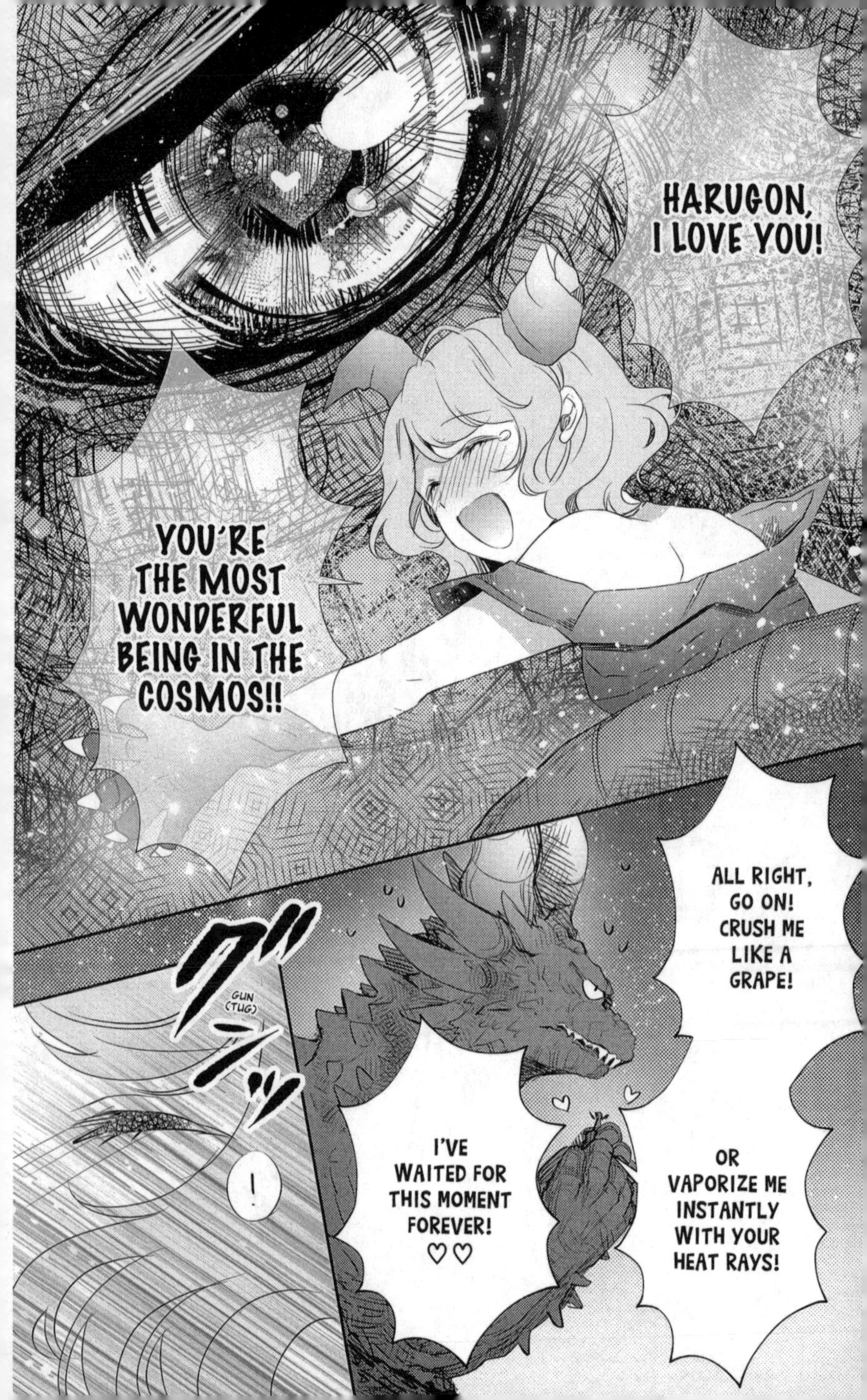
HARUGON, I LOVE YOU!
YOU'RE THE MOST WONDERFUL BEING IN THE COSMOS!!
ALL RIGHT, GO ON! CRUSH ME LIKE A GRAPE!
OR VAPORIZE ME INSTANTLY WITH YOUR HEAT RAYS!
I'VE WAITED FOR THIS MOMENT FOREVER! ♡♡
GUN (TUG)
!

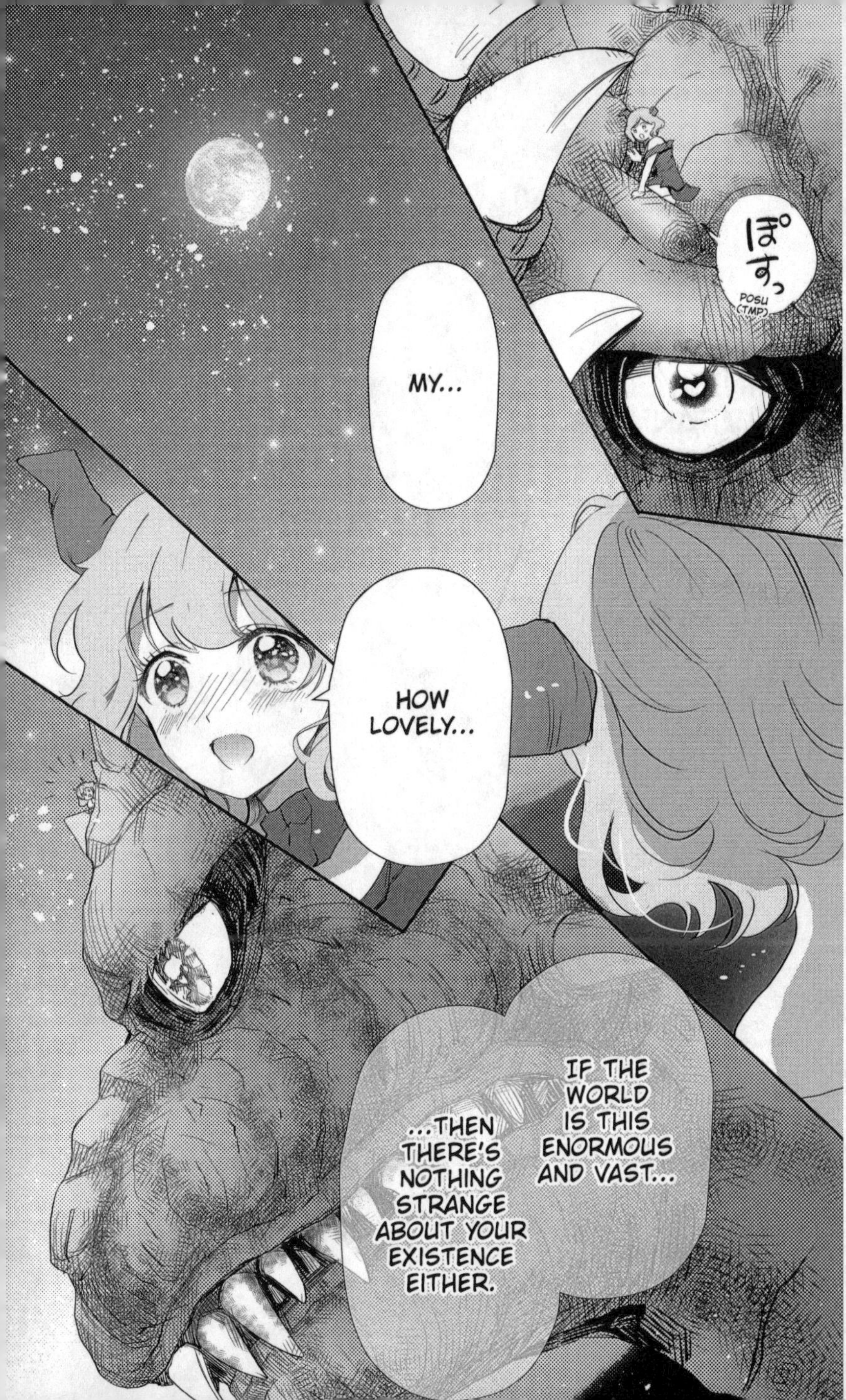
ぽすっ
POSU (TMP)
MY...
HOW LOVELY...
IF THE WORLD IS THIS ENORMOUS AND VAST...
...THEN THERE'S NOTHING STRANGE ABOUT YOUR EXISTENCE EITHER.

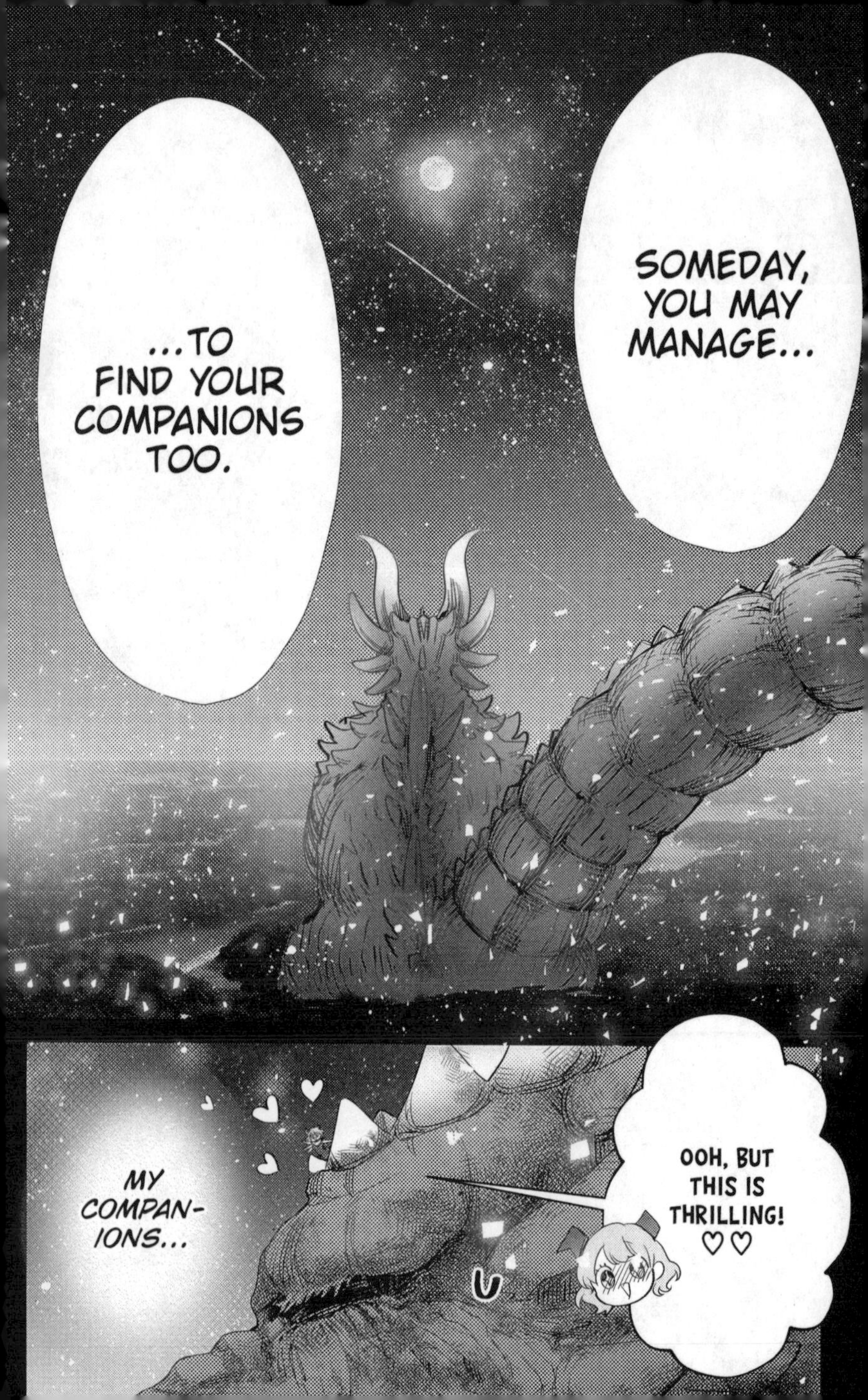
SOMEDAY, YOU MAY MANAGE...
...TO FIND YOUR COMPANIONS TOO.
OOH, BUT THIS IS THRILLING! ♡♡
MY COMPAN-IONS...

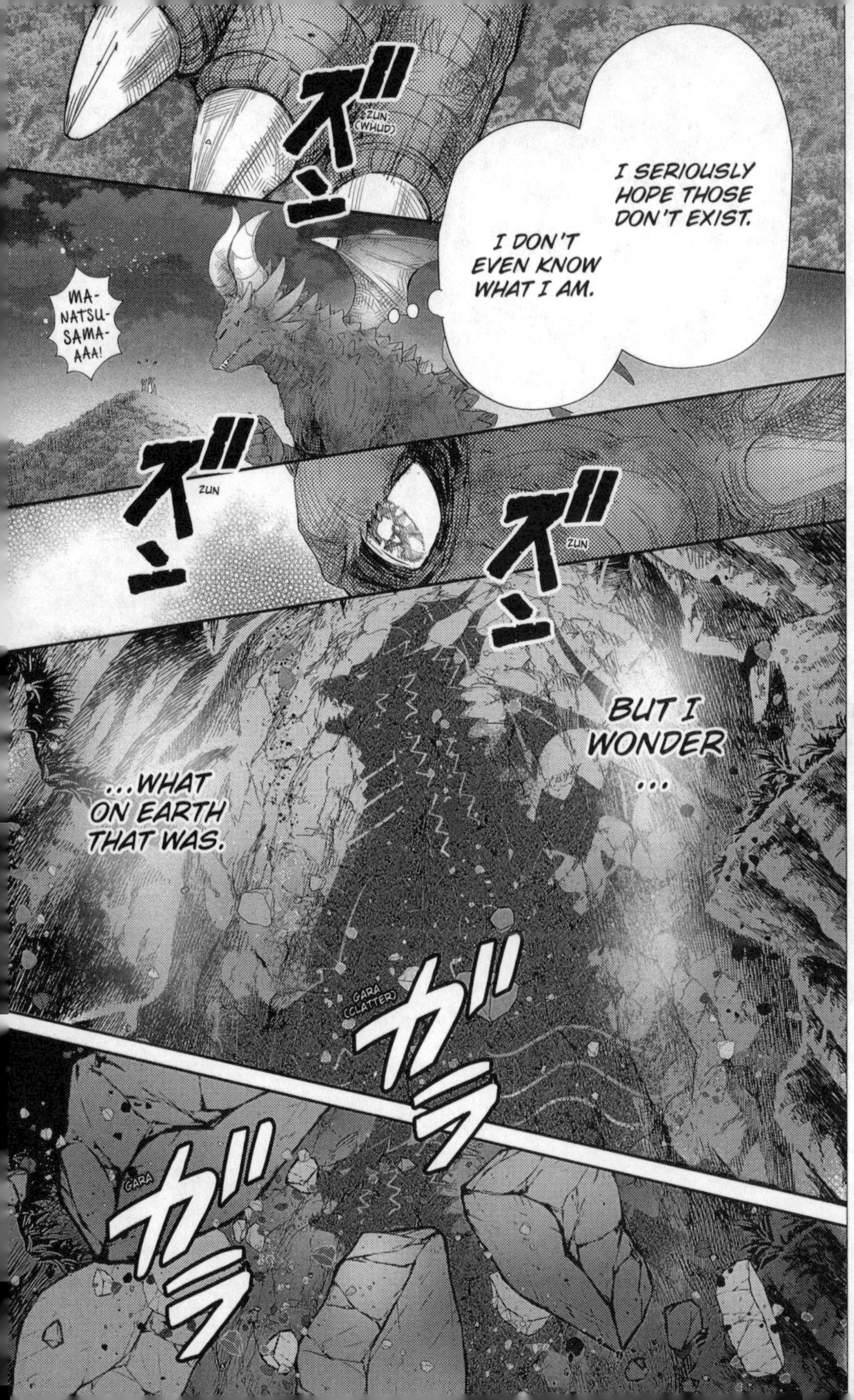
ZUN (WHUD)
I SERIOUSLY HOPE THOSE DON'T EXIST.
I DON'T EVEN KNOW WHAT I AM.
MA-NATSU-SAMA-AAA!
ZUN
ZUN
BUT I WONDER...
...WHAT ON EARTH THAT WAS.
GARA (CLATTER)
GARA

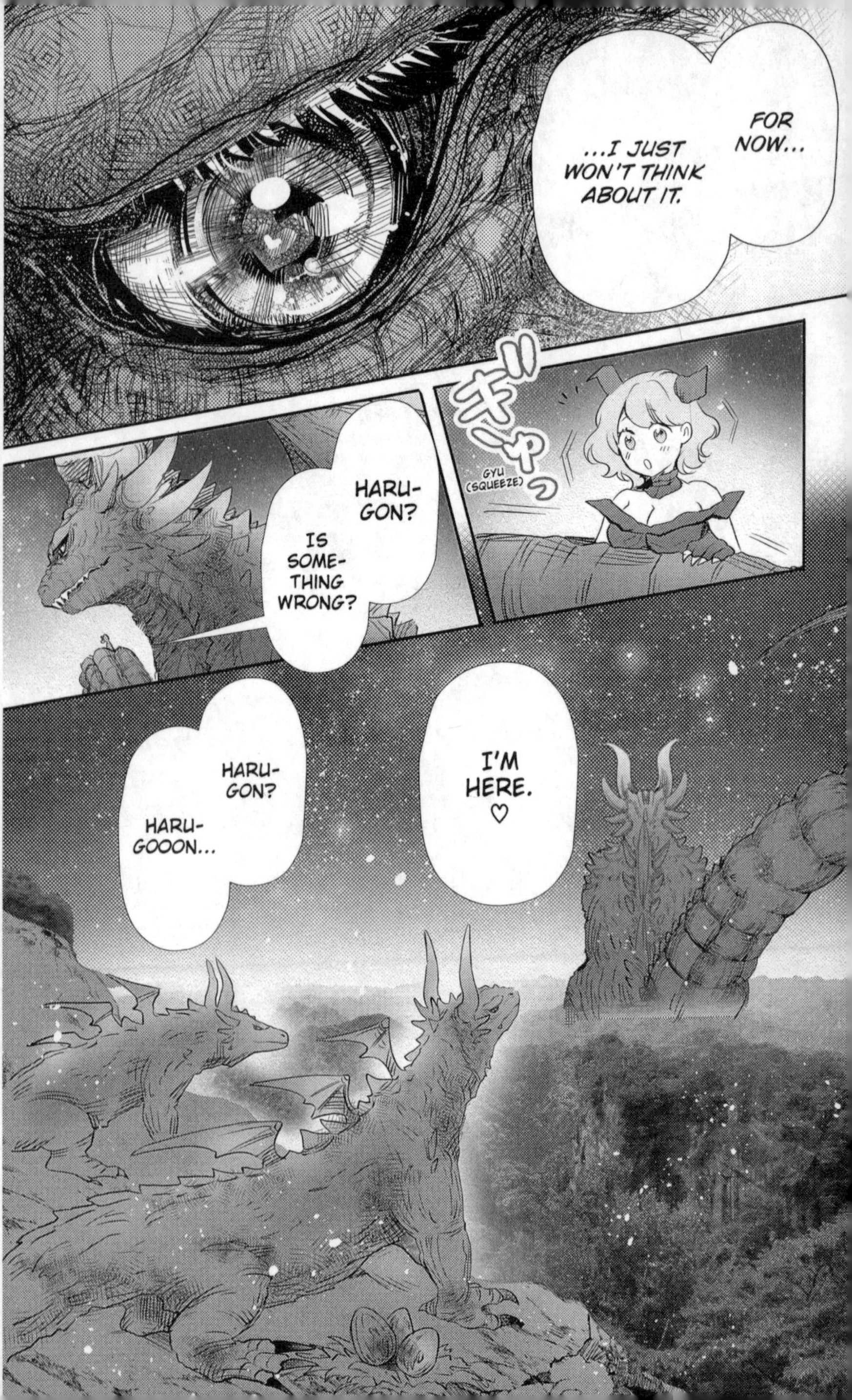
FOR NOW...
...I JUST WON'T THINK ABOUT IT.
ギュッ
GYU (SQUEEZE)
HARU-GON?
IS SOME-THING WRONG?
I'M HERE. ♡
HARU-GON?
HARU-GOOON...

KAIJU♥GIRL
CARAMELISE

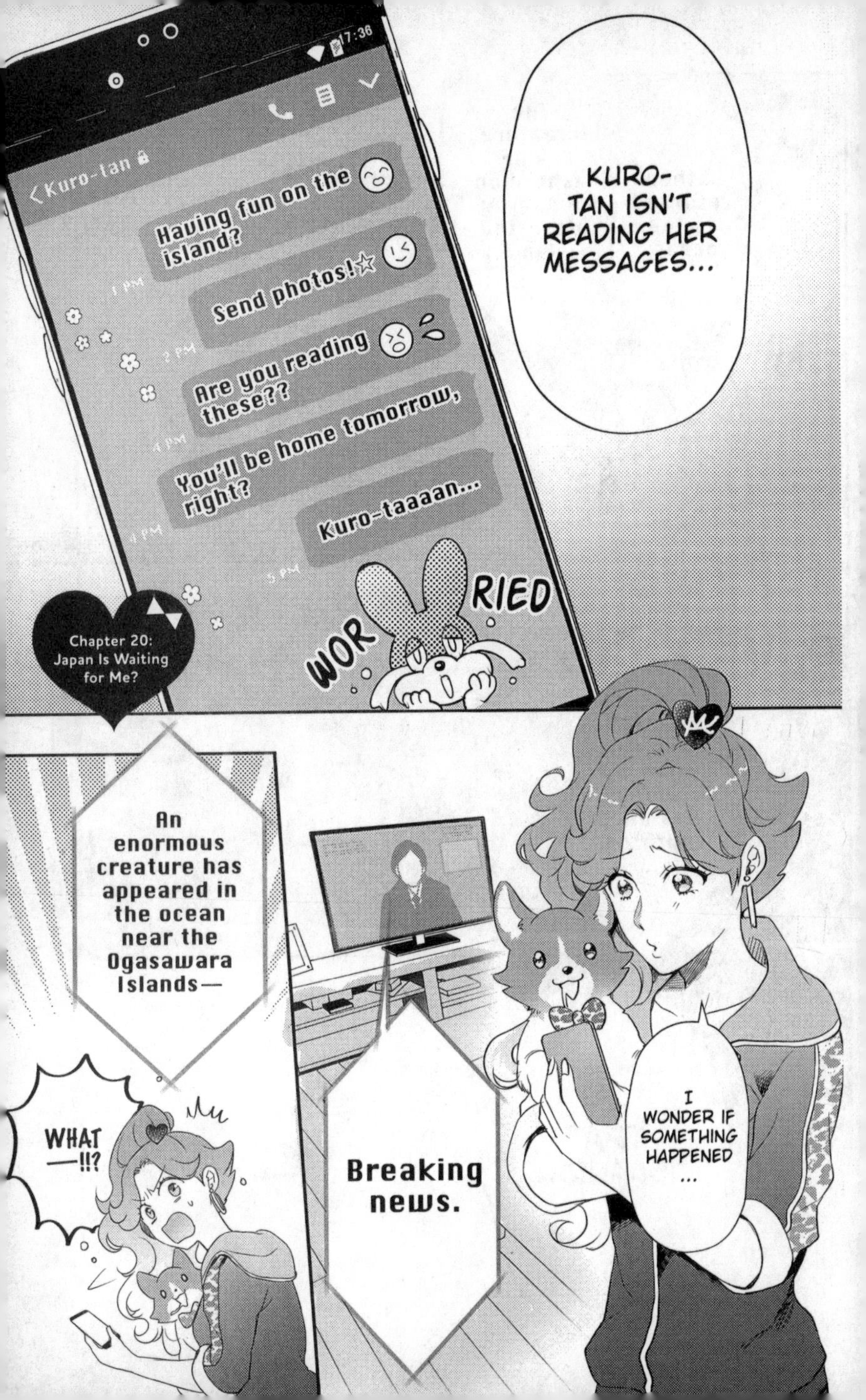
KURO-TAN ISN'T READING HER MESSAGES...
17:36
Kuro-tan
Having fun on the island?
Send photos!☆
Are you reading these??
You'll be home tomorrow, right?
Kuro-taaaan...
WOR RIED
Chapter 20: Japan Is Waiting for Me?
I WONDER IF SOMETHING HAPPENED...
Breaking news.
An enormous creature has appeared in the ocean near the Ogasawara Islands—
WHAT—!!?

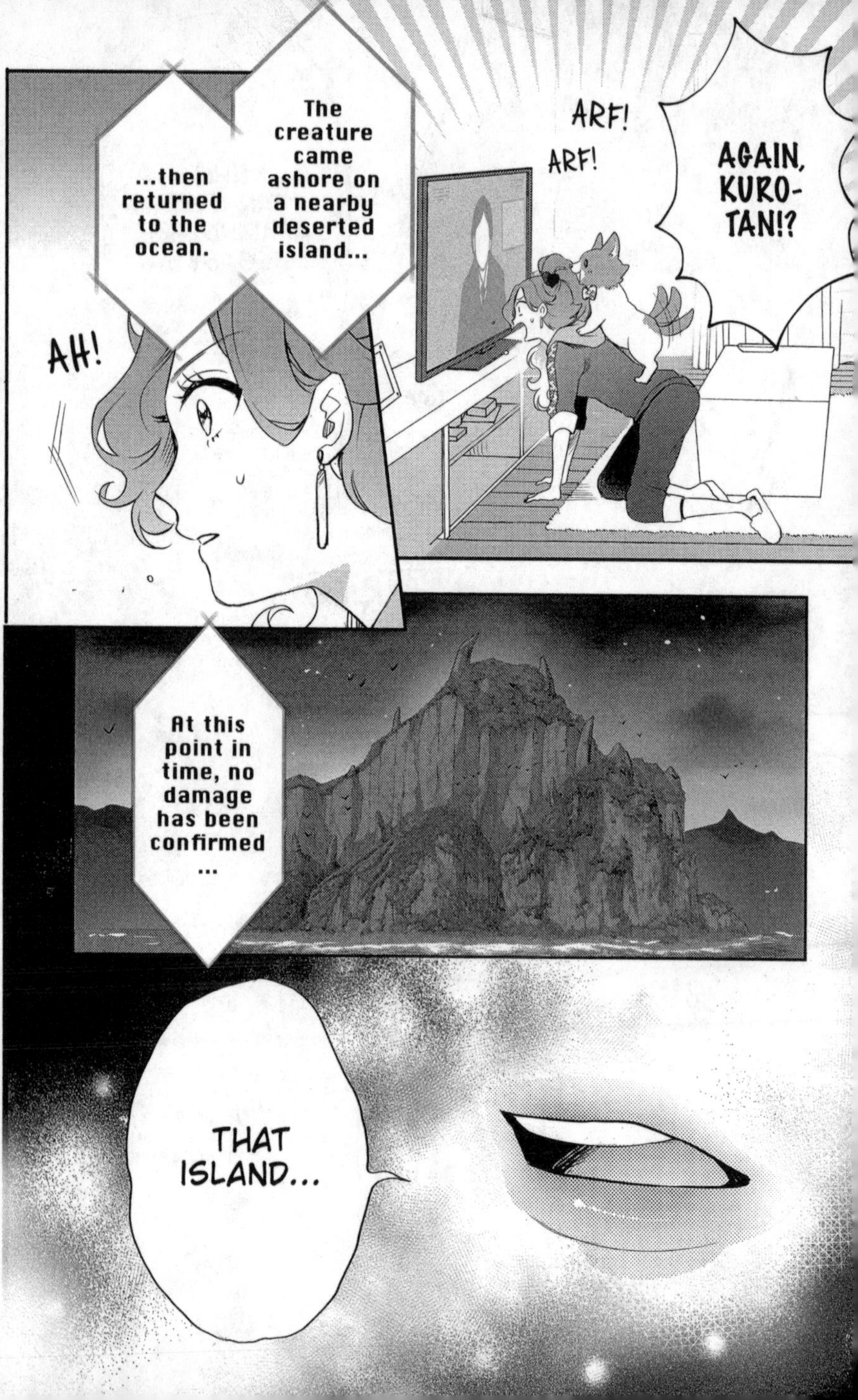
AGAIN, KURO-TAN!?
ARF!
ARF!
The creature came ashore on a nearby deserted island...
...then returned to the ocean.
AH!
At this point in time, no damage has been confirmed ...
THAT ISLAND...

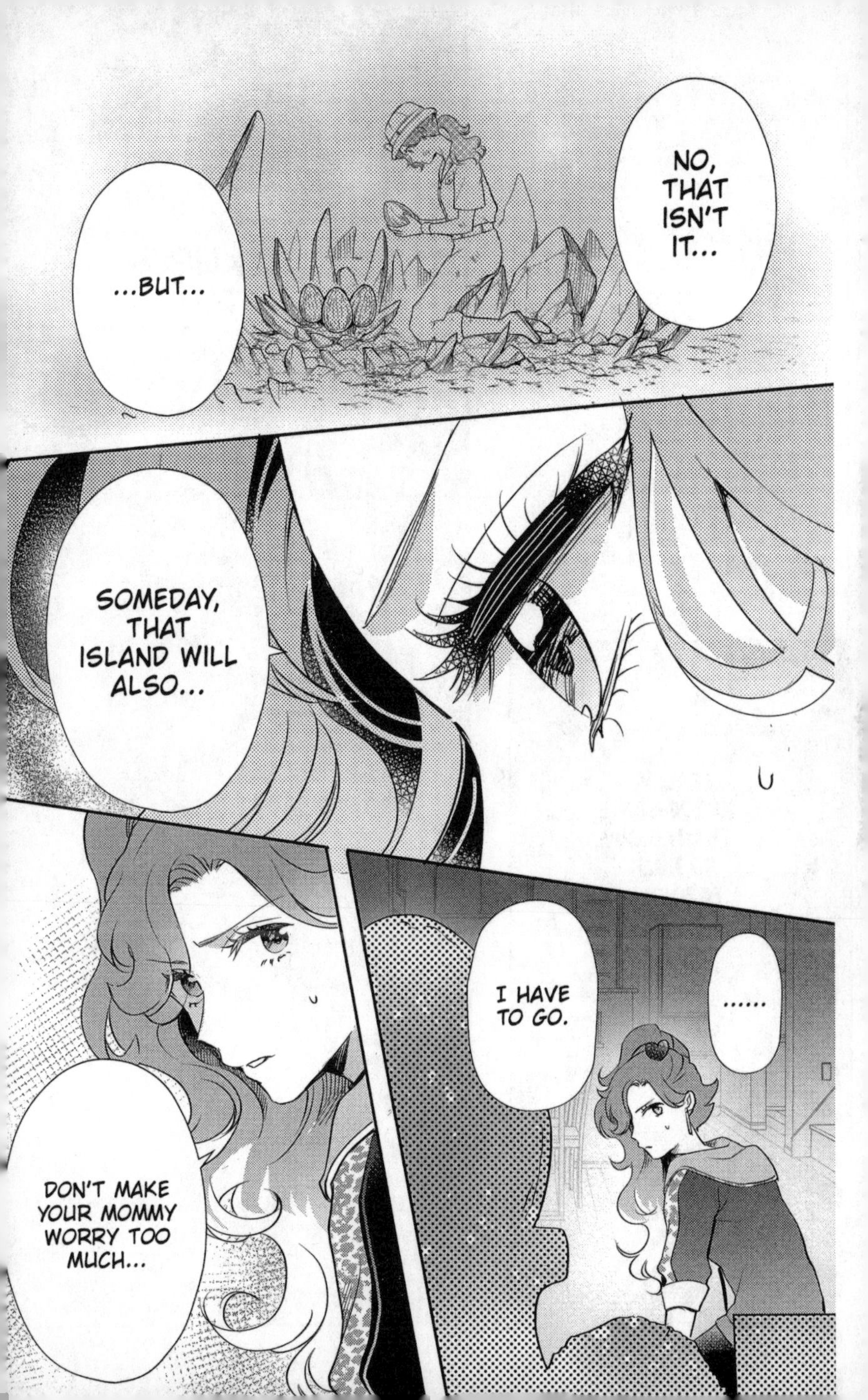
NO, THAT ISN'T IT...
...BUT...
SOMEDAY, THAT ISLAND WILL ALSO...
......
I HAVE TO GO.
DON'T MAKE YOUR MOMMY WORRY TOO MUCH...

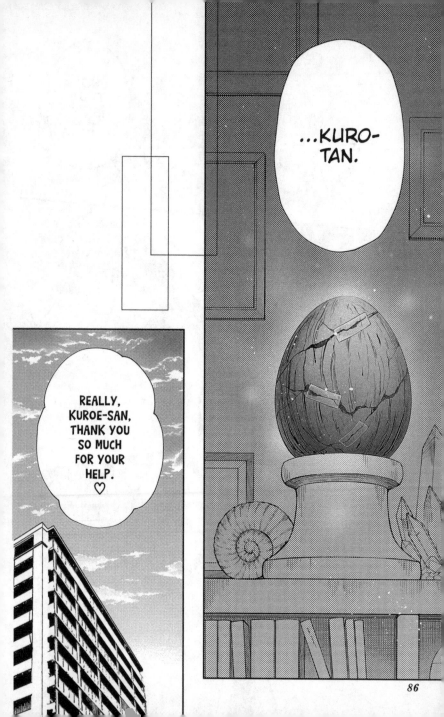

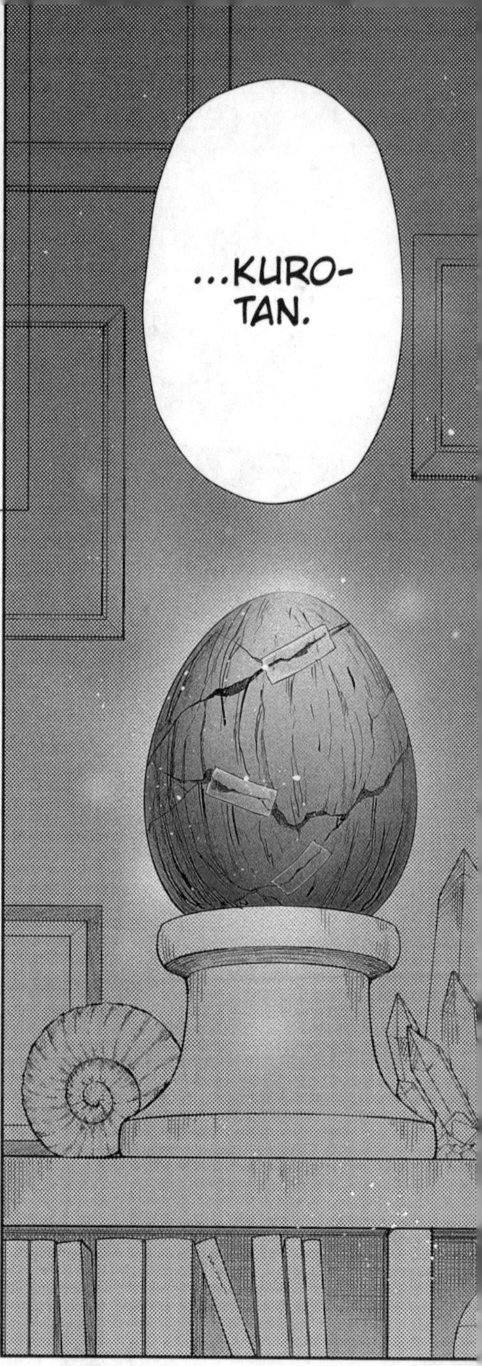
...KURO-TAN.

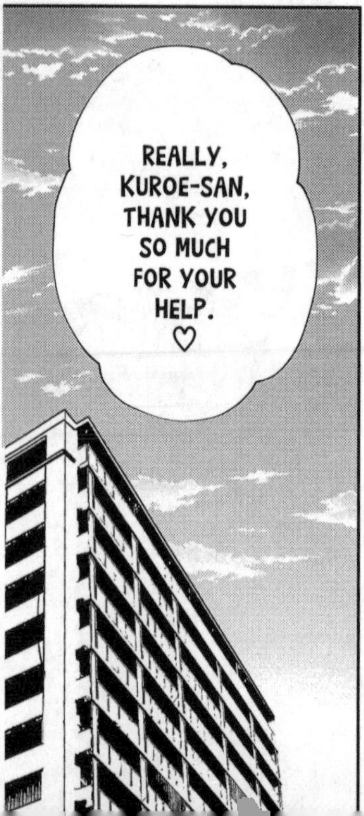
REALLY, KUROE-SAN, THANK YOU SO MUCH FOR YOUR HELP. ♡

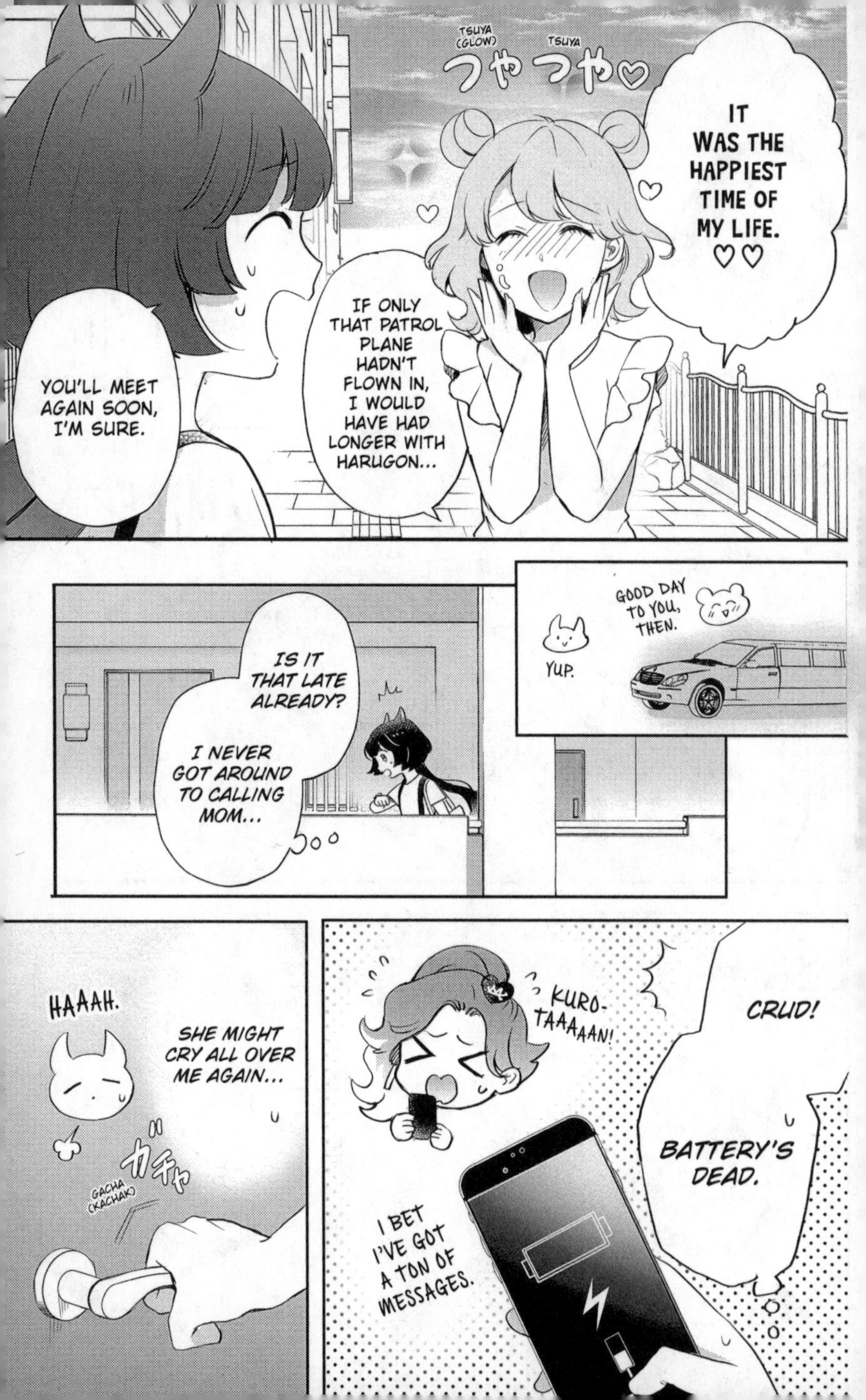
TSUYA (GLOW) TSUYA
つやつや♡
IT WAS THE HAPPIEST TIME OF MY LIFE. ♡♡
IF ONLY THAT PATROL PLANE HADN'T FLOWN IN, I WOULD HAVE HAD LONGER WITH HARUGON...
YOU'LL MEET AGAIN SOON, I'M SURE.
GOOD DAY TO YOU, THEN.
YUP.
IS IT THAT LATE ALREADY?
I NEVER GOT AROUND TO CALLING MOM...
CRUD!
BATTERY'S DEAD.
KURO-TAAAAAN!
I BET I'VE GOT A TON OF MESSAGES.
HAAAH.
SHE MIGHT CRY ALL OVER ME AGAIN...
ガチャ
GACHA (KACHAK)

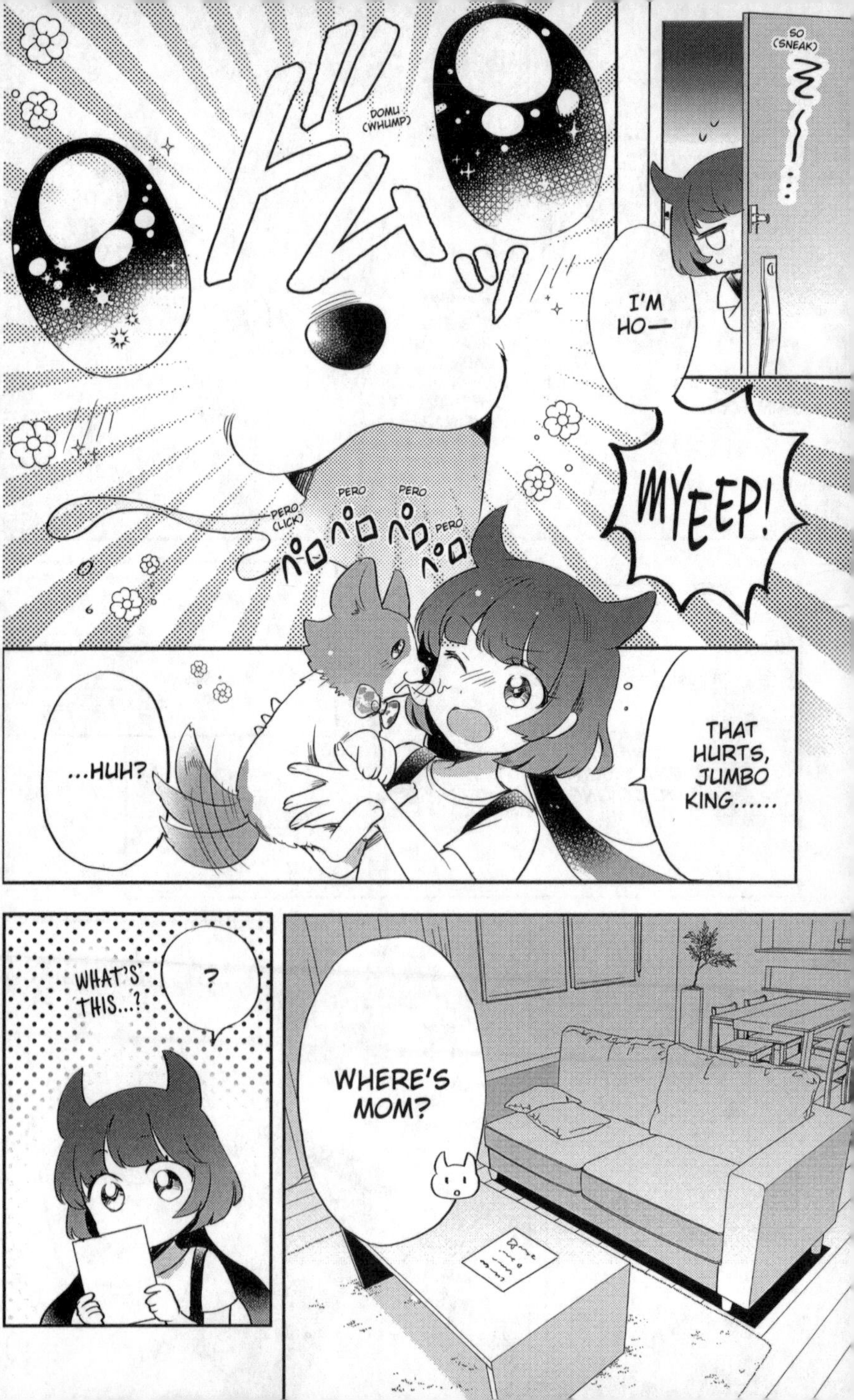
SO (SNEAK)
I'M HO—
MYEEP!
DOMU (WHUMP)
PERO PERO PERO (LICK) PERO
THAT HURTS, JUMBO KING......
...HUH?
WHERE'S MOM?
?
WHAT'S THIS...?

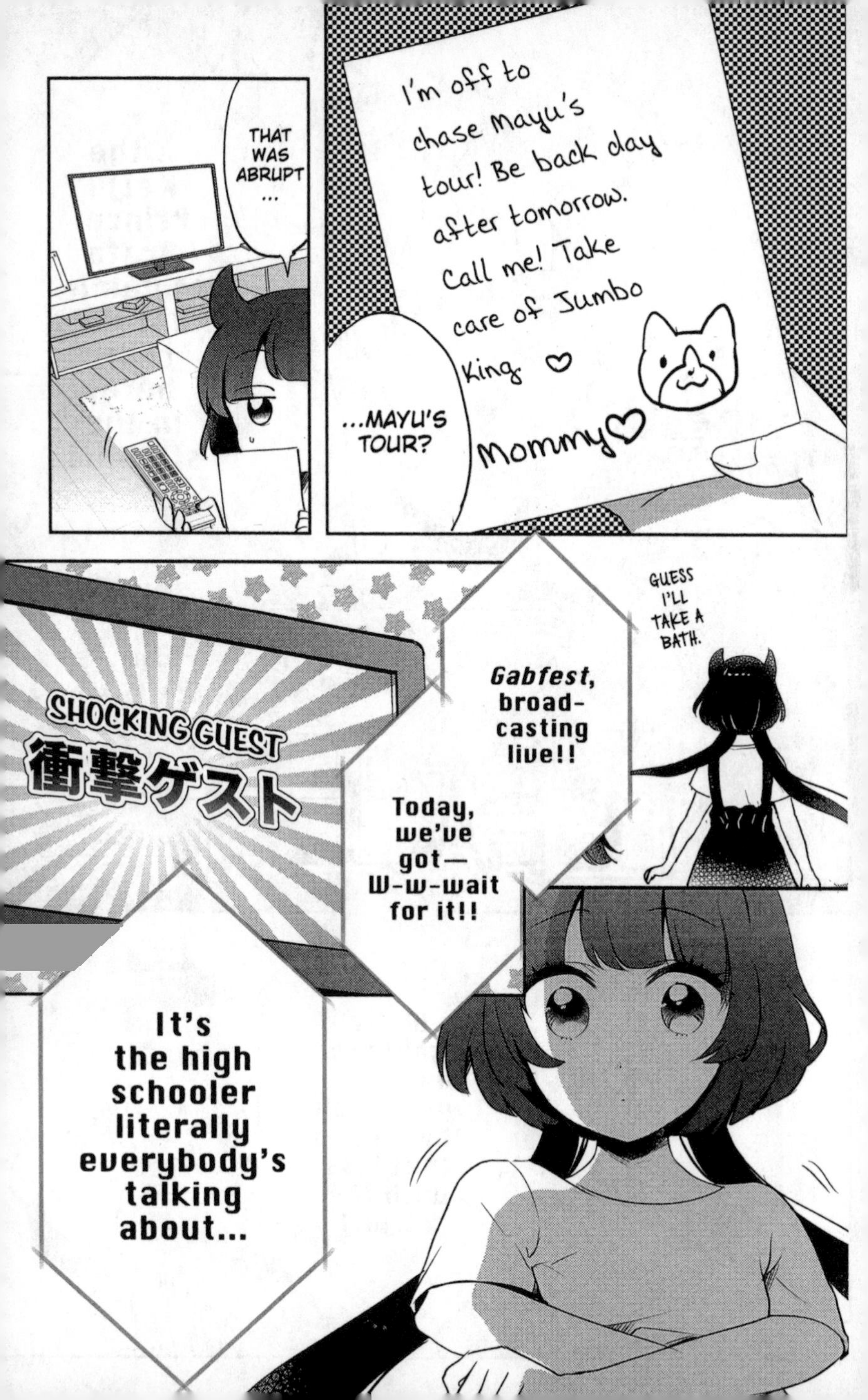
I'm off to chase Mayu's tour! Be back day after tomorrow. Call me! Take care of Jumbo King ♡
Mommy♡
...MAYU'S TOUR?
THAT WAS ABRUPT...
GUESS I'LL TAKE A BATH.
Gabfest, broad-casting live!!
Today, we've got— W-w-wait for it!!
SHOCKING GUEST
衝撃ゲスト
It's the high schooler literally everybody's talking about...

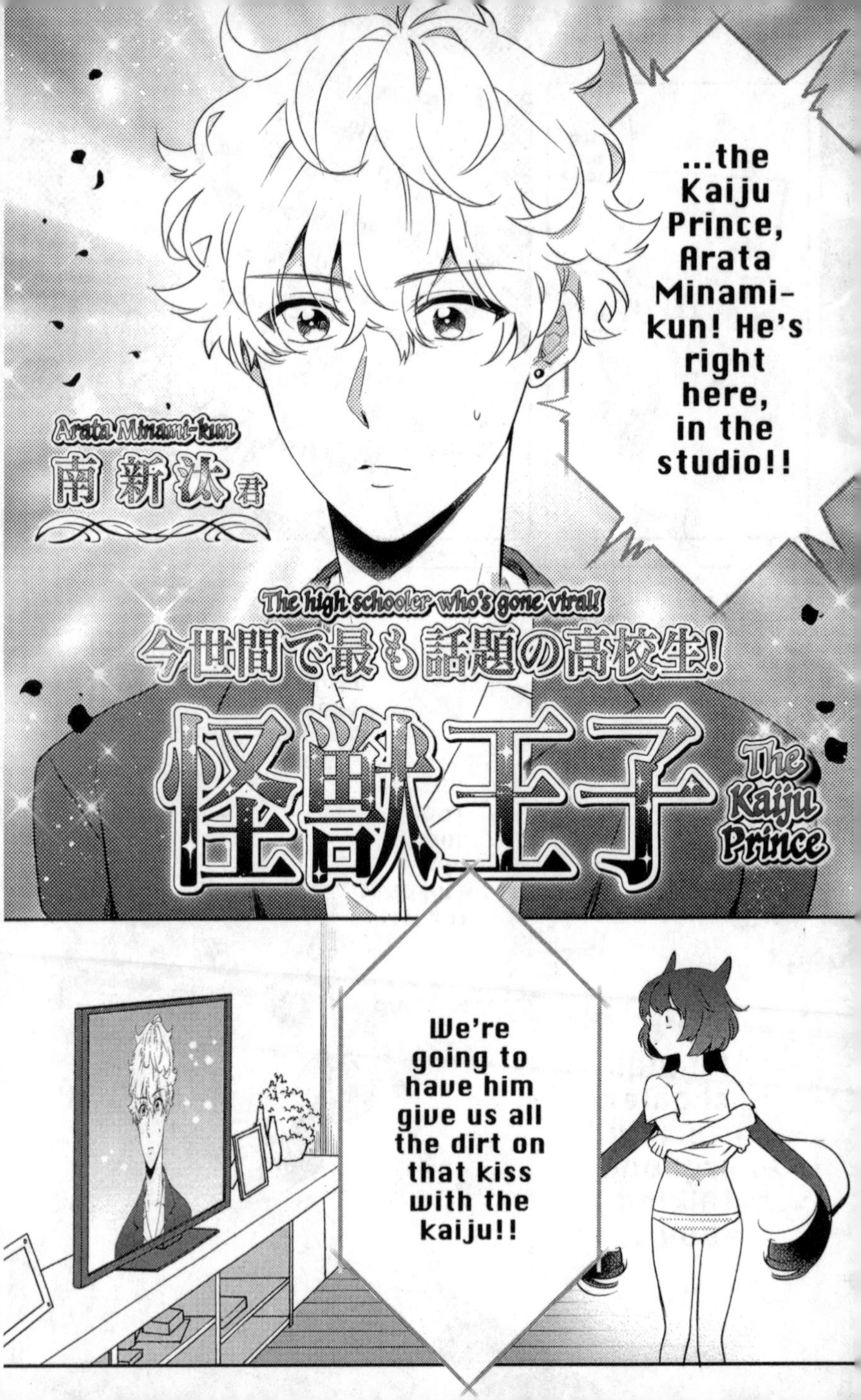
...the Kaiju Prince, Arata Minami-kun! He's right here, in the studio!!
Arata Minami-kun
南新汰君
The high schooler who's gone viral!
今世間で最も話題の高校生!
怪獣王子
The Kaiju Prince
We're going to have him give us all the dirt on that kiss with the kaiju!!

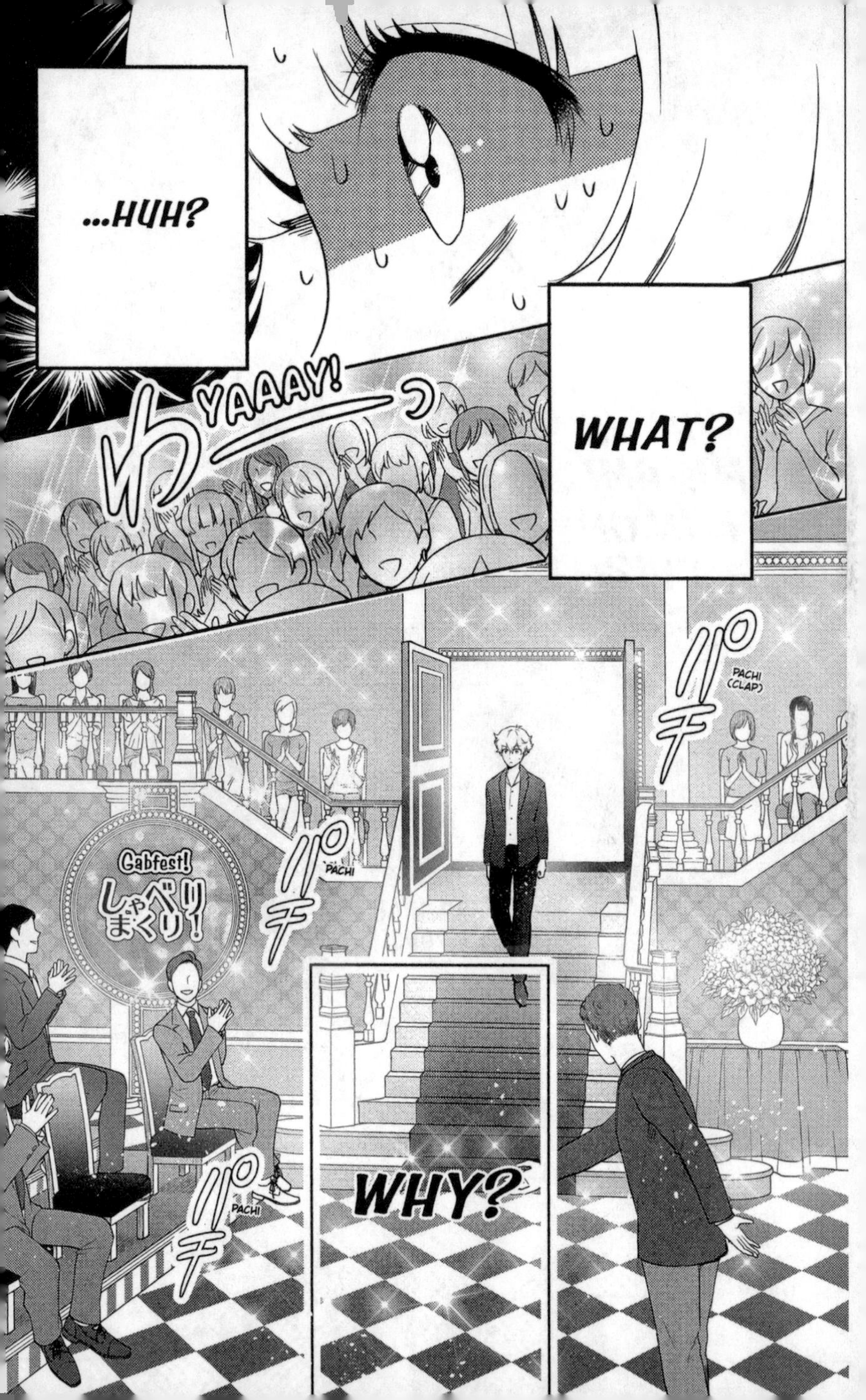
...HUH?
WHAT?
YAAAY!
PACHI (CLAP)
Gabfest!
しゃべりまくり!
PACHI
PACHI!
WHY?

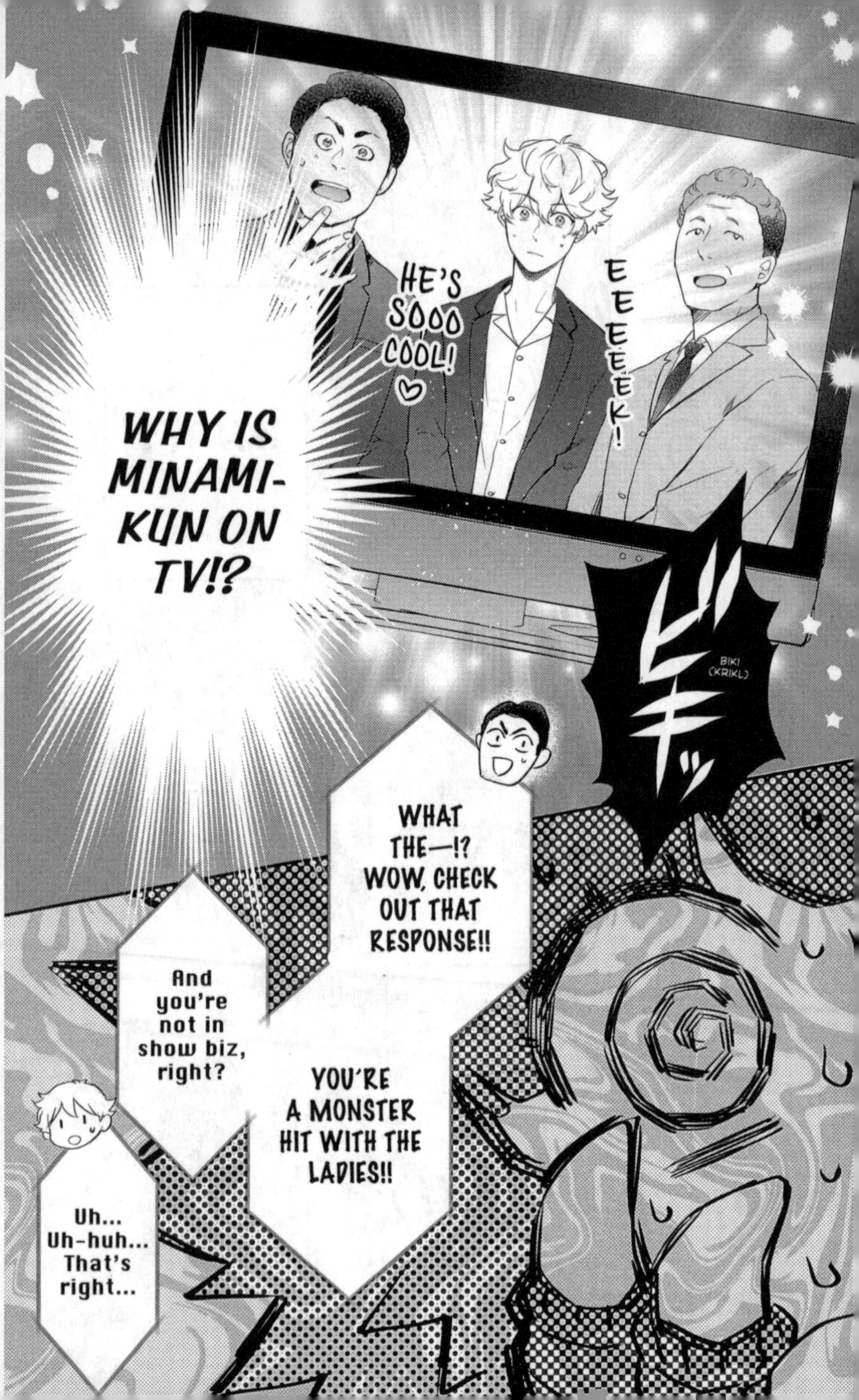
EEEEEEK!
HE'S SOOO COOL! ♡
WHY IS MINAMI-KUN ON TV!?
BIKI (KRIKL)
WHAT THE—!? WOW, CHECK OUT THAT RESPONSE!!
YOU'RE A MONSTER HIT WITH THE LADIES!!
And you're not in show biz, right?
Uh... Uh-huh... That's right...

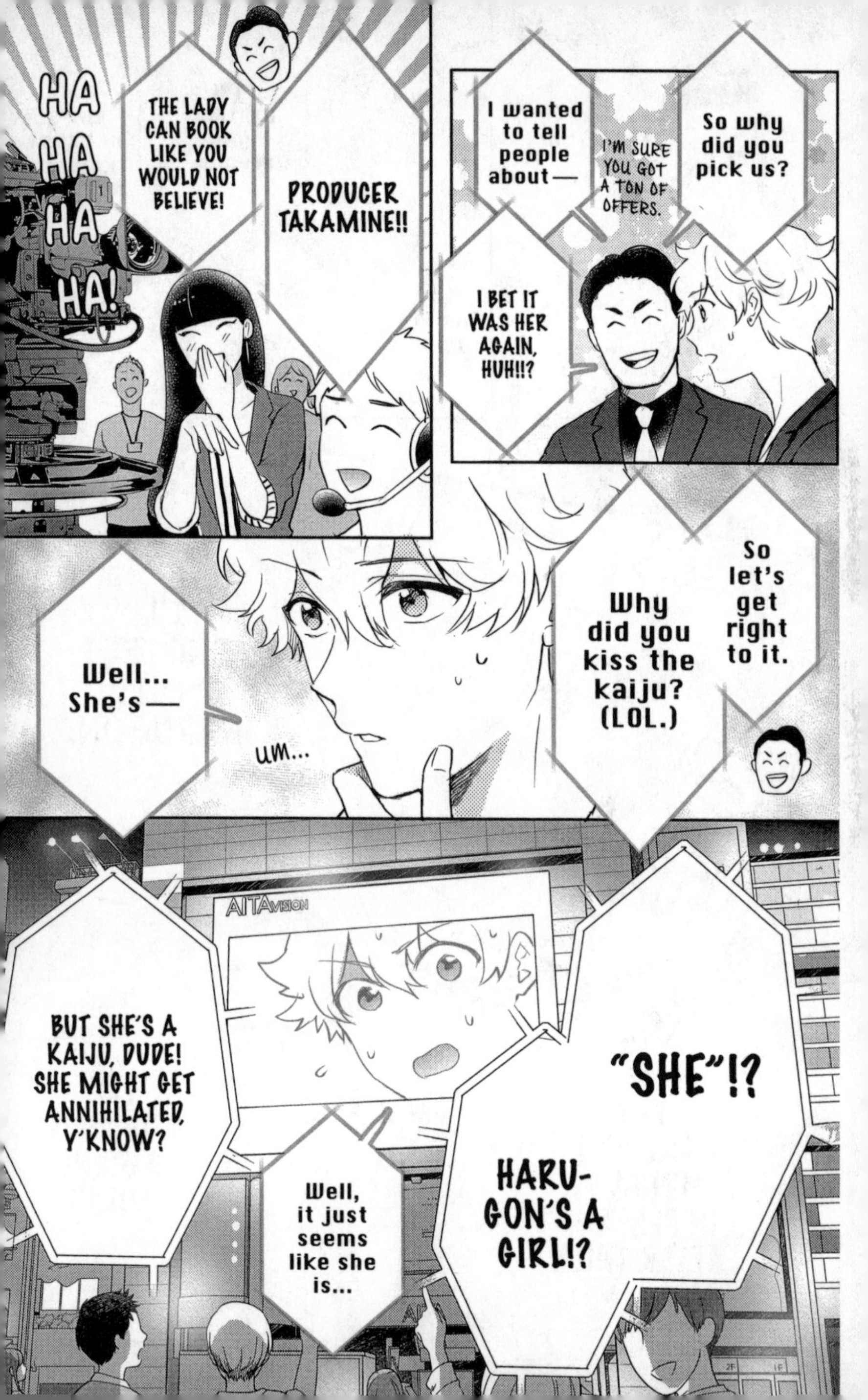
So why did you pick us?
I'M SURE YOU GOT A TON OF OFFERS.
I wanted to tell people about—
I BET IT WAS HER AGAIN, HUH!!?
PRODUCER TAKAMINE!!
THE LADY CAN BOOK LIKE YOU WOULD NOT BELIEVE!
HA HA HA HA!
So let's get right to it.
Why did you kiss the kaiju? (LOL.)
UM...
Well... She's—
AITAVISION
"SHE"!?
HARU-GON'S A GIRL!?
Well, it just seems like she is...
BUT SHE'S A KAIJU, DUDE! SHE MIGHT GET ANNIHILATED, Y'KNOW?

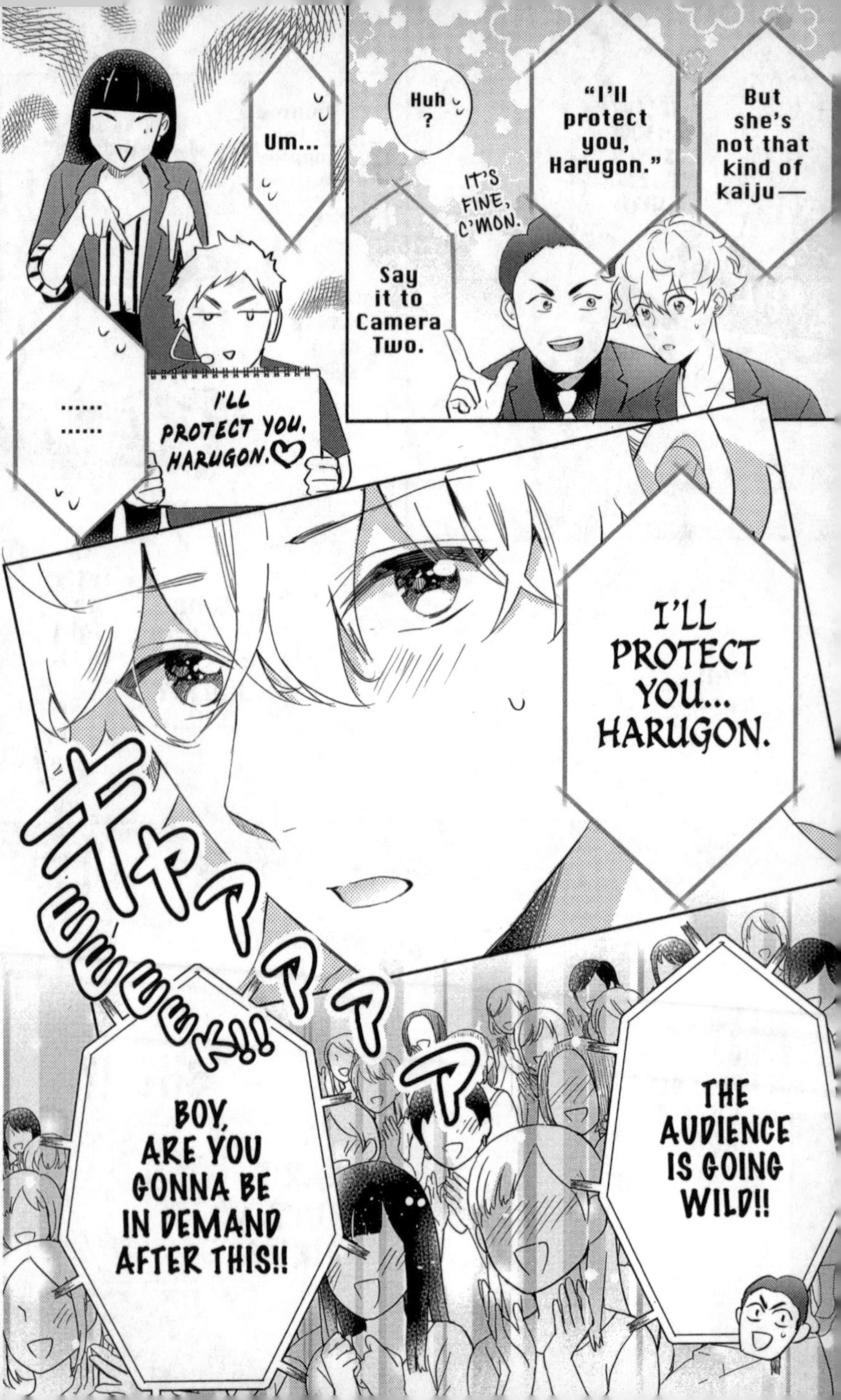
But she's not that kind of kaiju—
"I'll protect you, Harugon."
Huh?
IT'S FINE, C'MON.
Say it to Camera Two.
Um...
......
......
I'LL PROTECT YOU, HARUGON.♡
I'LL PROTECT YOU... HARUGON.
キャアアア
EEEEEK!!
THE AUDIENCE IS GOING WILD!!
BOY, ARE YOU GONNA BE IN DEMAND AFTER THIS!!

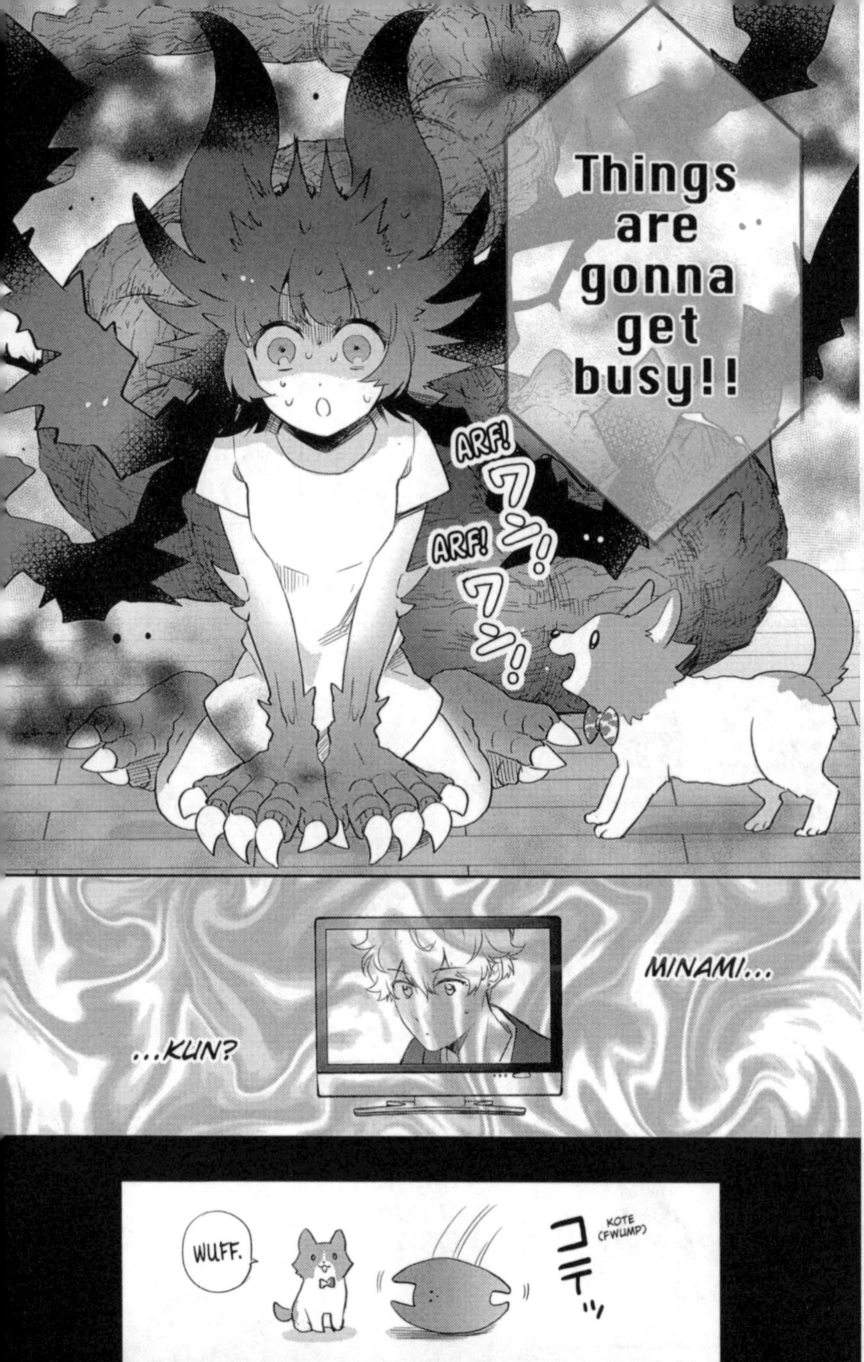
Things are gonna get busy!!
ARF!
ワン!
ARF!
ワン!
MINAMI...
...KUN?
KOTE (FWUMP)
コテッ
WUFF.

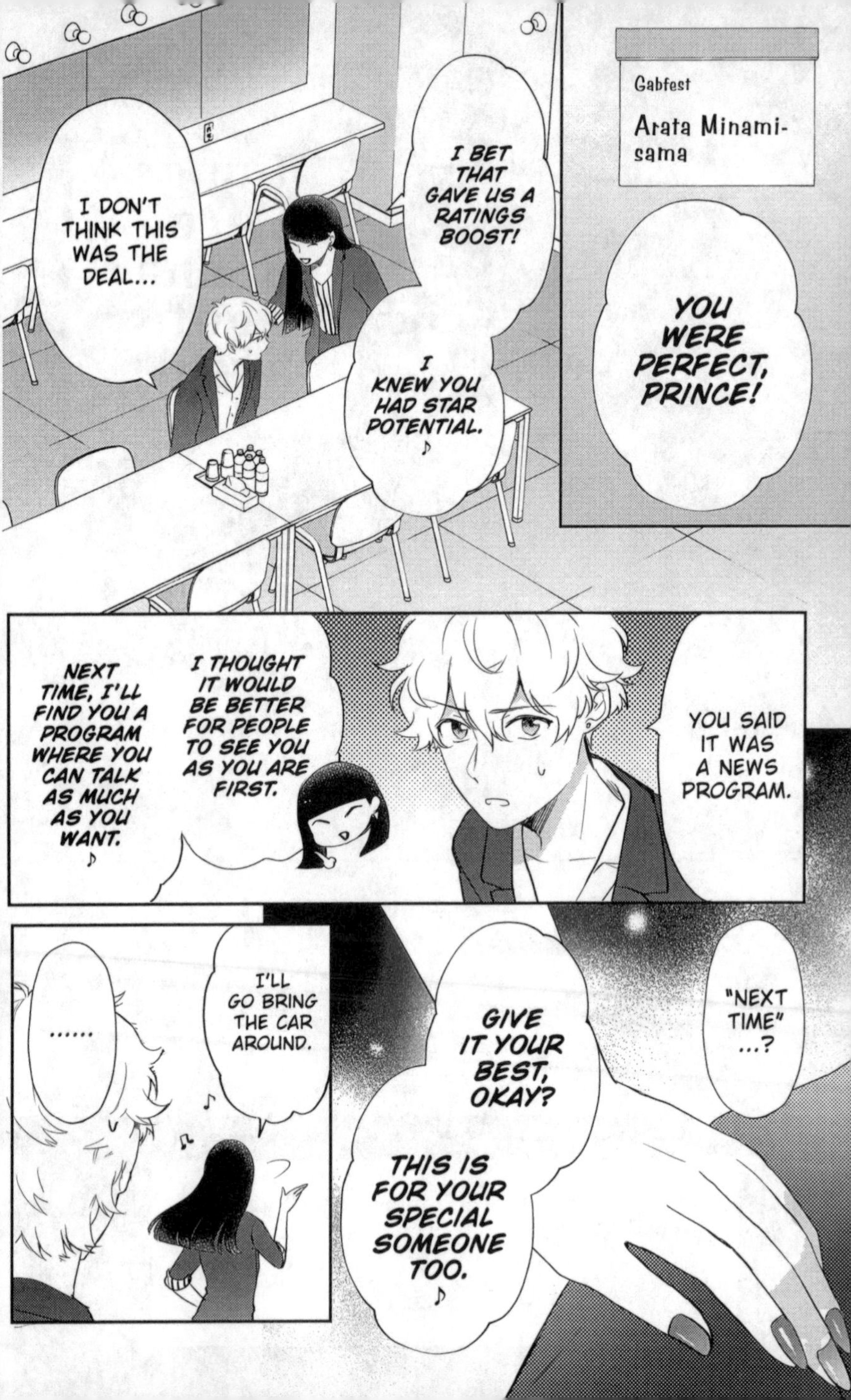
Gabfest
Arata Minami-sama
YOU WERE PERFECT, PRINCE!
I BET THAT GAVE US A RATINGS BOOST!
I KNEW YOU HAD STAR POTENTIAL. ♪
I DON'T THINK THIS WAS THE DEAL...
YOU SAID IT WAS A NEWS PROGRAM.
I THOUGHT IT WOULD BE BETTER FOR PEOPLE TO SEE YOU AS YOU ARE FIRST.
NEXT TIME, I'LL FIND YOU A PROGRAM WHERE YOU CAN TALK AS MUCH AS YOU WANT. ♪
"NEXT TIME"...?
GIVE IT YOUR BEST, OKAY?
THIS IS FOR YOUR SPECIAL SOMEONE TOO. ♪
I'LL GO BRING THE CAR AROUND.
......

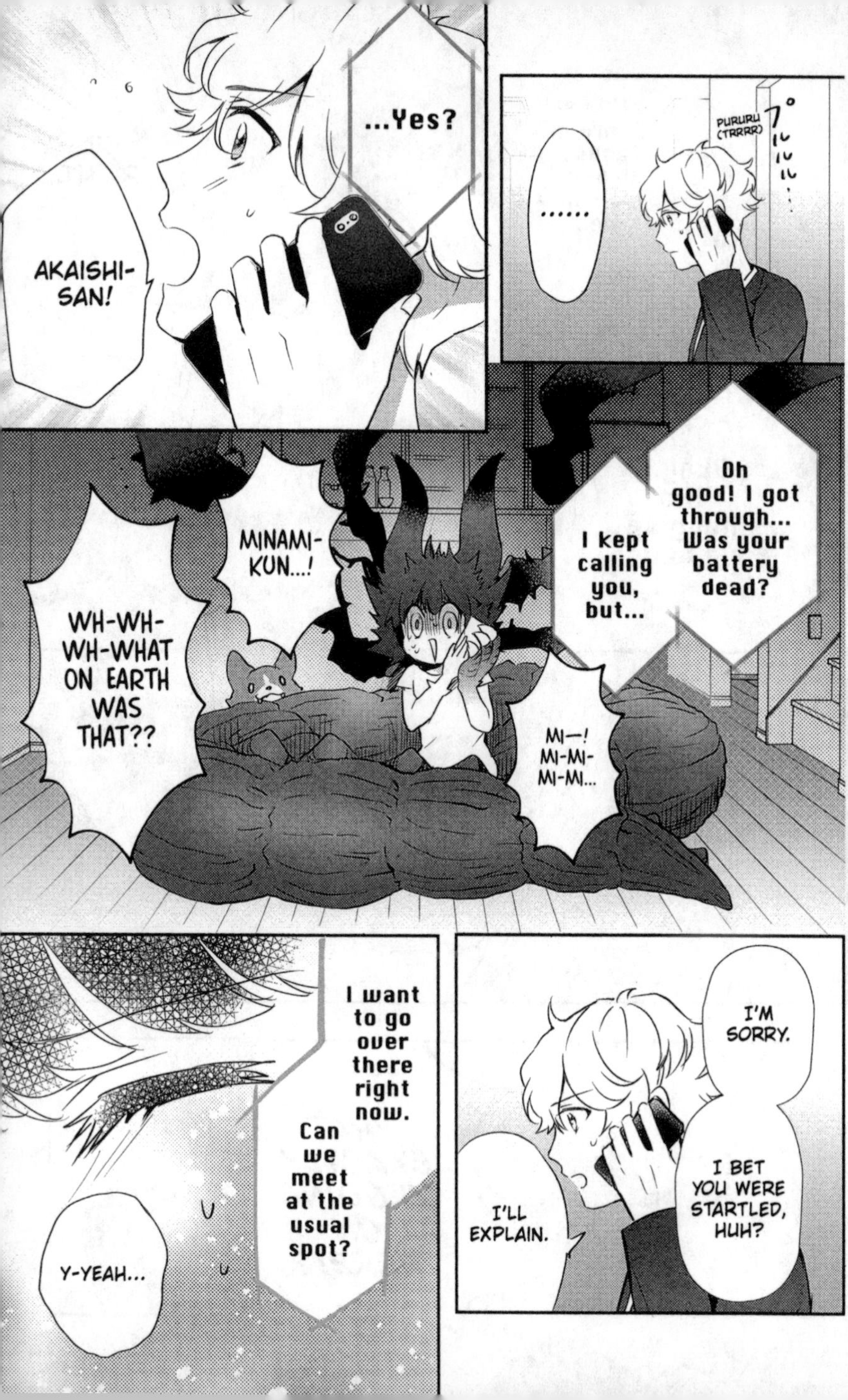
PURURU (TRRRR)
プルルル…
......
...Yes?
AKAISHI-SAN!
Oh good! I got through... Was your battery dead?
I kept calling you, but...
MINAMI-KUN...!
MI—! MI-MI-MI-MI...
WH-WH-WH-WHAT ON EARTH WAS THAT??
I'M SORRY.
I BET YOU WERE STARTLED, HUH?
I'LL EXPLAIN.
I want to go over there right now.
Can we meet at the usual spot?
Y-YEAH...

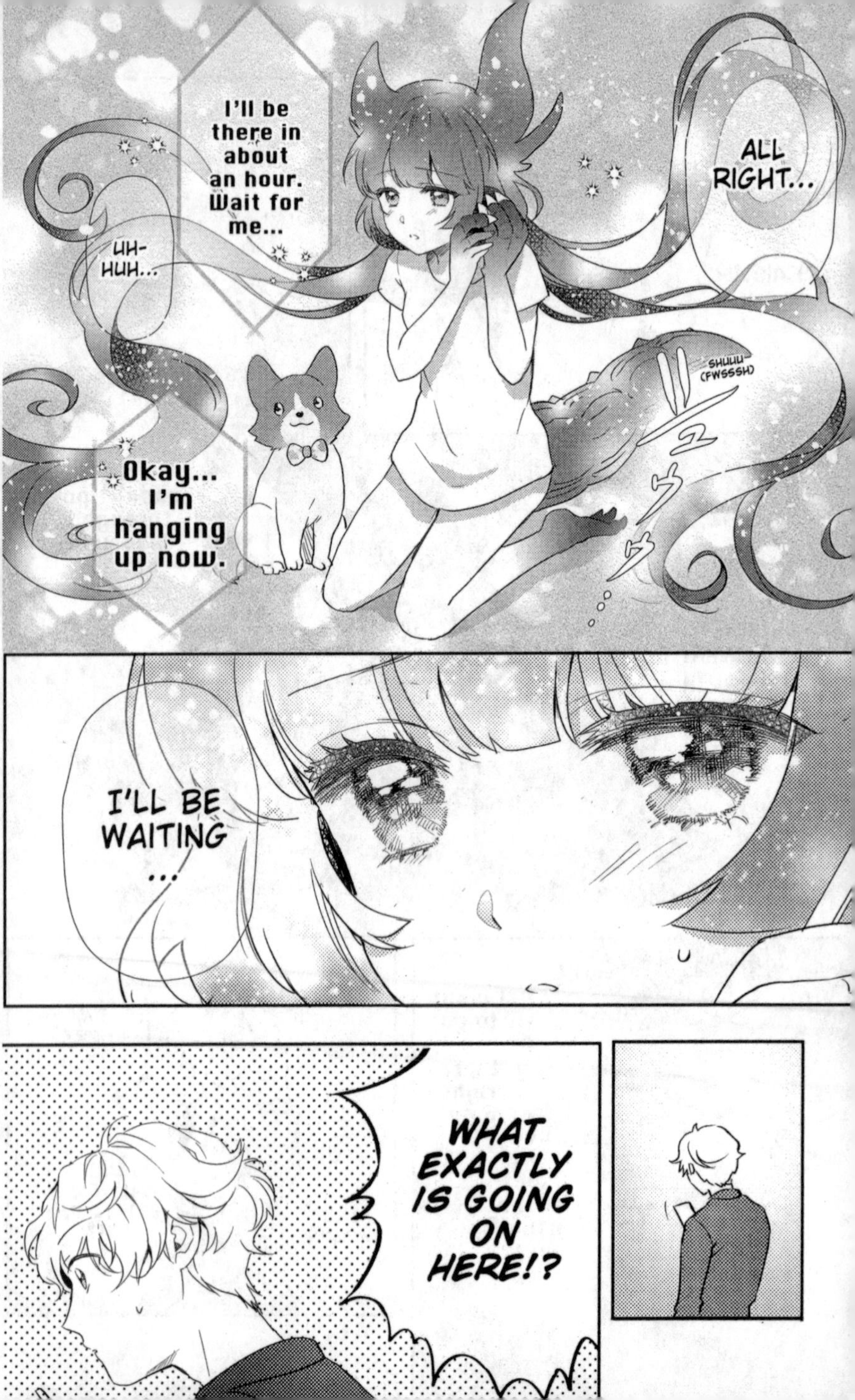
ALL RIGHT...
I'll be there in about an hour. Wait for me...
UH-HUH...
SHUUU (FWSSSH)
Okay... I'm hanging up now.
I'LL BE WAITING...
WHAT EXACTLY IS GOING ON HERE!?

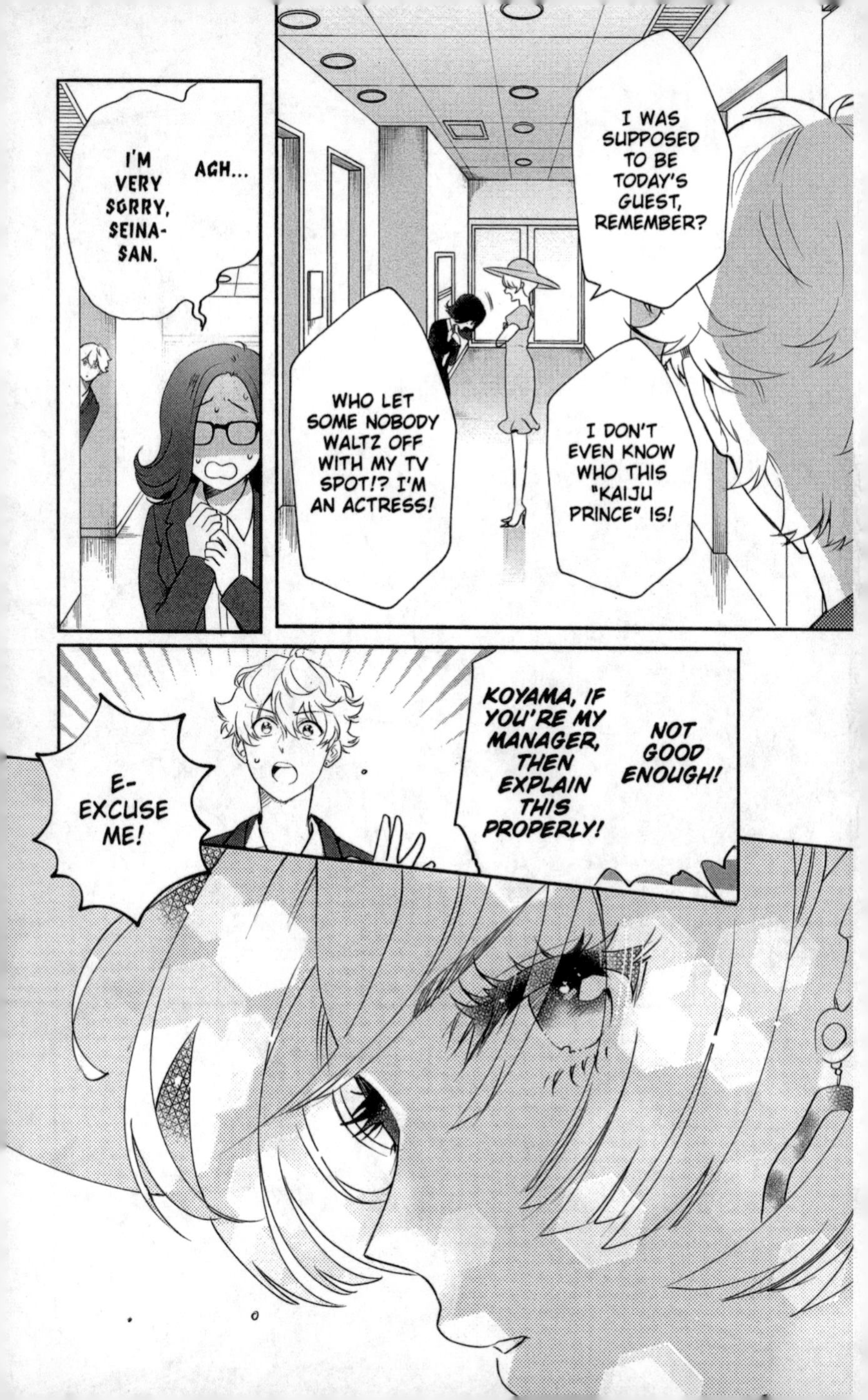
I WAS SUPPOSED TO BE TODAY'S GUEST, REMEMBER?
I DON'T EVEN KNOW WHO THIS "KAIJU PRINCE" IS!
WHO LET SOME NOBODY WALTZ OFF WITH MY TV SPOT!? I'M AN ACTRESS!
AGH...
I'M VERY SORRY, SEINA-SAN.
NOT GOOD ENOUGH!
KOYAMA, IF YOU'RE MY MANAGER, THEN EXPLAIN THIS PROPERLY!
E-EXCUSE ME!

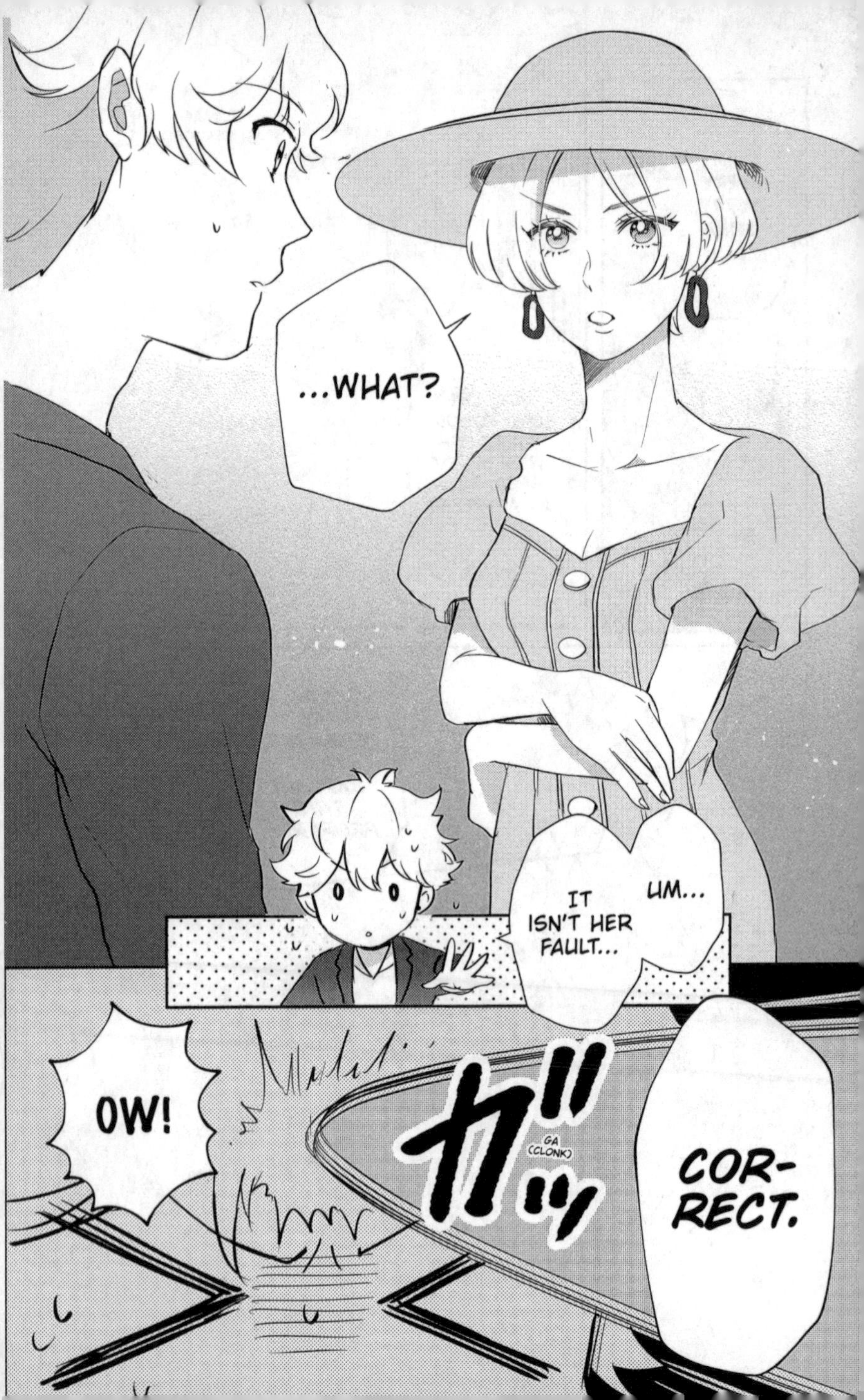
...WHAT?
UM...
IT ISN'T HER FAULT...
COR-RECT.
GA (CLONK)
OW!

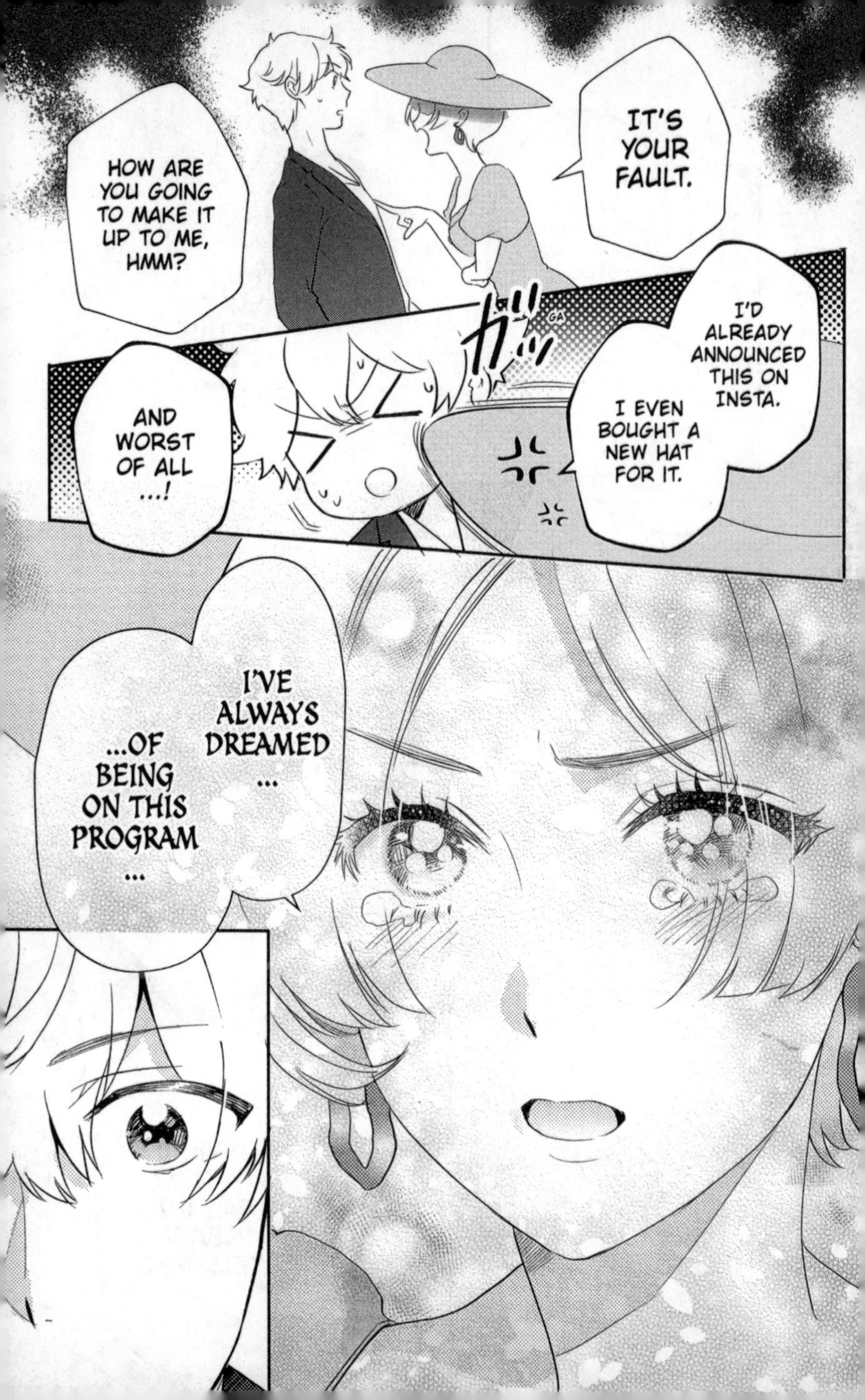
IT'S YOUR FAULT.
HOW ARE YOU GOING TO MAKE IT UP TO ME, HMM?
GA
I'D ALREADY ANNOUNCED THIS ON INSTA.
I EVEN BOUGHT A NEW HAT FOR IT.
AND WORST OF ALL ...!
I'VE ALWAYS DREAMED ...
...OF BEING ON THIS PROGRAM ...

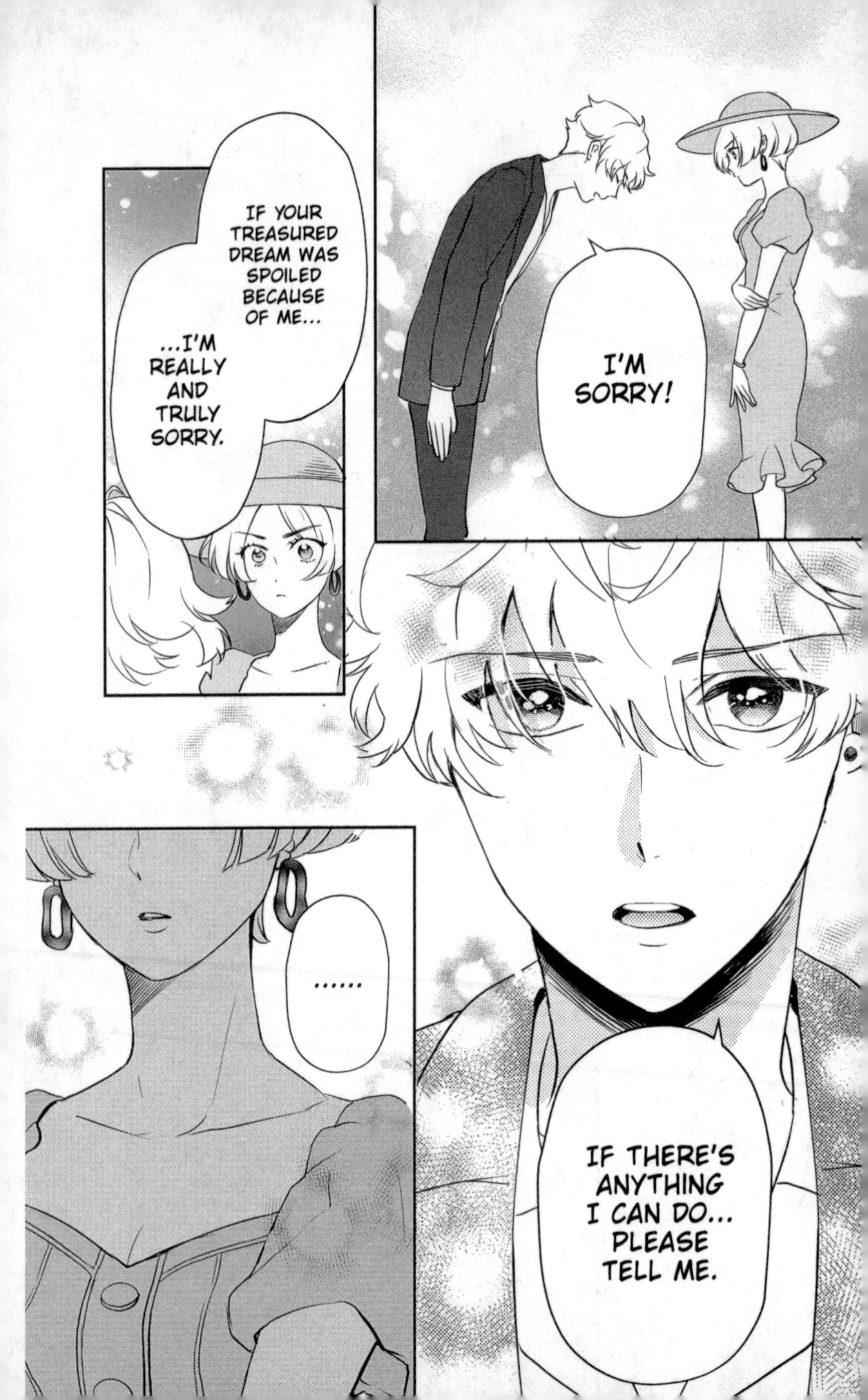
I'M SORRY!
IF YOUR TREASURED DREAM WAS SPOILED BECAUSE OF ME...
...I'M REALLY AND TRULY SORRY.
IF THERE'S ANYTHING I CAN DO... PLEASE TELL ME.
......

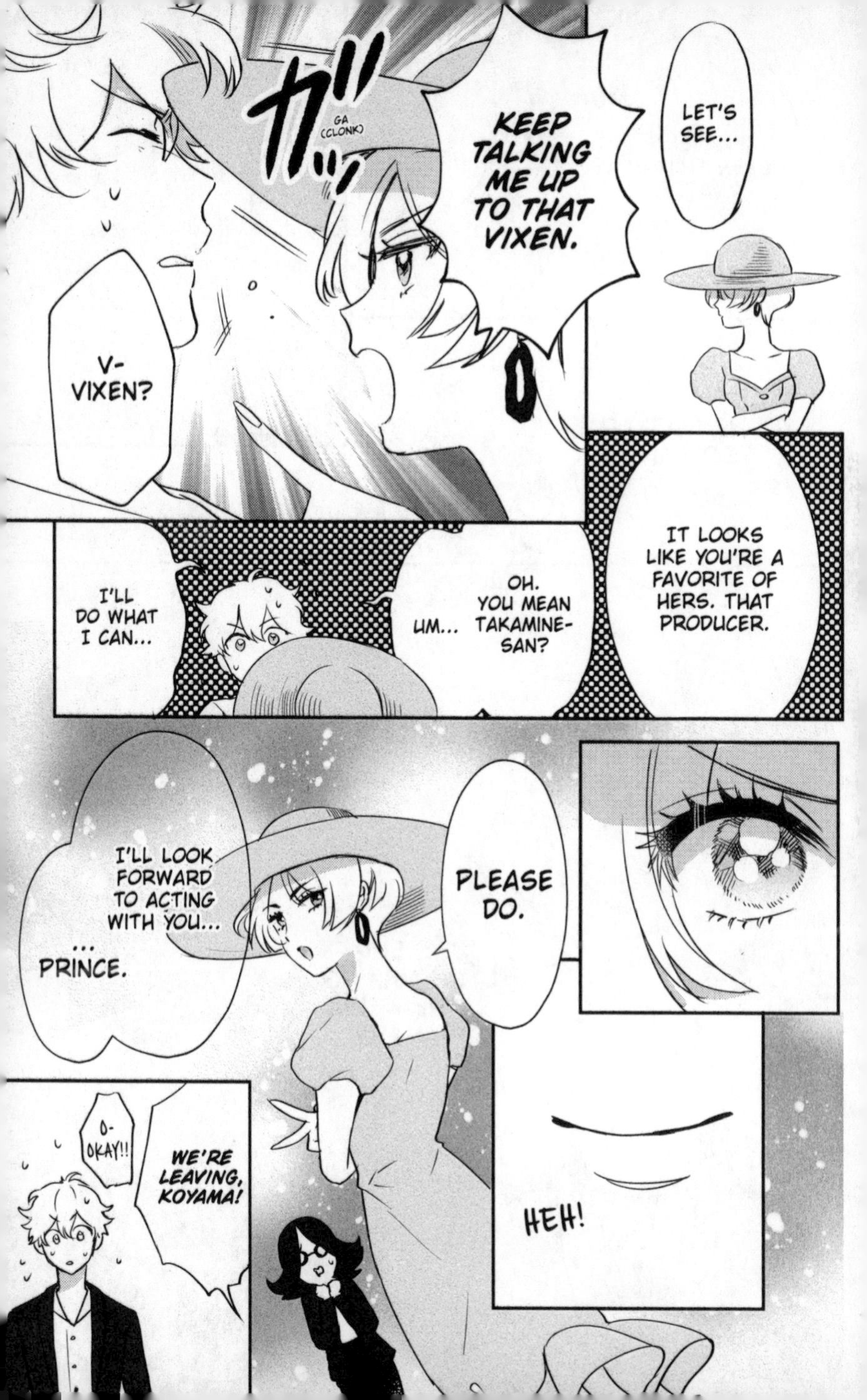
LET'S SEE...
KEEP TALKING ME UP TO THAT VIXEN.
GA (CLONK)
V-VIXEN?
IT LOOKS LIKE YOU'RE A FAVORITE OF HERS. THAT PRODUCER.
OH. YOU MEAN TAKAMINE-SAN?
UM...
I'LL DO WHAT I CAN...
PLEASE DO.
I'LL LOOK FORWARD TO ACTING WITH YOU... ...PRINCE.
HEH!
WE'RE LEAVING, KOYAMA!
O-OKAY!!

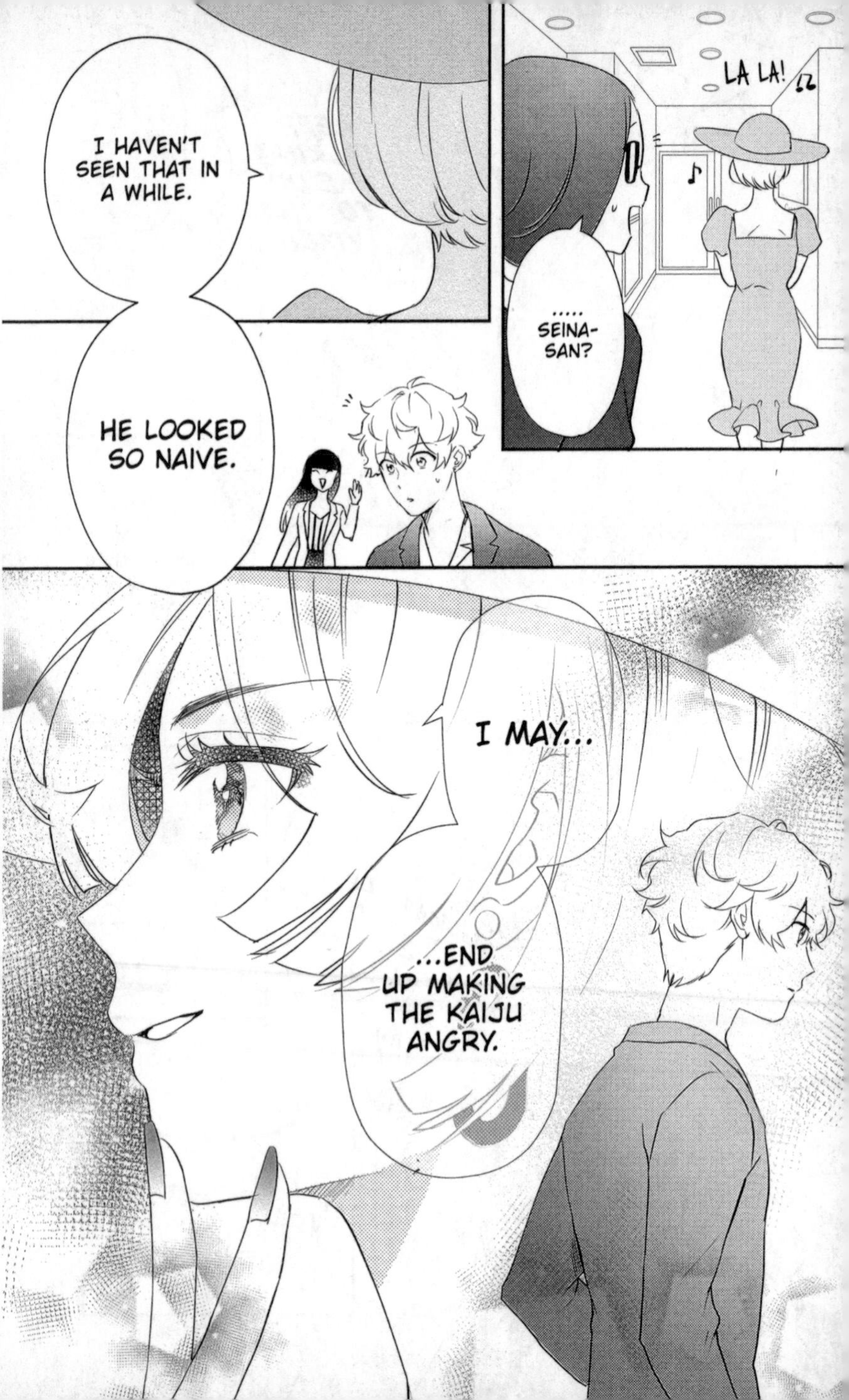
LA LA!
..... SEINA-SAN?
I HAVEN'T SEEN THAT IN A WHILE.
HE LOOKED SO NAIVE.
I MAY...
...END UP MAKING THE KAIJU ANGRY.

KAIJU♥GIRL
CARAMELISE

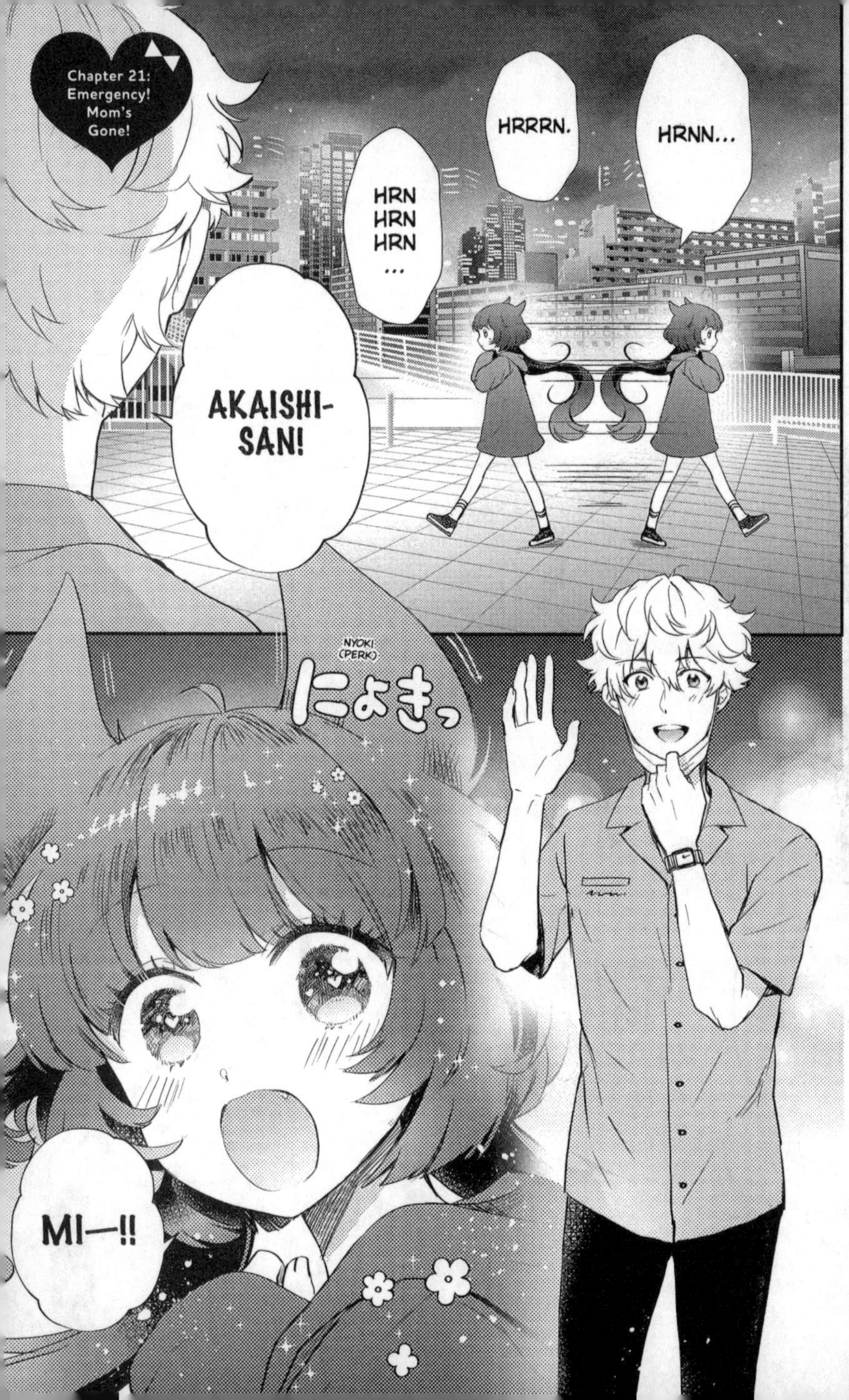
Chapter 21: Emergency! Mom's Gone!
HRNN...
HRRRN.
HRN HRN HRN ...
AKAISHI-SAN!
にょきっ
NYOKI (PERK)
MI—!!

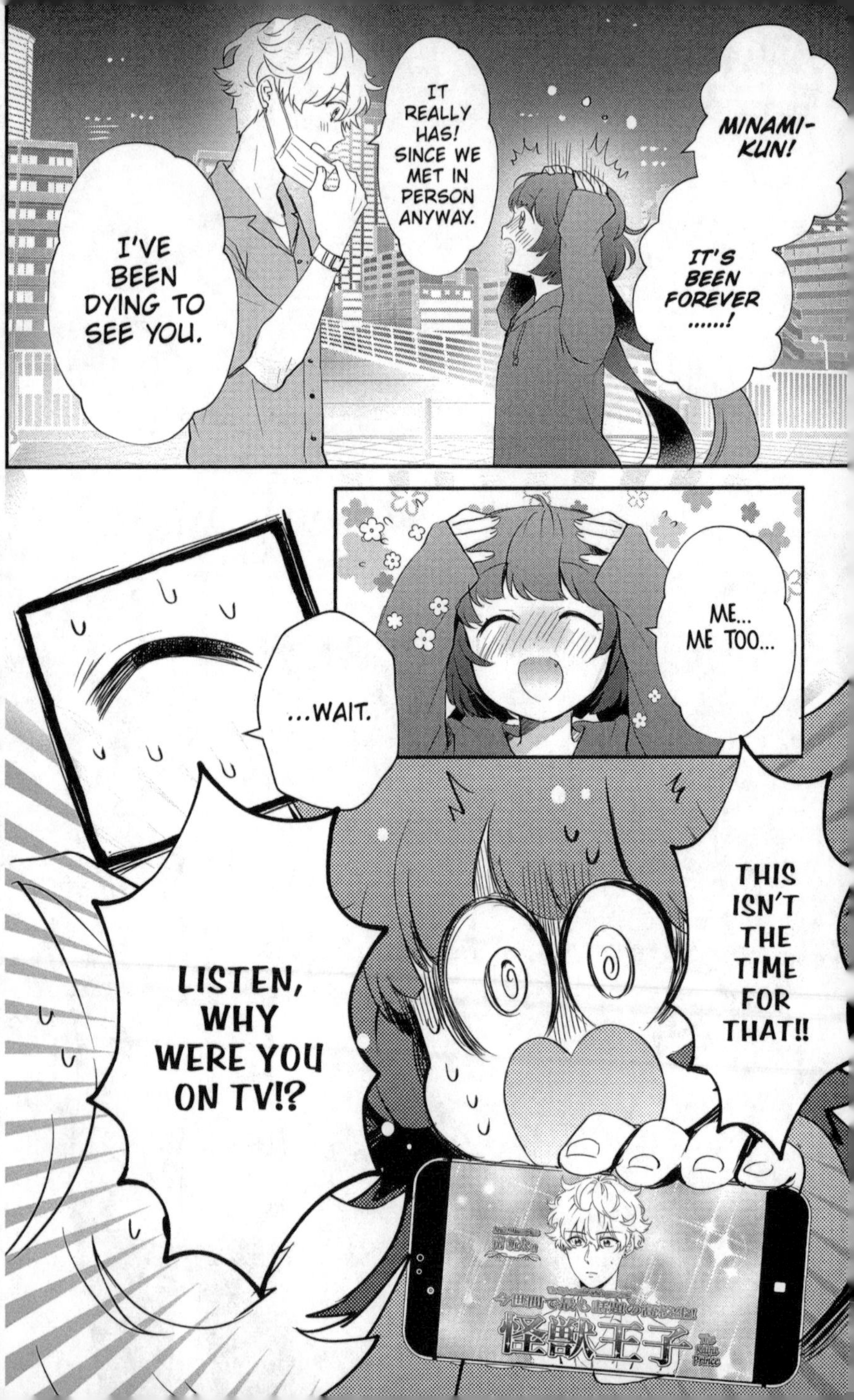
MINAMI-KUN!
IT'S BEEN FOREVER ......!
IT REALLY HAS! SINCE WE MET IN PERSON ANYWAY.
I'VE BEEN DYING TO SEE YOU.
ME... ME TOO...
...WAIT.
THIS ISN'T THE TIME FOR THAT!!
LISTEN, WHY WERE YOU ON TV!?
怪獣王子
The Kaiju Prince

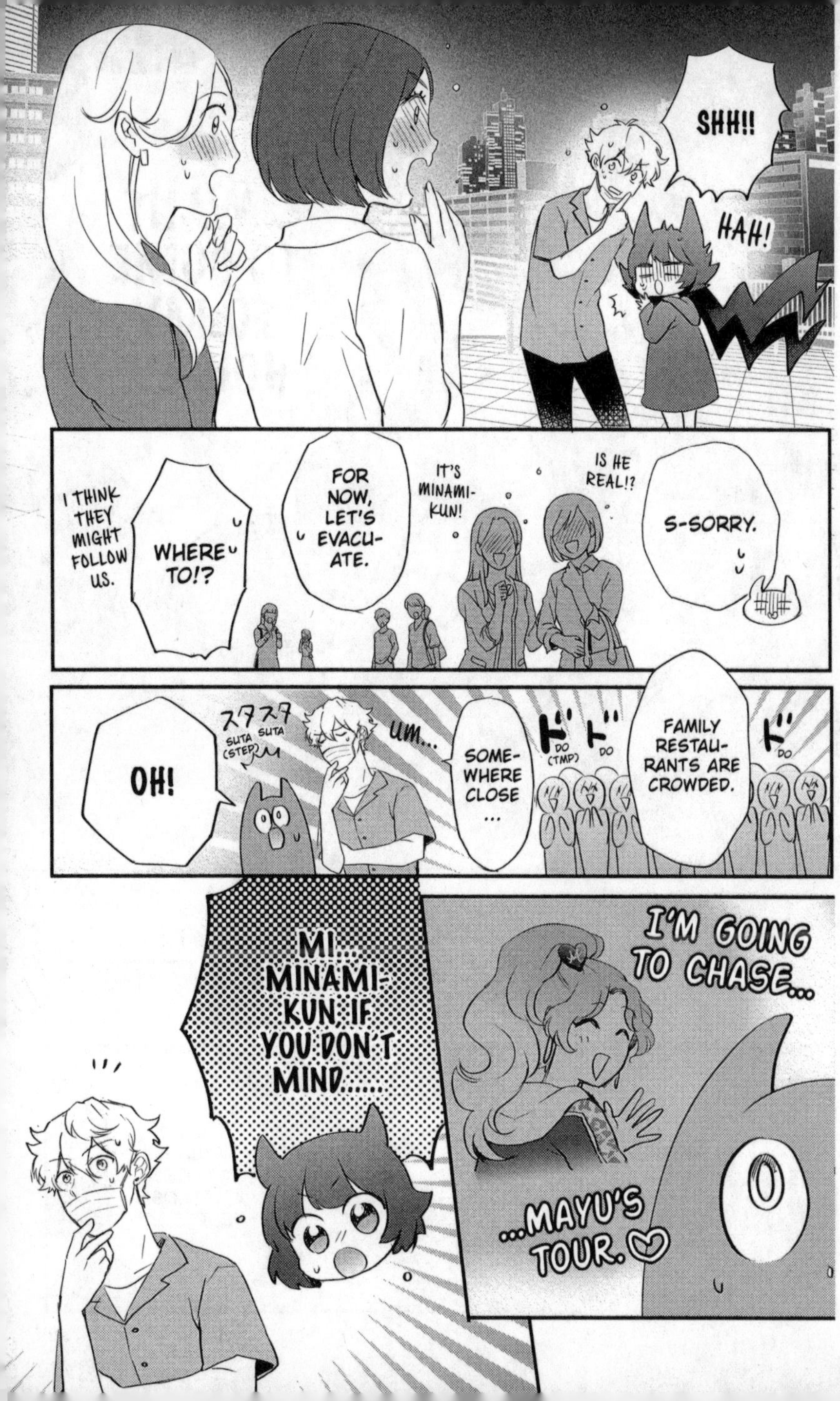
SHH!!
HAH!
S-SORRY.
IS HE REAL!?
IT'S MINAMI-KUN!
FOR NOW, LET'S EVACUATE.
WHERE TO!?
I THINK THEY MIGHT FOLLOW US.
ド DO
FAMILY RESTAURANTS ARE CROWDED.
ド ド DO (TMP) DO
SOMEWHERE CLOSE...
UM...
スタスタ SUTA SUTA (STEP)
OH!
I'M GOING TO CHASE...
...MAYU'S TOUR. ♡
MI... MINAMI-KUN IF YOU DON'T MIND......

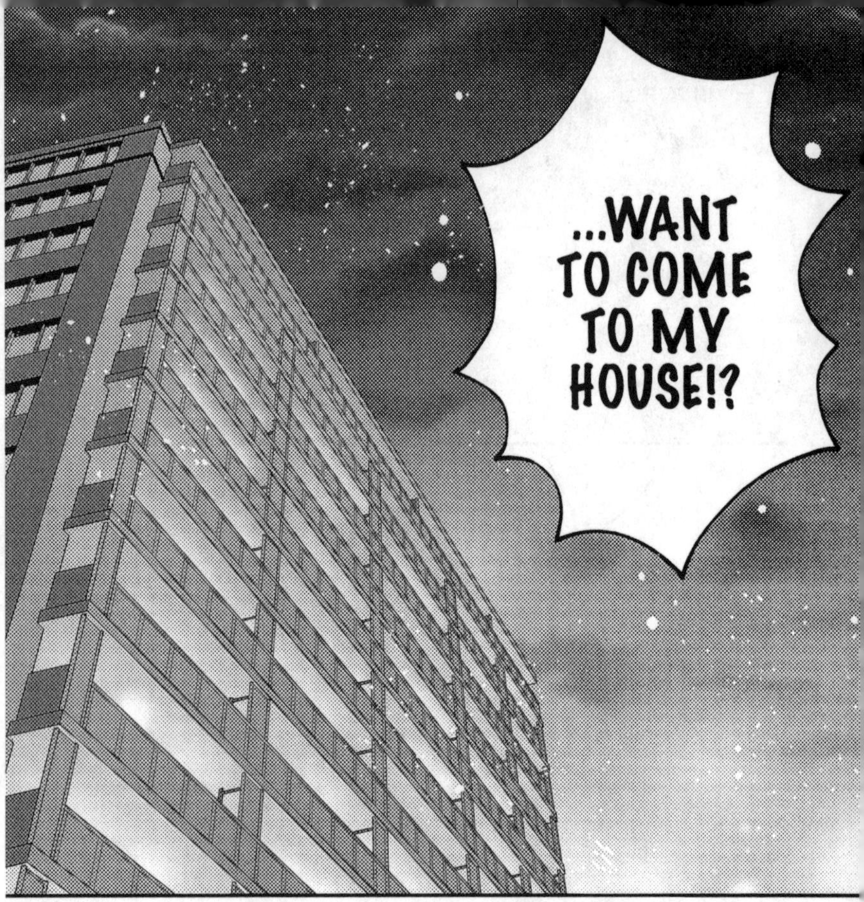
...WANT TO COME TO MY HOUSE!?

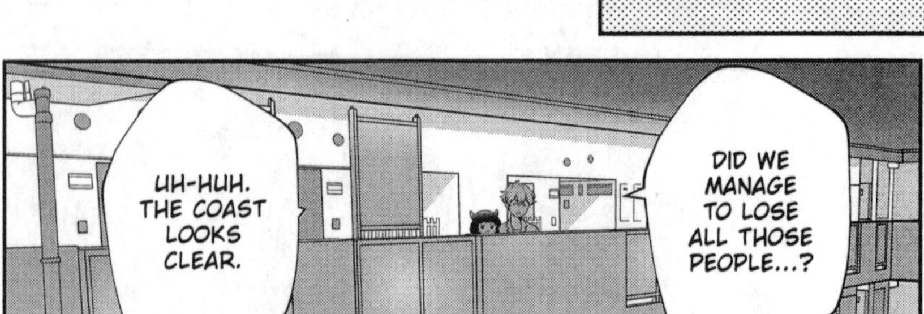
DID WE MANAGE TO LOSE ALL THOSE PEOPLE...?
UH-HUH. THE COAST LOOKS CLEAR.

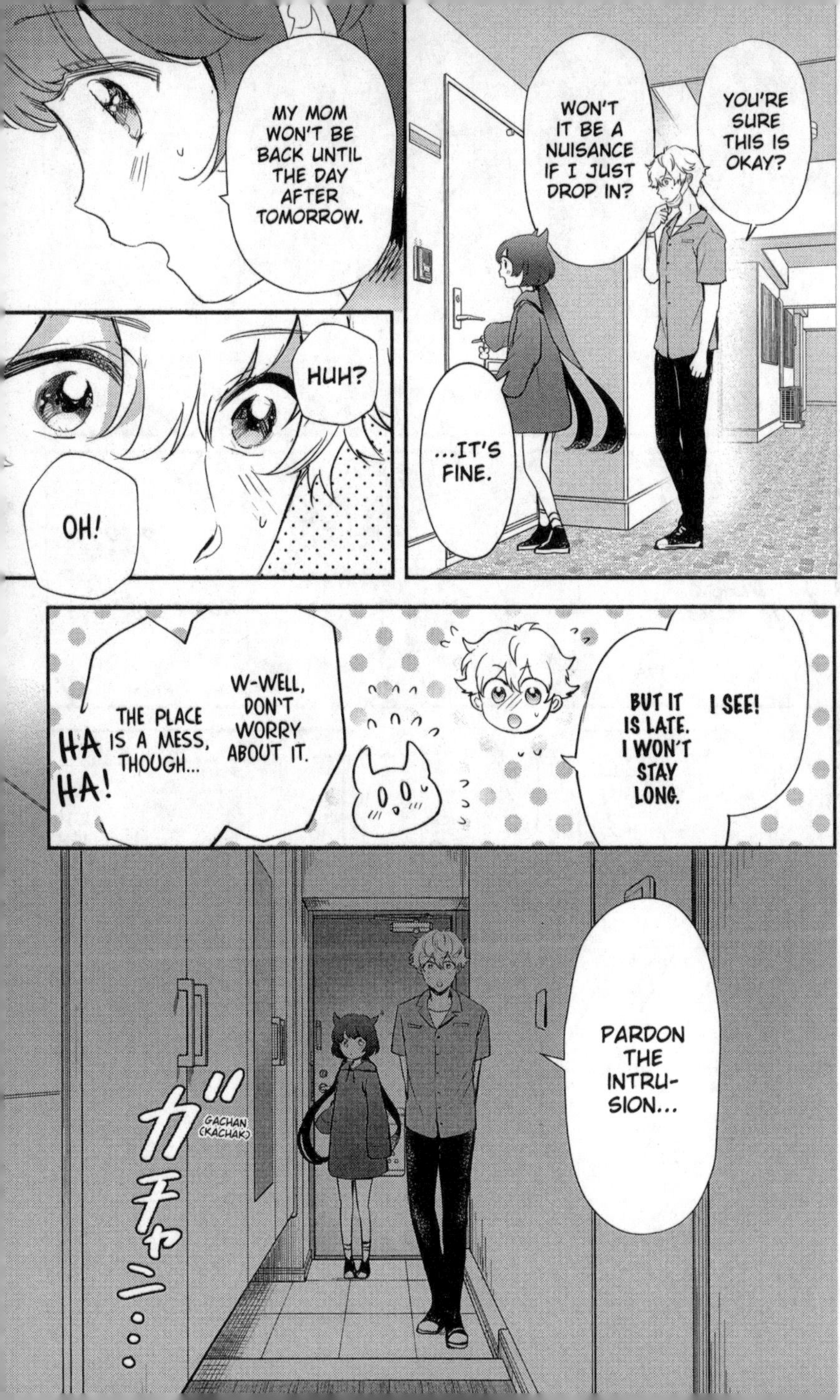
YOU'RE SURE THIS IS OKAY?
WON'T IT BE A NUISANCE IF I JUST DROP IN?
...IT'S FINE.
MY MOM WON'T BE BACK UNTIL THE DAY AFTER TOMORROW.
HUH?
OH!
I SEE!
BUT IT IS LATE. I WON'T STAY LONG.
W-WELL, DON'T WORRY ABOUT IT.
THE PLACE IS A MESS, THOUGH...
HA HA!
PARDON THE INTRU-SION...
ガチャン…
GACHAN (KACHAK)

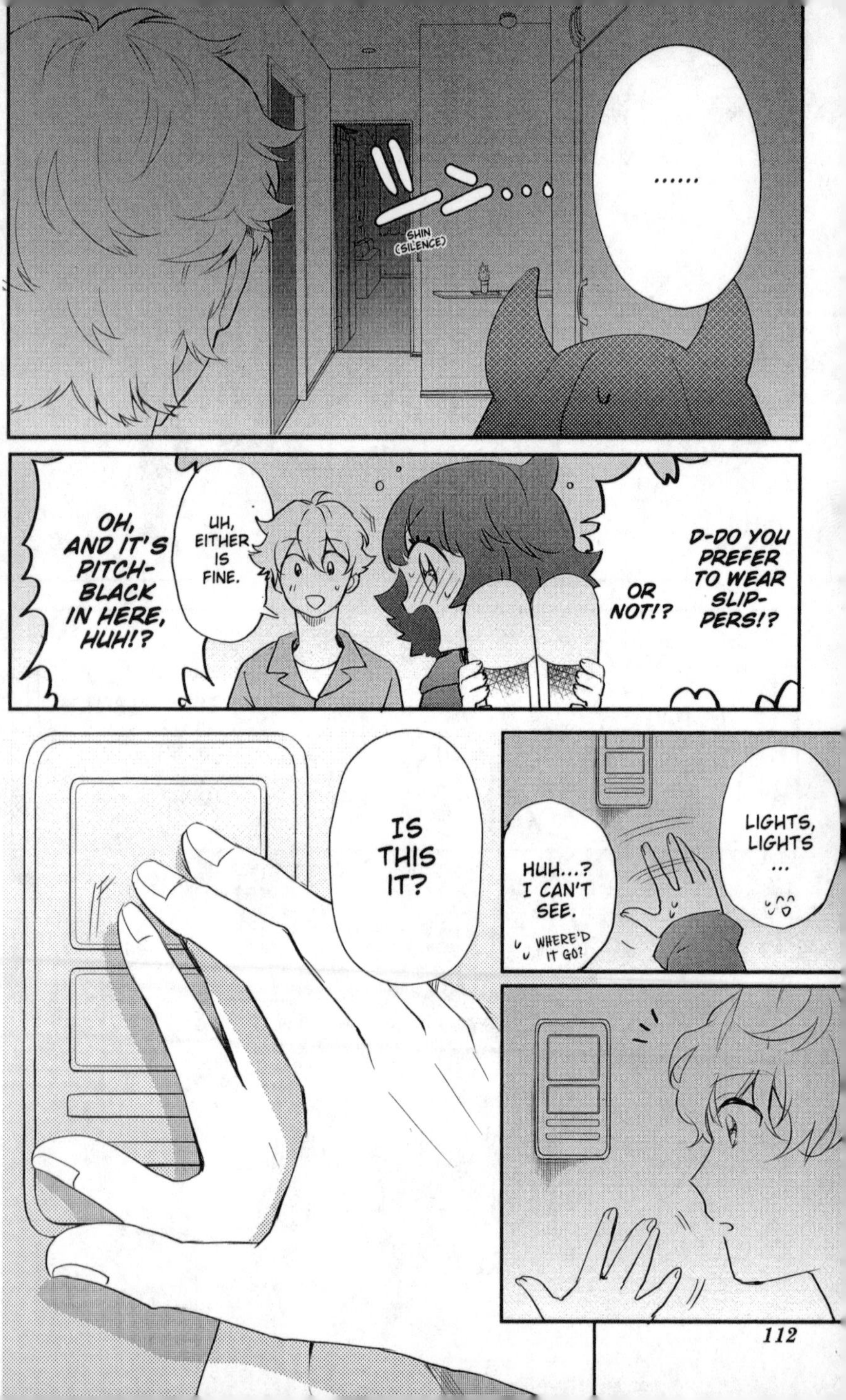
......
SHIN (SILENCE)
D-DO YOU PREFER TO WEAR SLIP-PERS!?
OR NOT!?
UH, EITHER IS FINE.
OH, AND IT'S PITCH-BLACK IN HERE, HUH!?
LIGHTS, LIGHTS ...
HUH...? I CAN'T SEE.
WHERE'D IT GO?
IS THIS IT?

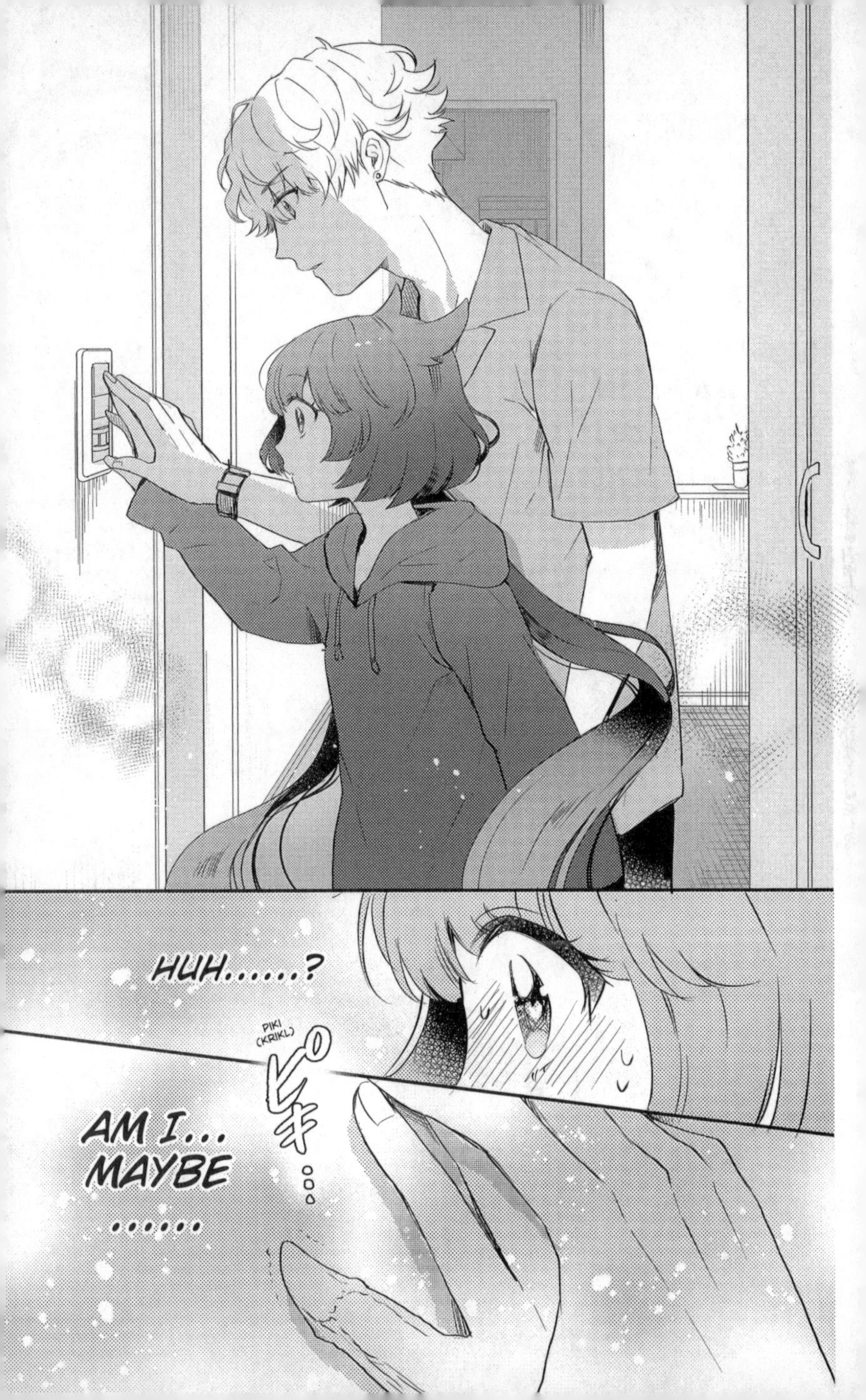
HUH......?
PIKI (KRIKL)
ピキ…
AM I... MAYBE
......

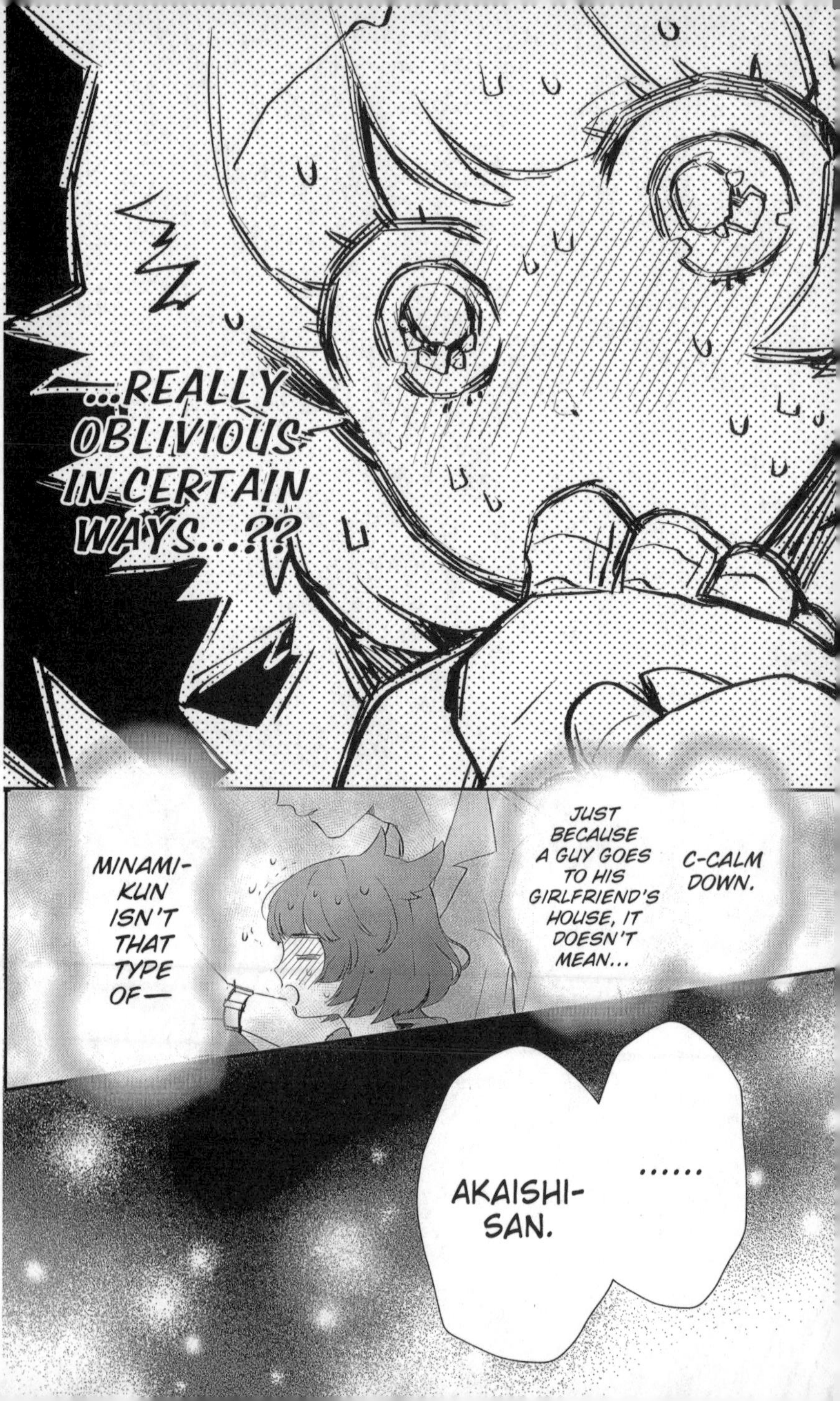
...REALLY OBLIVIOUS IN CERTAIN WAYS...??
C-CALM DOWN.
JUST BECAUSE A GUY GOES TO HIS GIRLFRIEND'S HOUSE, IT DOESN'T MEAN...
MINAMI-KUN ISN'T THAT TYPE OF—
......
AKAISHI-SAN.

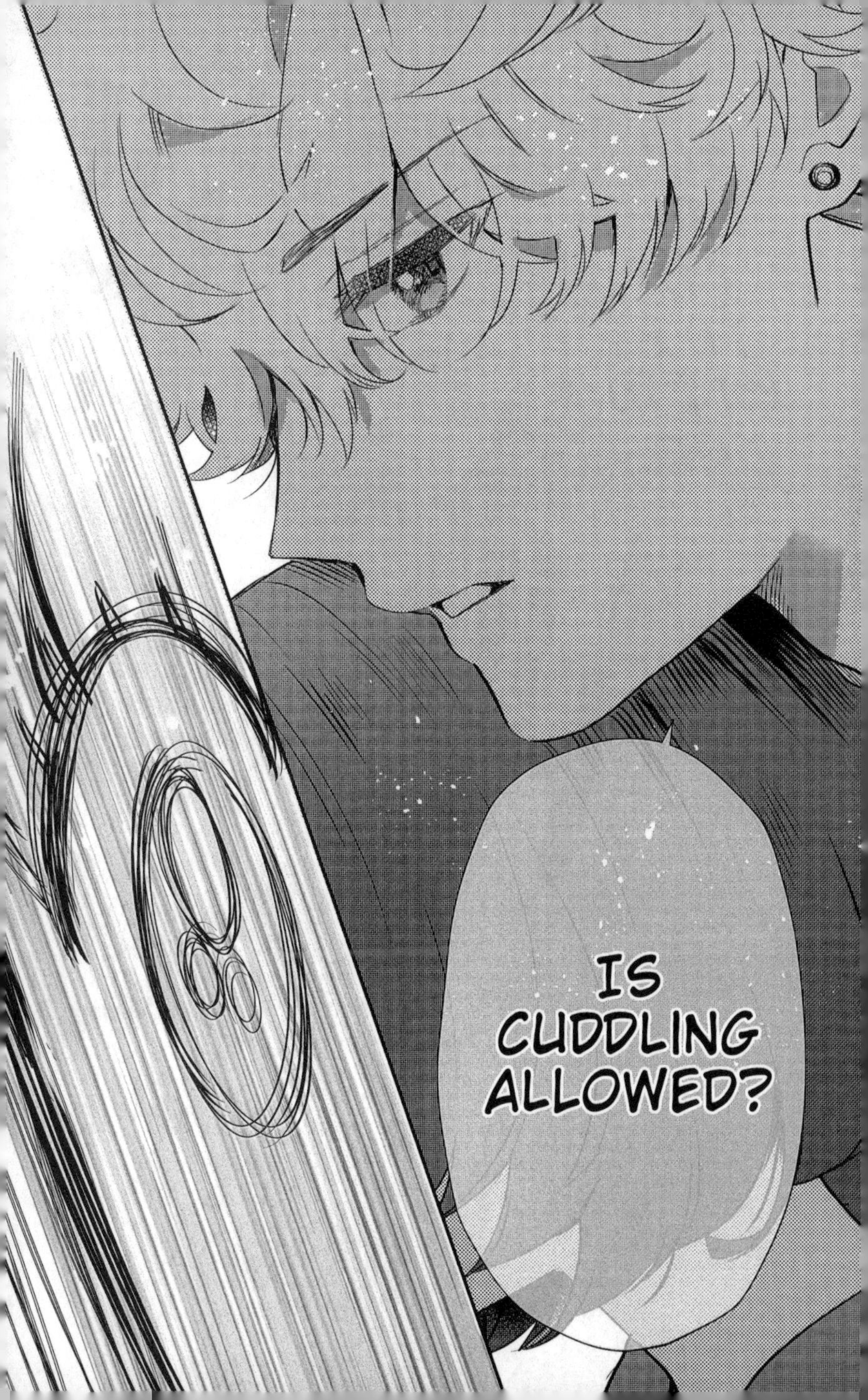
IS CUDDLING ALLOWED?

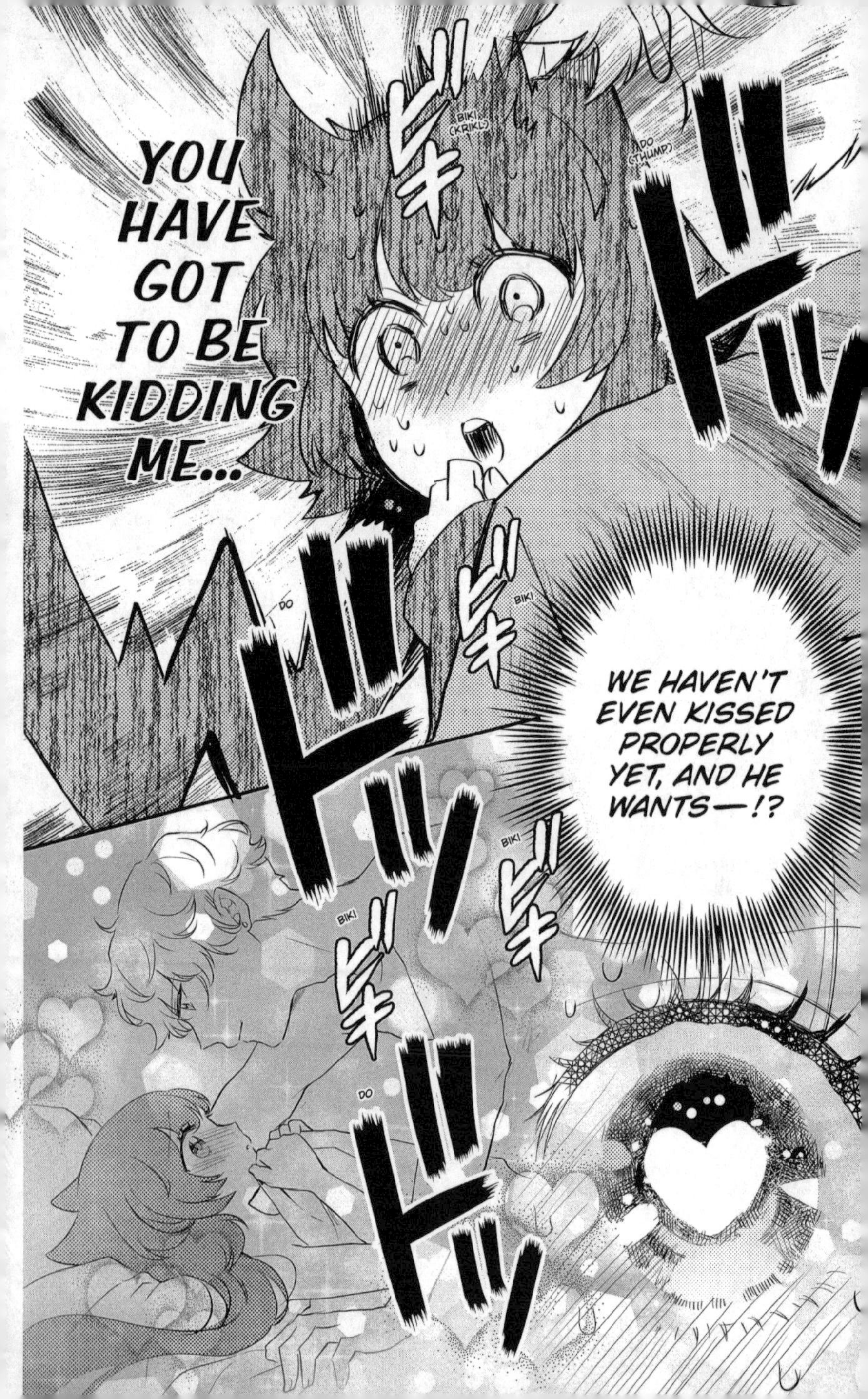
DO (THUMP)
BIKI (KRIKL)
YOU HAVE GOT TO BE KIDDING ME...
WE HAVEN'T EVEN KISSED PROPERLY YET, AND HE WANTS—!?
BIKI
DO
BIKI
BIKI
DO

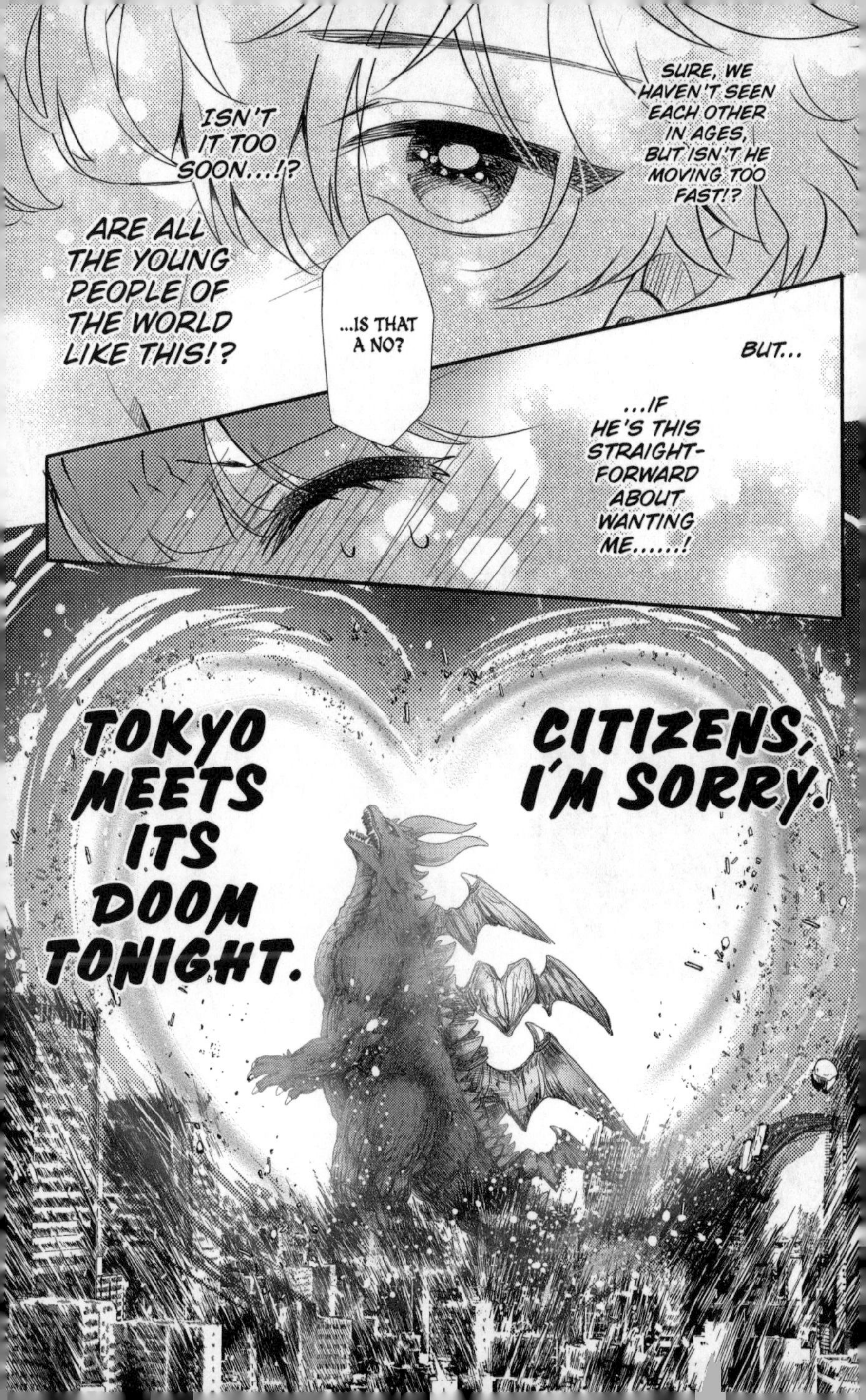
SURE, WE HAVEN'T SEEN EACH OTHER IN AGES, BUT ISN'T HE MOVING TOO FAST!?
ISN'T IT TOO SOON...!?
ARE ALL THE YOUNG PEOPLE OF THE WORLD LIKE THIS!?
...IS THAT A NO?
BUT...
...IF HE'S THIS STRAIGHT-FORWARD ABOUT WANTING ME......!
CITIZENS, I'M SORRY.
TOKYO MEETS ITS DOOM TONIGHT.

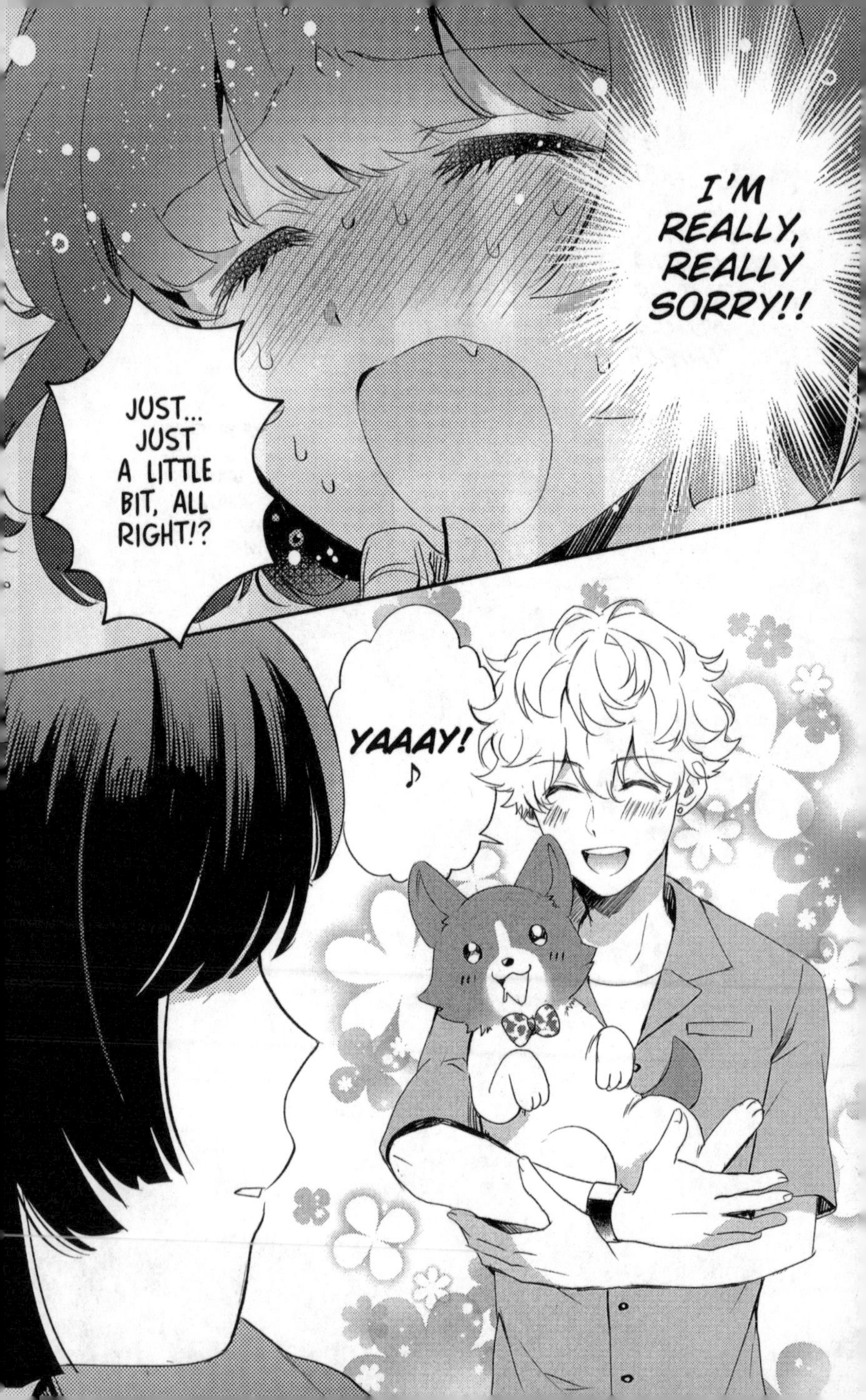
I'M REALLY, REALLY SORRY!!
JUST... JUST A LITTLE BIT, ALL RIGHT!?
YAAAY! ♪

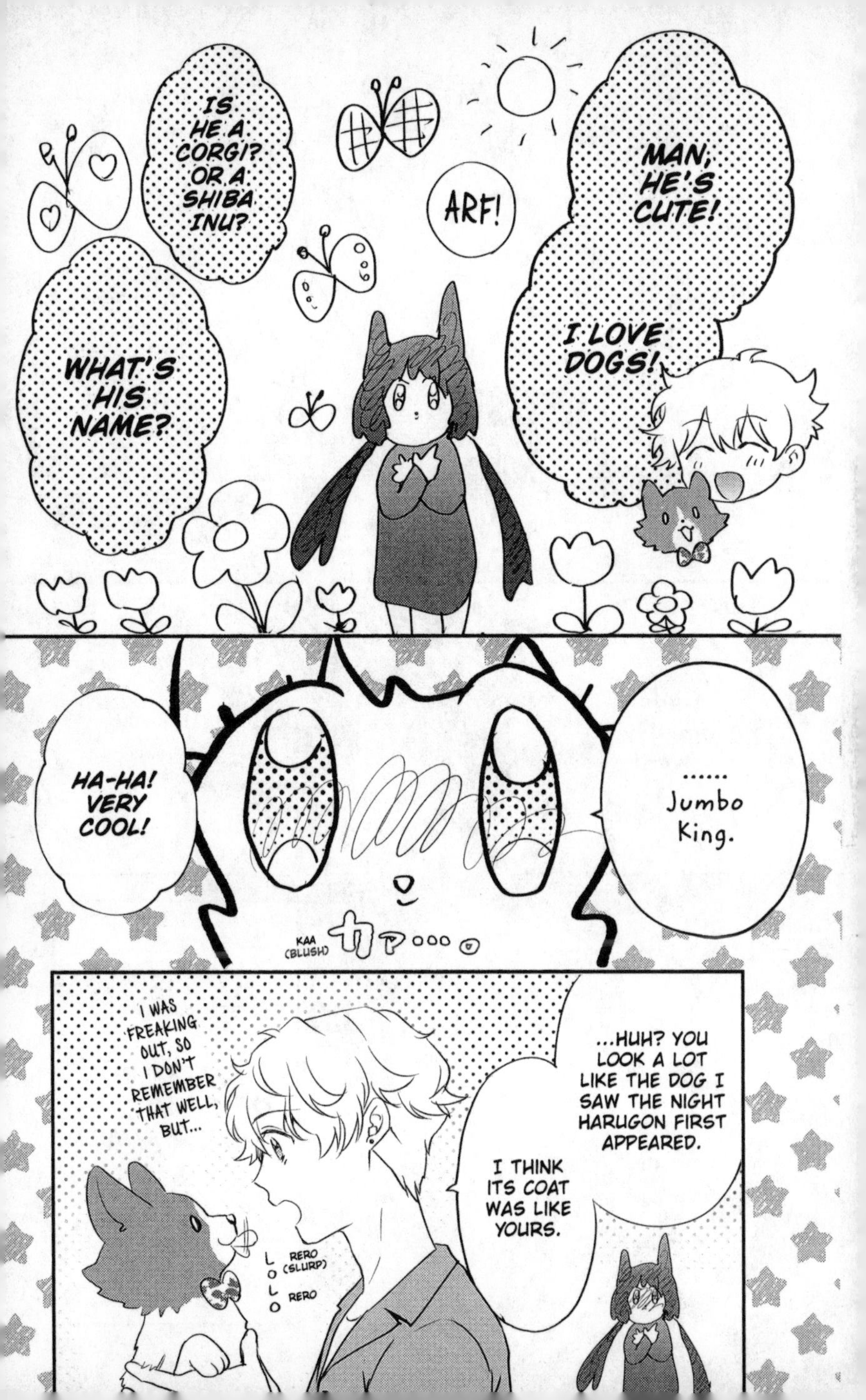
MAN, HE'S CUTE!
IS HE A CORGI? OR A SHIBA INU?
ARF!
I LOVE DOGS!
WHAT'S HIS NAME?
...... Jumbo King.
HA-HA! VERY COOL!
KAA (BLUSH)
...HUH? YOU LOOK A LOT LIKE THE DOG I SAW THE NIGHT HARUGON FIRST APPEARED.
I THINK ITS COAT WAS LIKE YOURS.
I WAS FREAKING OUT, SO I DON'T REMEMBER THAT WELL, BUT...
RERO (SLURP)
RERO

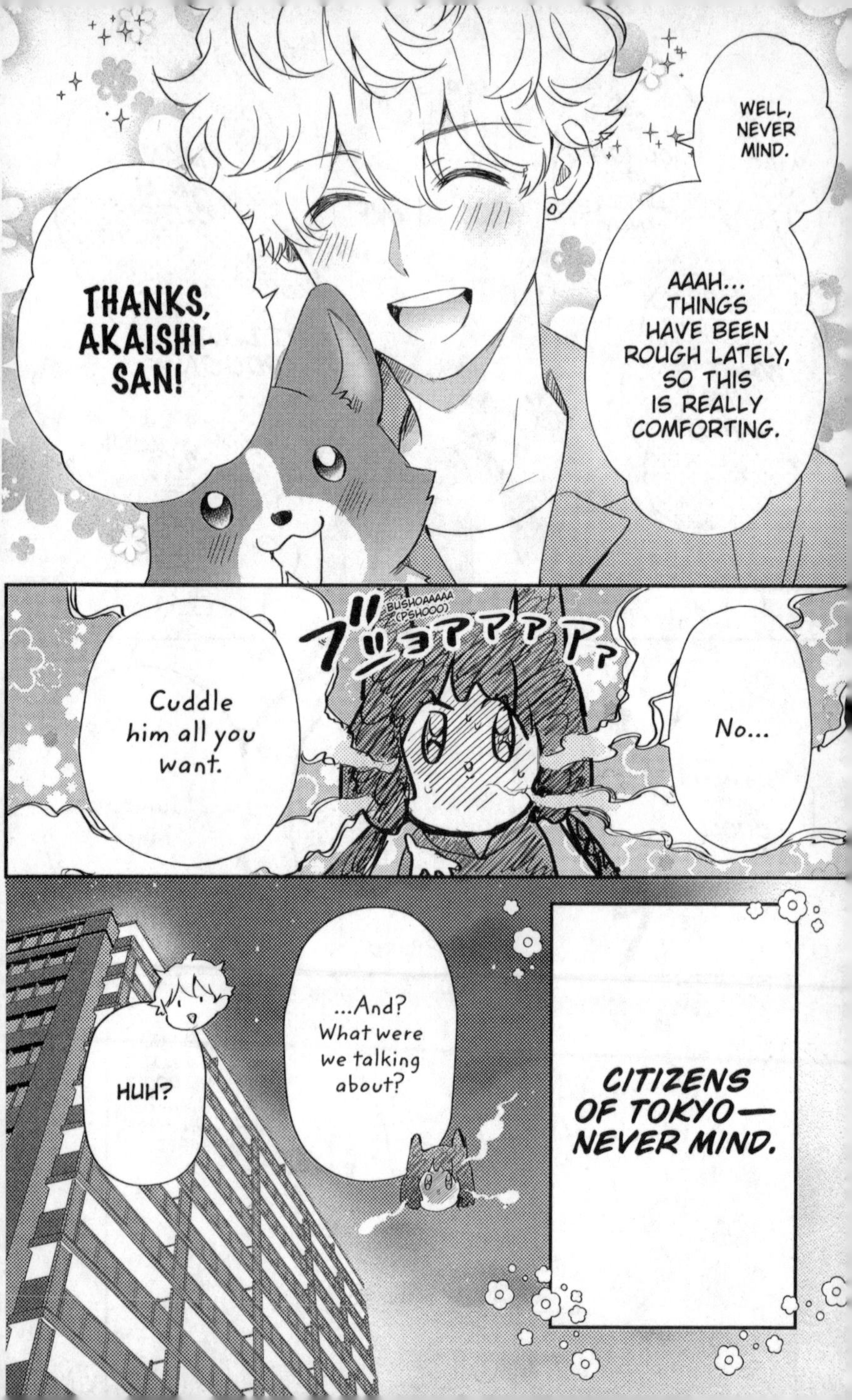
WELL, NEVER MIND.
AAAH... THINGS HAVE BEEN ROUGH LATELY, SO THIS IS REALLY COMFORTING.
THANKS, AKAISHI-SAN!
No...
ブシュアアアアァ
BUSHOAAAAA (PSHOOO)
Cuddle him all you want.
CITIZENS OF TOKYO— NEVER MIND.
...And? What were we talking about?
HUH?

KAIJU♥GIRL
CARAMELISE

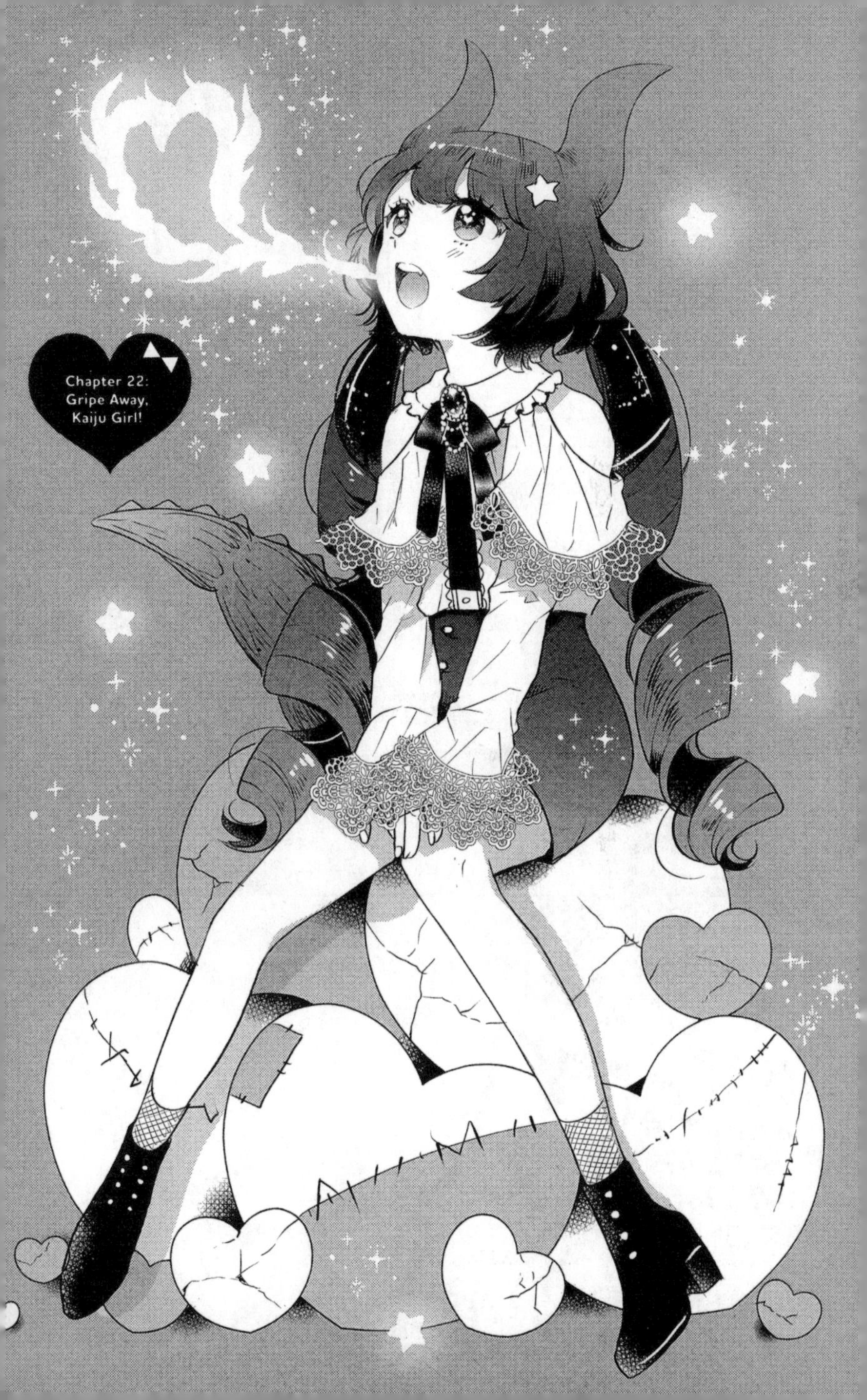
Chapter 22:
Gripe Away,
Kaiju Girl!

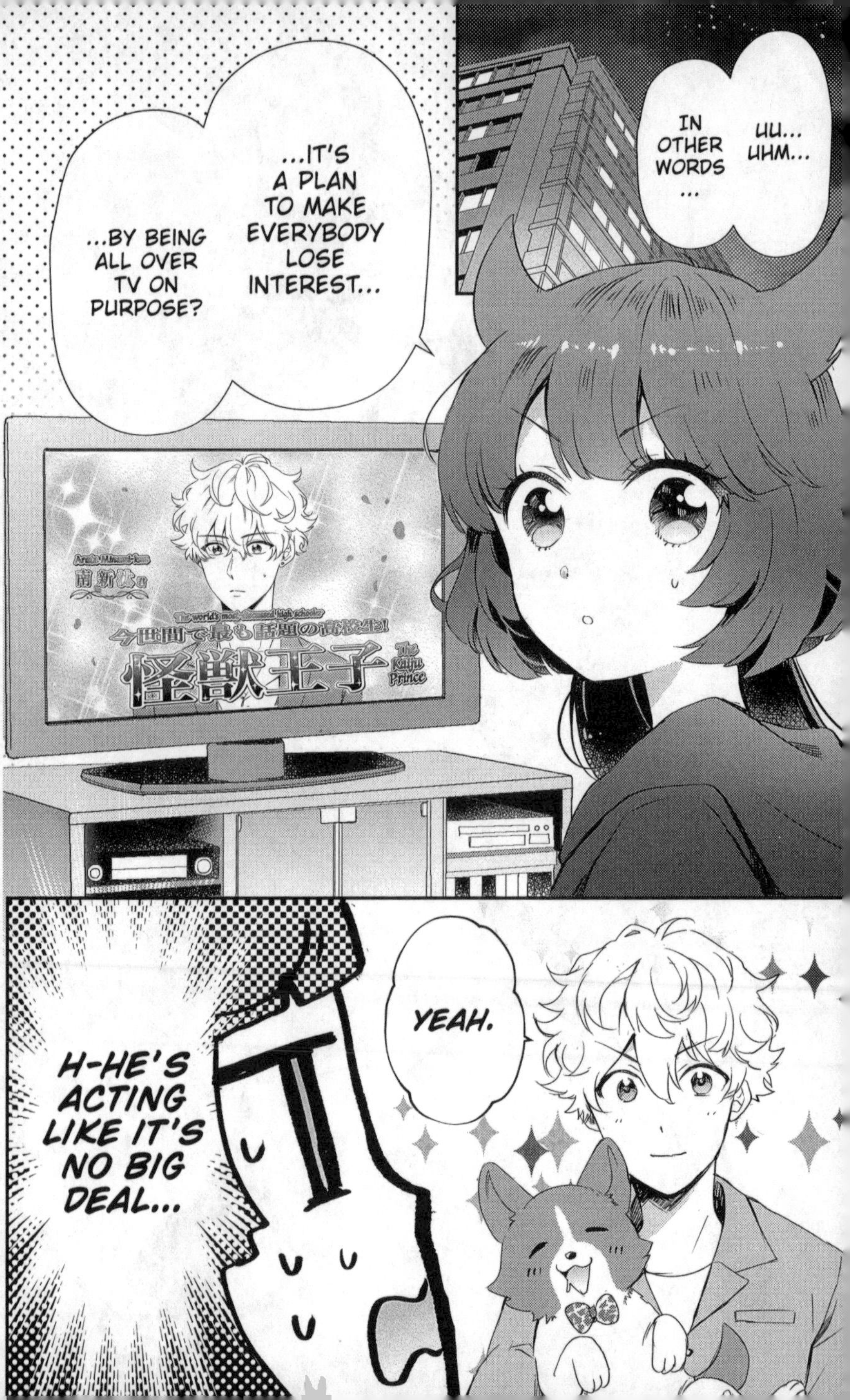
UU... UHM...
IN OTHER WORDS...
...IT'S A PLAN TO MAKE EVERYBODY LOSE INTEREST...
...BY BEING ALL OVER TV ON PURPOSE?
今世間で最も話題の高校生!
怪獣王子
The Kaiju Prince
YEAH.
H-HE'S ACTING LIKE IT'S NO BIG DEAL...

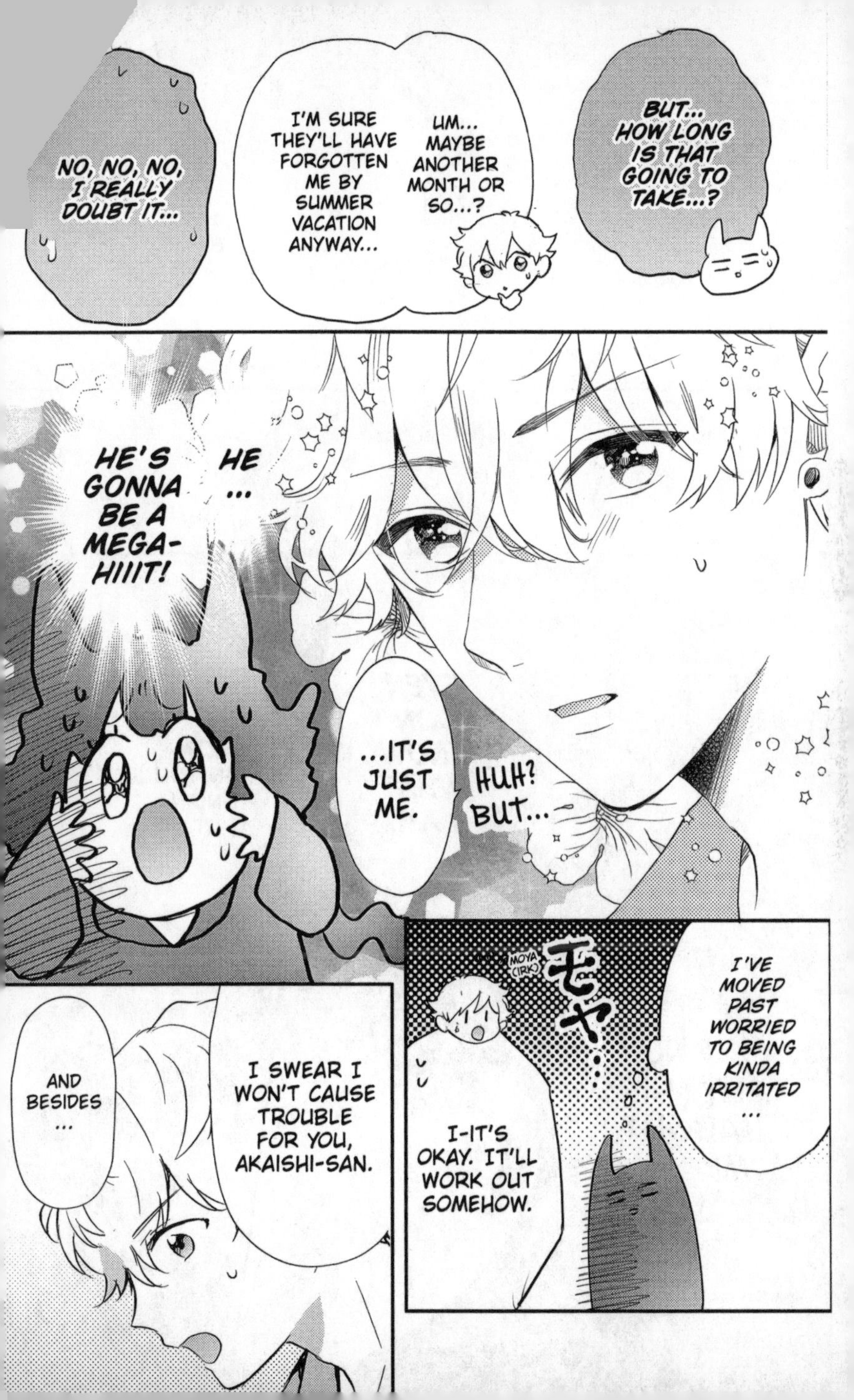
BUT... HOW LONG IS THAT GOING TO TAKE...?
UM... MAYBE ANOTHER MONTH OR SO...?
I'M SURE THEY'LL HAVE FORGOTTEN ME BY SUMMER VACATION ANYWAY...
NO, NO, NO, I REALLY DOUBT IT...
HUH? BUT...
...IT'S JUST ME.
HE ...
HE'S GONNA BE A MEGA-HIIIT!
I'VE MOVED PAST WORRIED TO BEING KINDA IRRITATED ...
MOYA (IRK)
モヤ...
I-IT'S OKAY. IT'LL WORK OUT SOMEHOW.
I SWEAR I WON'T CAUSE TROUBLE FOR YOU, AKAISHI-SAN.
AND BESIDES ...

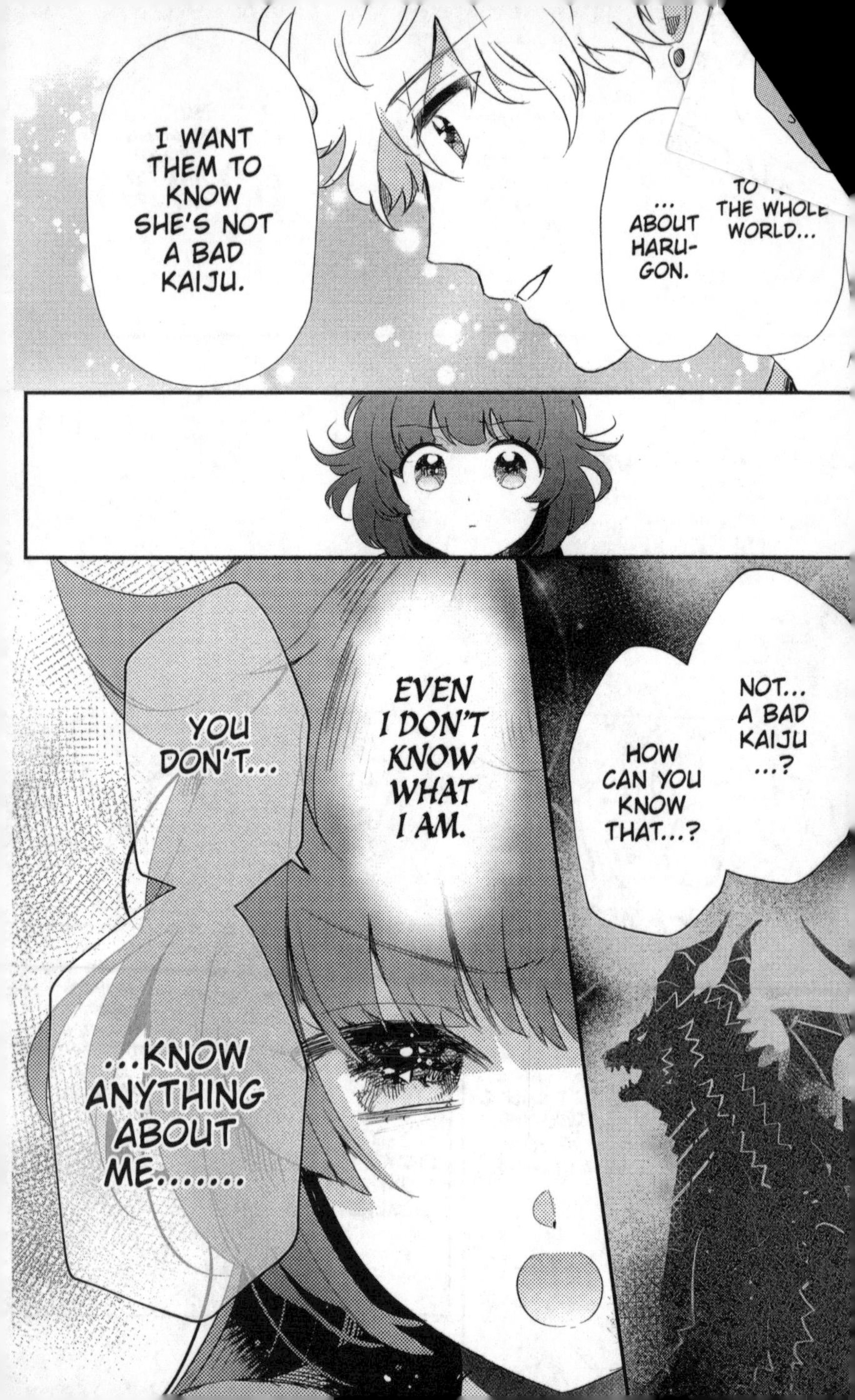
TO T THE WHOLE WORLD...
...ABOUT HARU-GON.
I WANT THEM TO KNOW SHE'S NOT A BAD KAIJU.
NOT... A BAD KAIJU ...?
HOW CAN YOU KNOW THAT...?
EVEN I DON'T KNOW WHAT I AM.
YOU DON'T...
...KNOW ANYTHING ABOUT ME.......

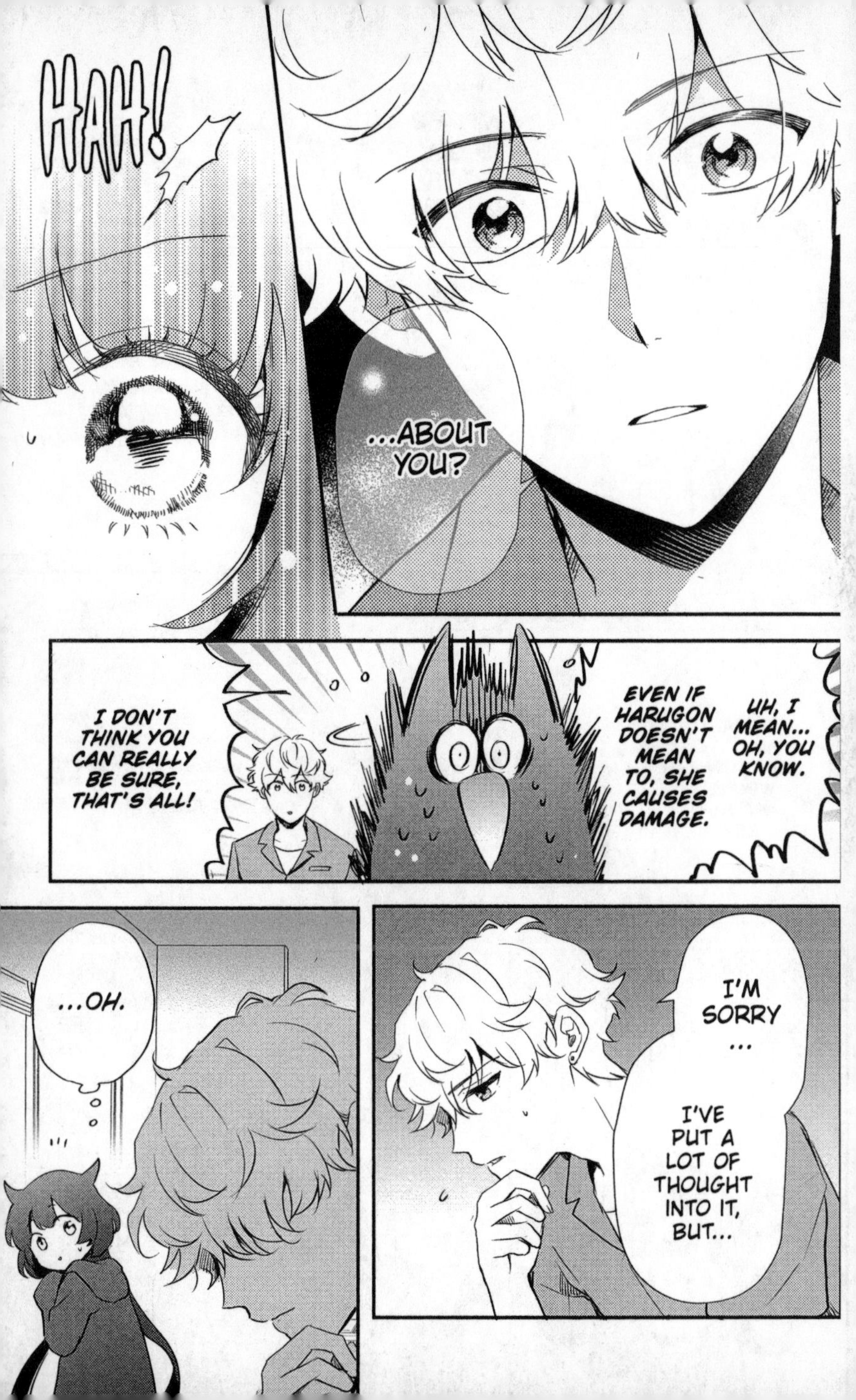
...ABOUT YOU?
HAH!
UH, I MEAN... OH, YOU KNOW.
EVEN IF HARUGON DOESN'T MEAN TO, SHE CAUSES DAMAGE.
I DON'T THINK YOU CAN REALLY BE SURE, THAT'S ALL!
I'M SORRY...
I'VE PUT A LOT OF THOUGHT INTO IT, BUT...
...OH.

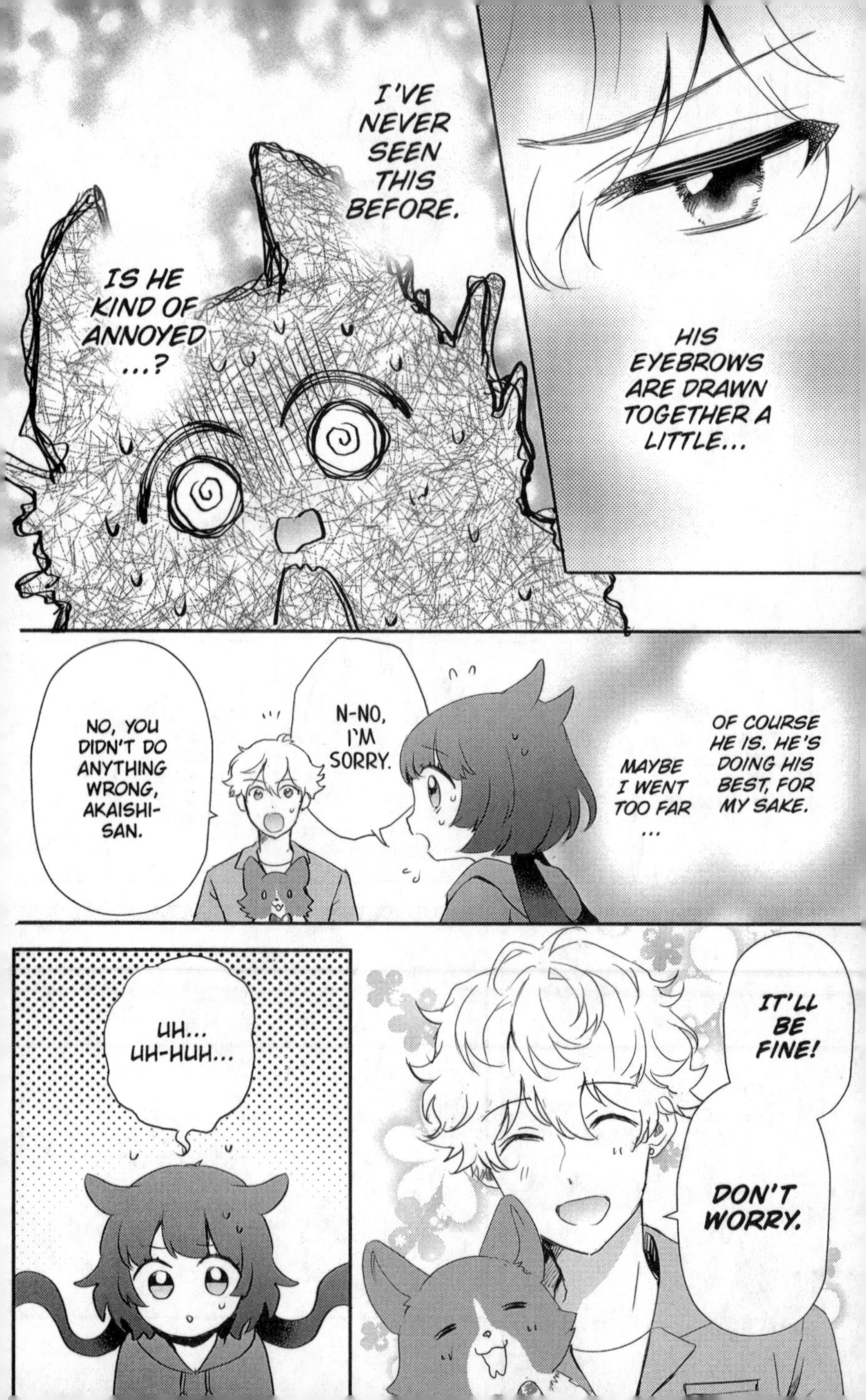
HIS EYEBROWS ARE DRAWN TOGETHER A LITTLE...
I'VE NEVER SEEN THIS BEFORE.
IS HE KIND OF ANNOYED ...?
OF COURSE HE IS. HE'S DOING HIS BEST, FOR MY SAKE.
MAYBE I WENT TOO FAR ...
N-NO, I'M SORRY.
NO, YOU DIDN'T DO ANYTHING WRONG, AKAISHI-SAN.
IT'LL BE FINE!
DON'T WORRY.
UH... UH-HUH...

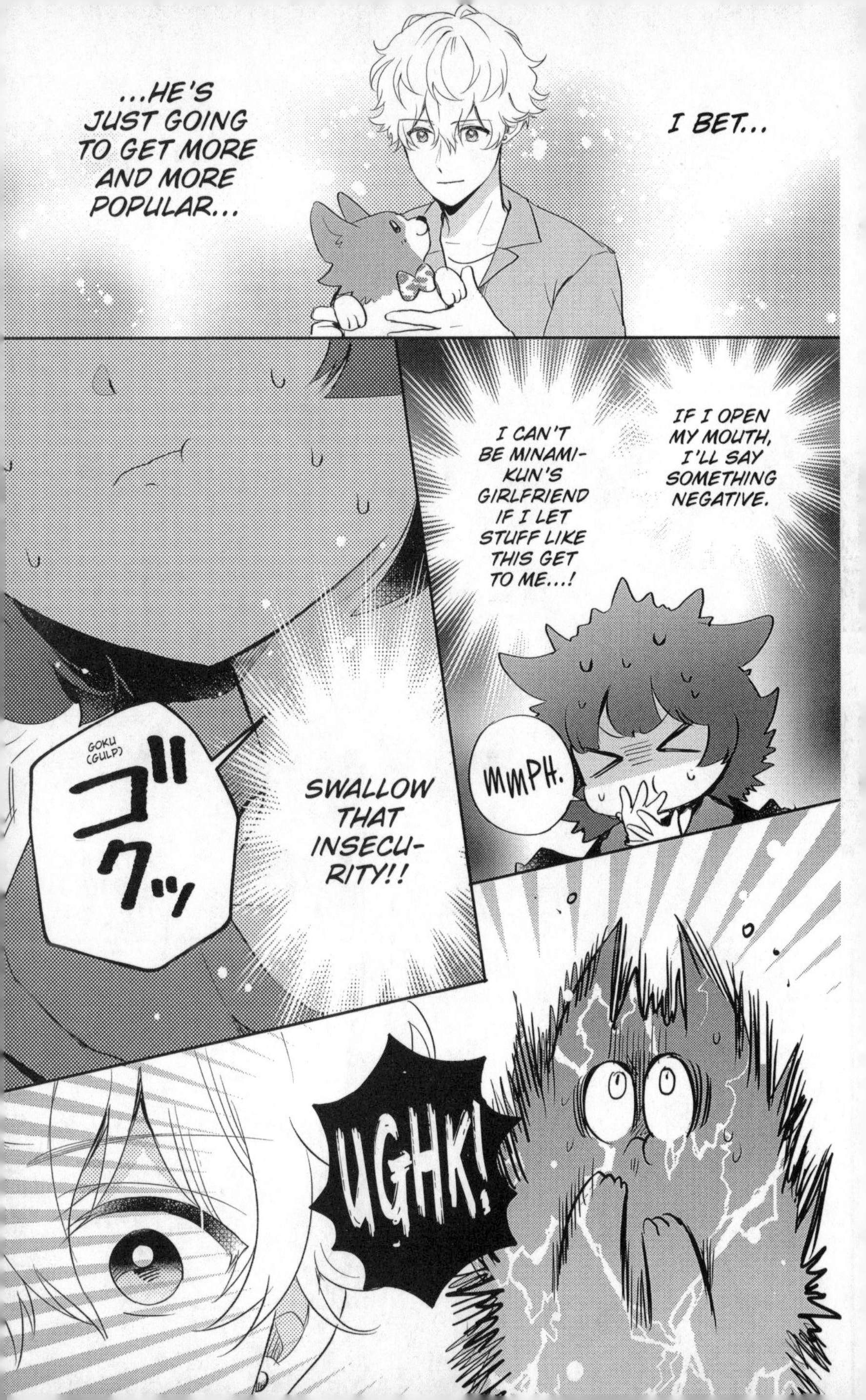
I BET...
...HE'S JUST GOING TO GET MORE AND MORE POPULAR...
IF I OPEN MY MOUTH, I'LL SAY SOMETHING NEGATIVE.
I CAN'T BE MINAMI-KUN'S GIRLFRIEND IF I LET STUFF LIKE THIS GET TO ME...!
MMPH.
SWALLOW THAT INSECU-RITY!!
ゴクッ
GOKU (GULP)
UGHK!

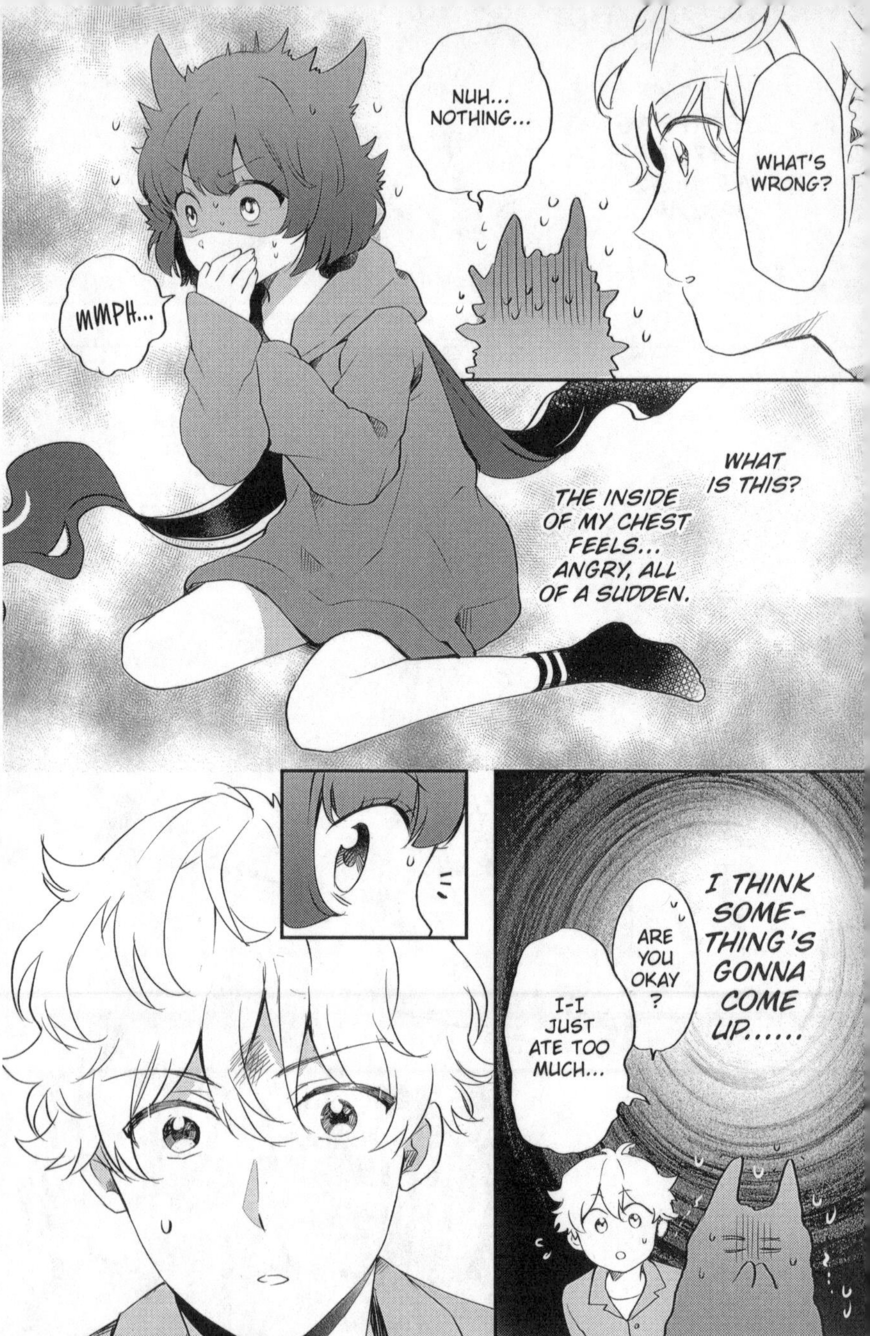
WHAT'S WRONG?
NUH... NOTHING...
MMPH...
WHAT IS THIS?
THE INSIDE OF MY CHEST FEELS... ANGRY, ALL OF A SUDDEN.
ARE YOU OKAY?
I THINK SOME-THING'S GONNA COME UP......
I-I JUST ATE TOO MUCH...

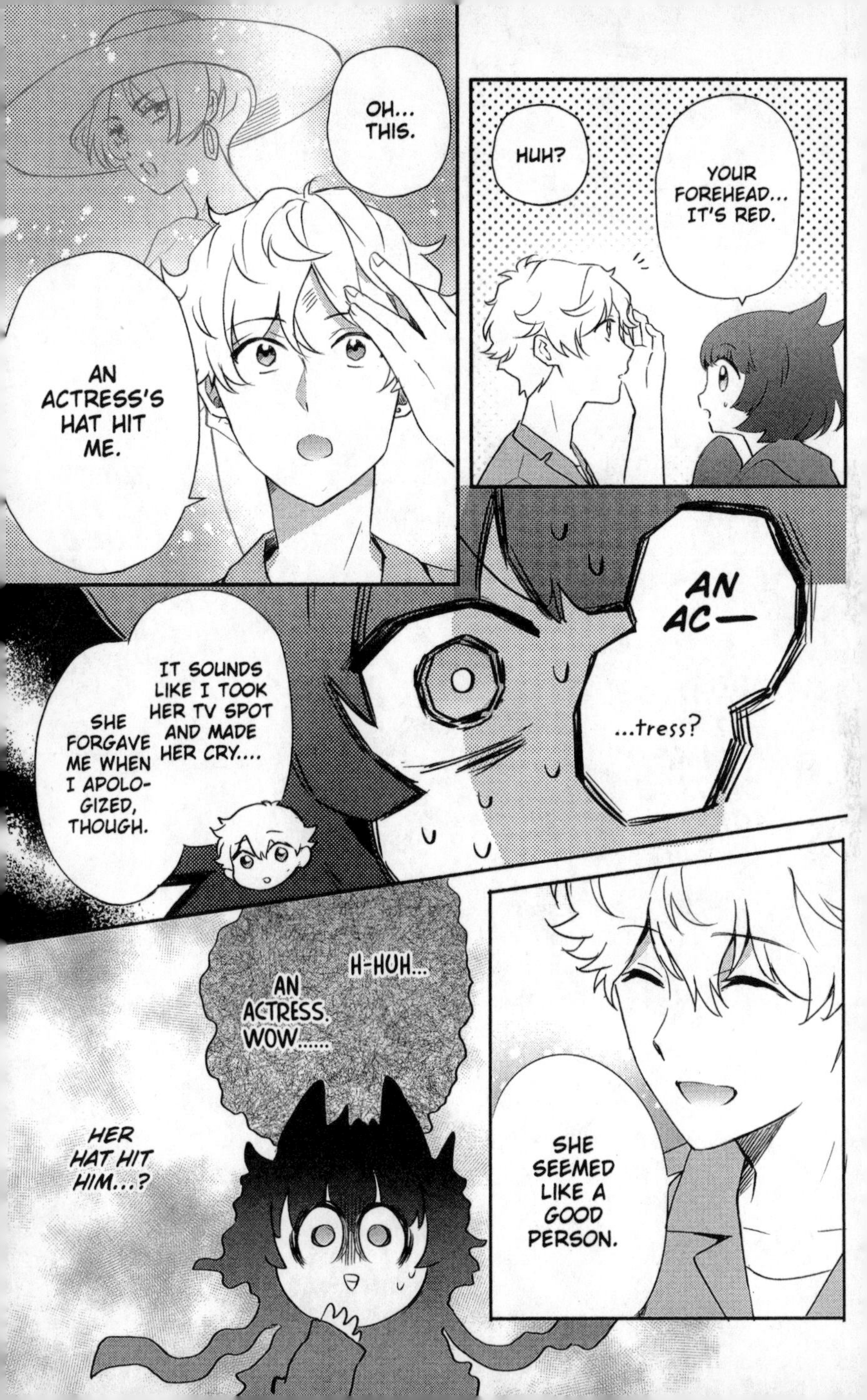
YOUR FOREHEAD... IT'S RED.
HUH?
OH... THIS.
AN ACTRESS'S HAT HIT ME.
AN AC—
...tress?
IT SOUNDS LIKE I TOOK HER TV SPOT AND MADE HER CRY....
SHE FORGAVE ME WHEN I APOLOGIZED, THOUGH.
SHE SEEMED LIKE A GOOD PERSON.
H-HUH...
AN ACTRESS. WOW......
HER HAT HIT HIM...?

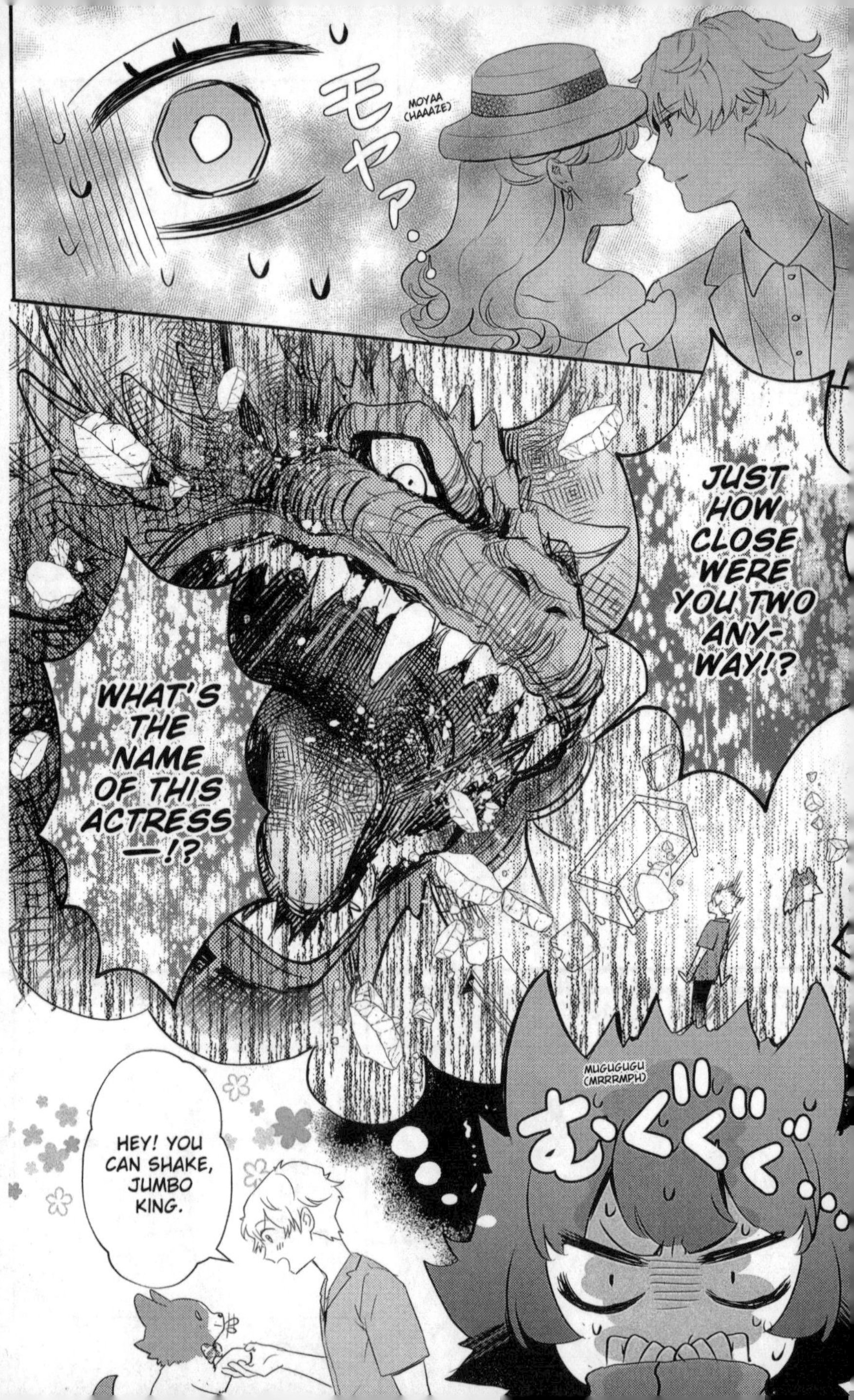
モヤァ
MOYAA (HAAAZE)
JUST HOW CLOSE WERE YOU TWO ANY-WAY!?
WHAT'S THE NAME OF THIS ACTRESS—!?
むぐぐ
MUGUGUGU (MRRRMPH)
HEY! YOU CAN SHAKE, JUMBO KING.

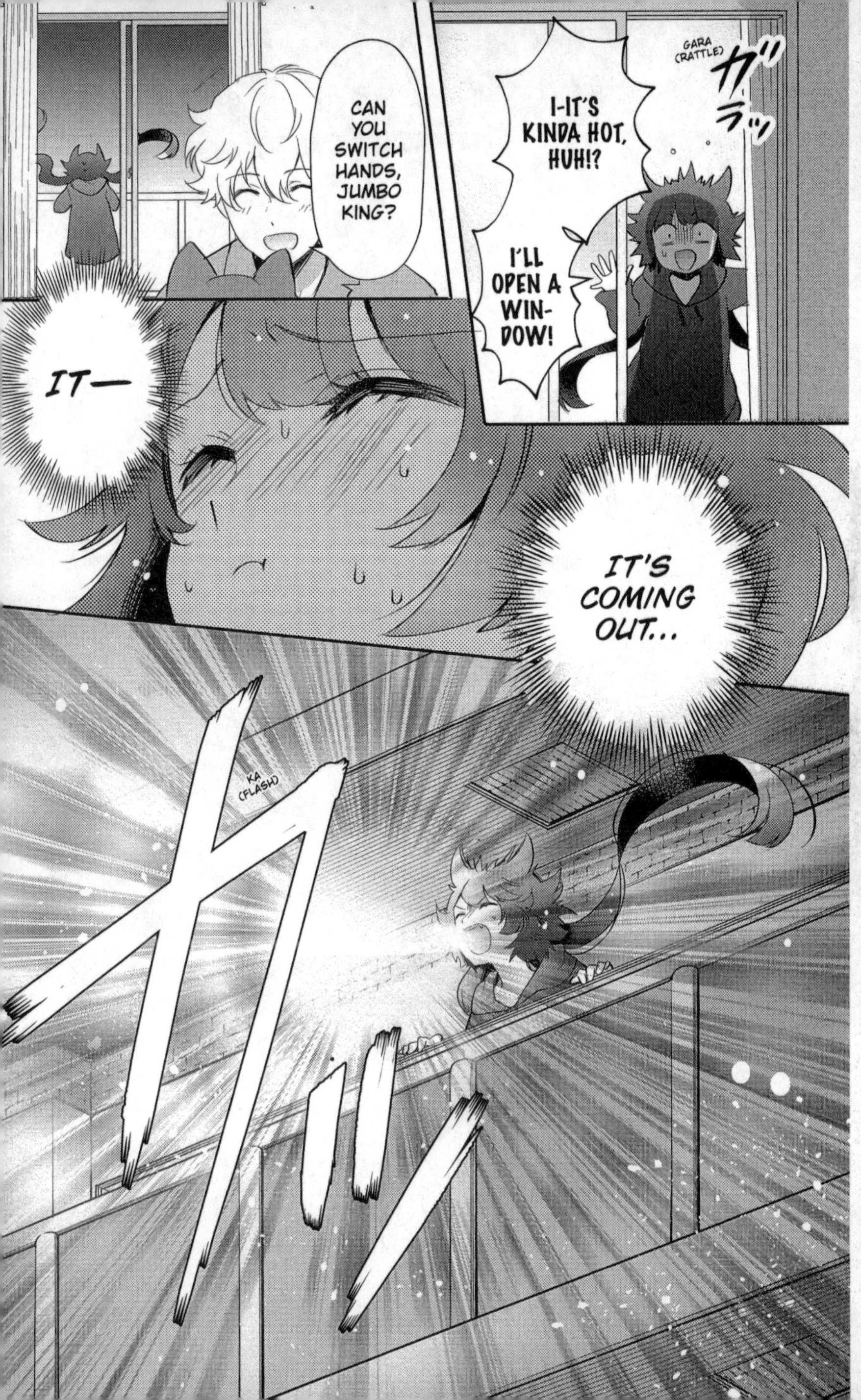
GARA (RATTLE)
I-IT'S KINDA HOT, HUH!?
I'LL OPEN A WIN-DOW!
CAN YOU SWITCH HANDS, JUMBO KING?
IT—
IT'S COMING OUT...
KA (FLASH)

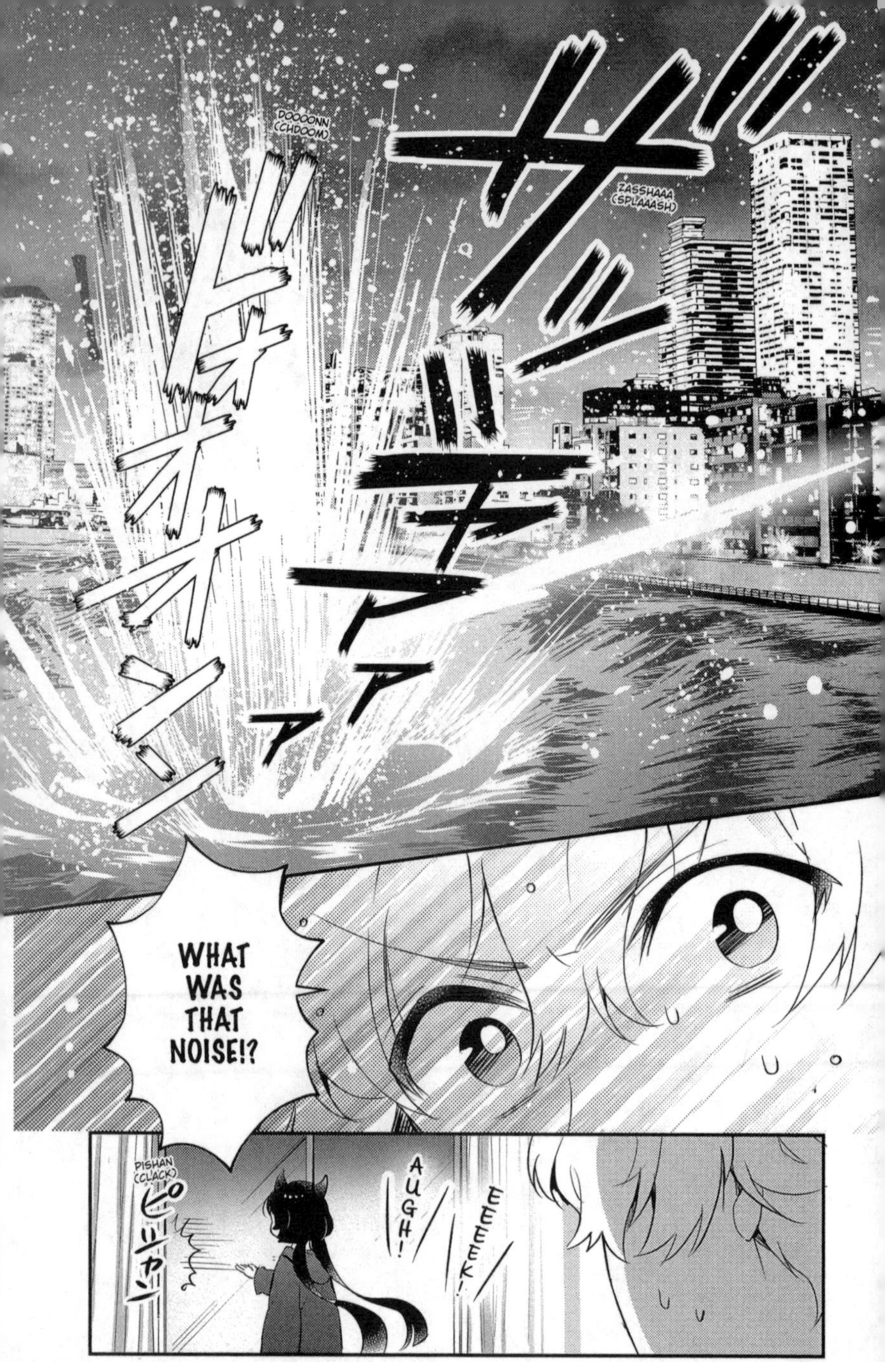
ZASSHAAA (SPLAAASH)
DOOOONN (CHDOOM)
WHAT WAS THAT NOISE!?
EEEEEK!
AUGH!
PISHAN (CLACK)

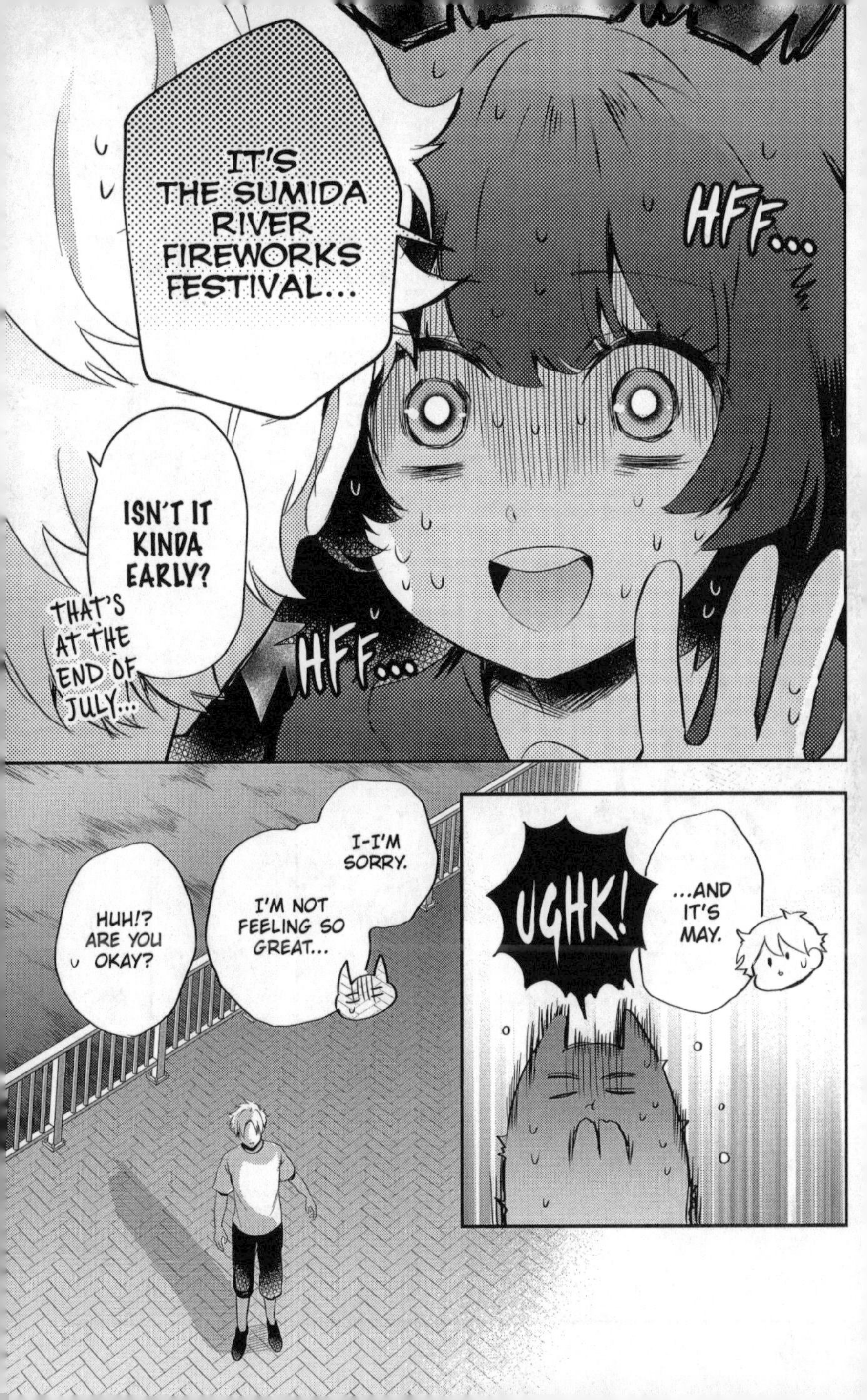
HFF...
IT'S THE SUMIDA RIVER FIREWORKS FESTIVAL...
ISN'T IT KINDA EARLY?
HFF...
THAT'S AT THE END OF JULY..!
...AND IT'S MAY.
UGHK!
I-I'M SORRY.
I'M NOT FEELING SO GREAT...
HUH!? ARE YOU OKAY?

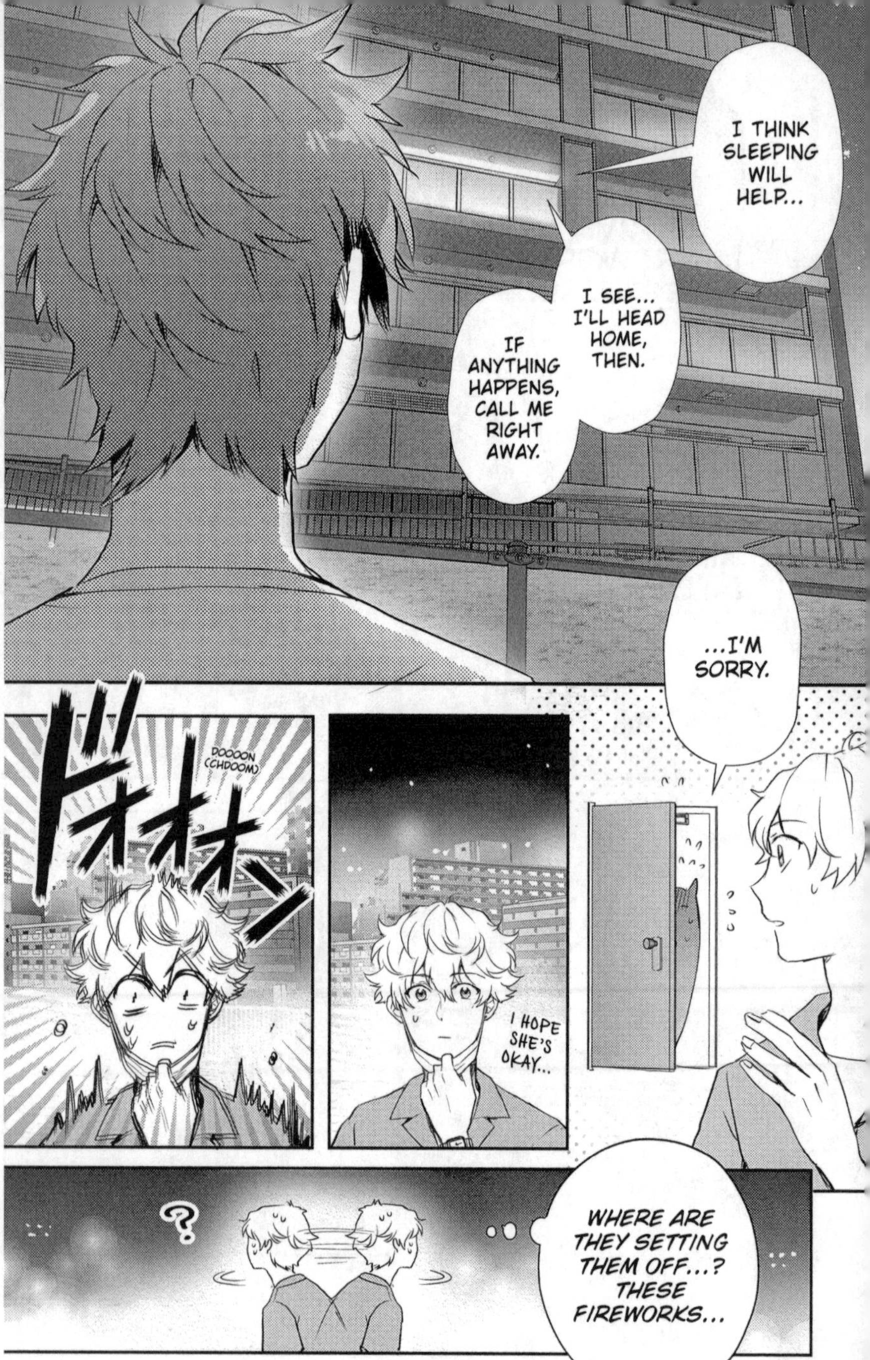
I THINK SLEEPING WILL HELP...
I SEE... I'LL HEAD HOME, THEN.
IF ANYTHING HAPPENS, CALL ME RIGHT AWAY.
...I'M SORRY.
I HOPE SHE'S OKAY...
ドオオン
DOOOON (CHDOOM)
WHERE ARE THEY SETTING THEM OFF...? THESE FIREWORKS...

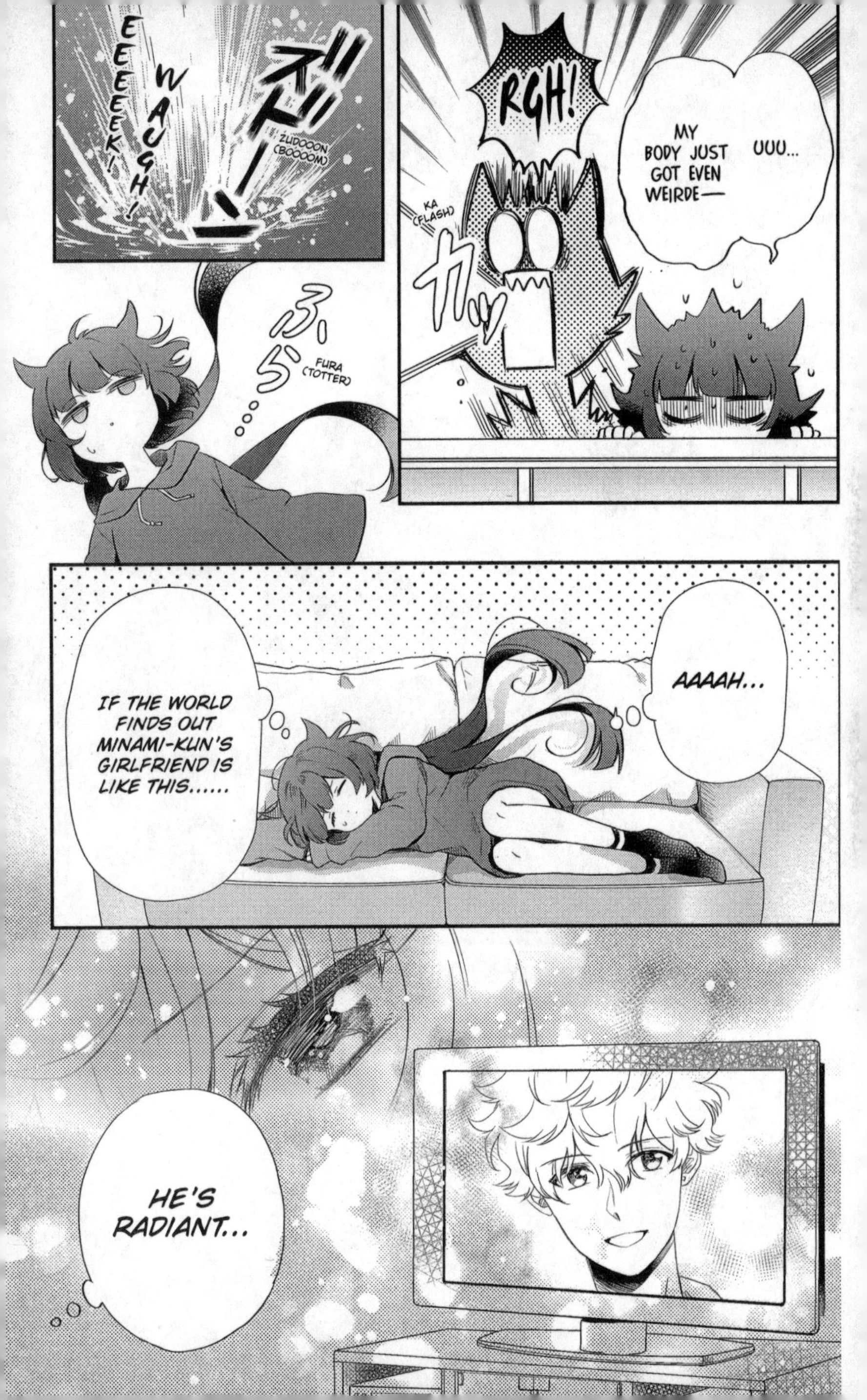
UUU...
MY BODY JUST GOT EVEN WEIRDE—
RGH!
KA (FLASH)
ZUDOOON (BOOOOM)
WAUGH!
EEEEEEK!
FURA (TOTTER)
AAAAH...
IF THE WORLD FINDS OUT MINAMI-KUN'S GIRLFRIEND IS LIKE THIS......
HE'S RADIANT...

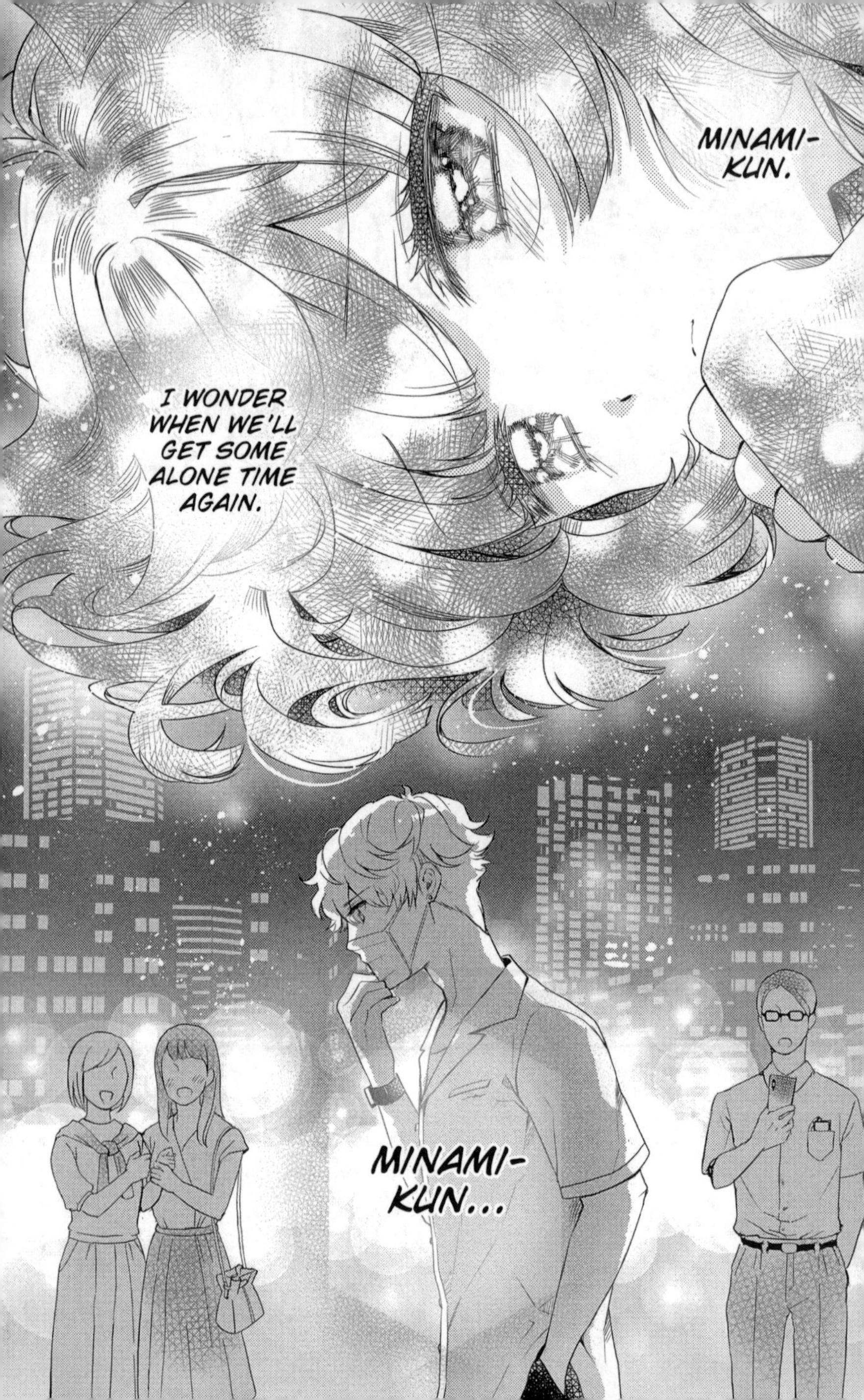
MINAMI-
KUN.
I WONDER
WHEN WE'LL
GET SOME
ALONE TIME
AGAIN.
MINAMI-
KUN...

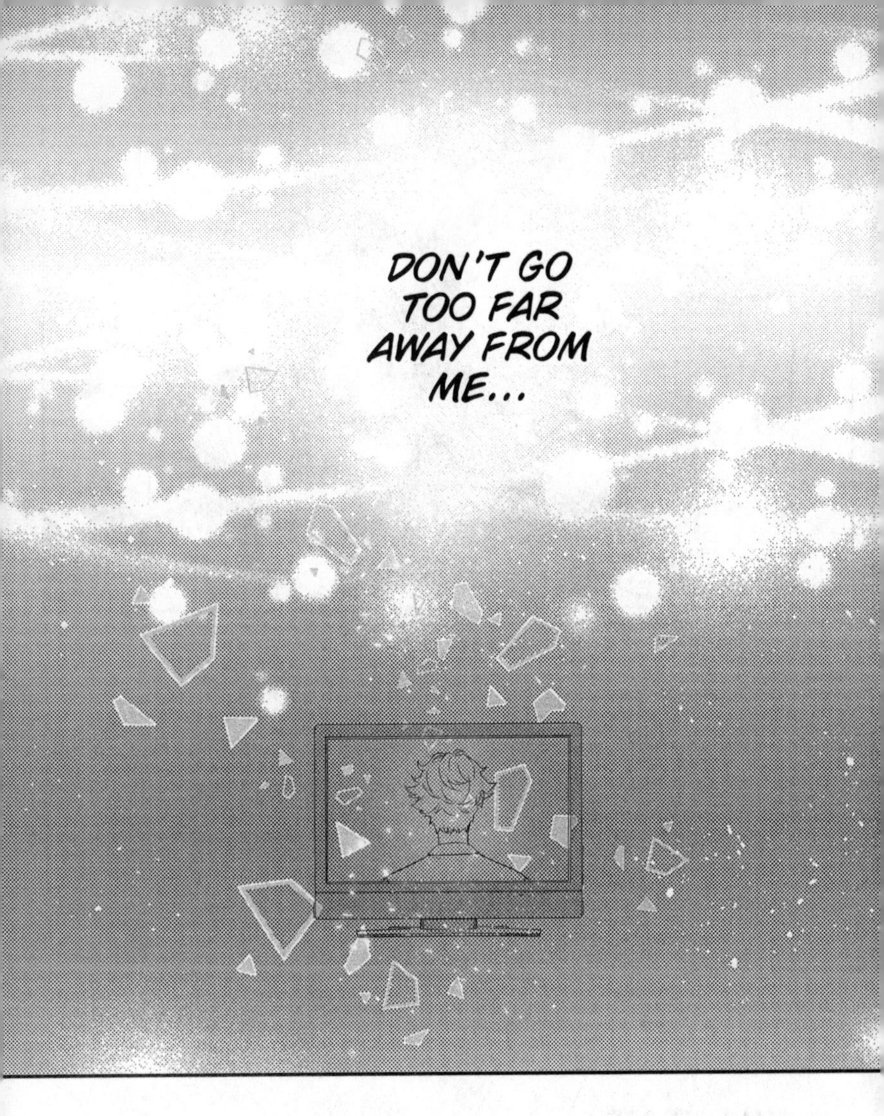
DON'T GO TOO FAR AWAY FROM ME...

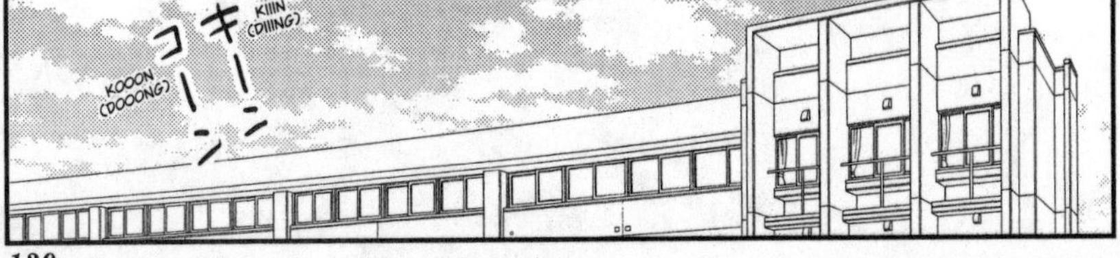
キーン
KIIN (DIIING)
コーン
KOOON (DOOONG)

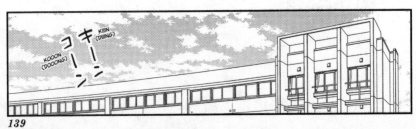

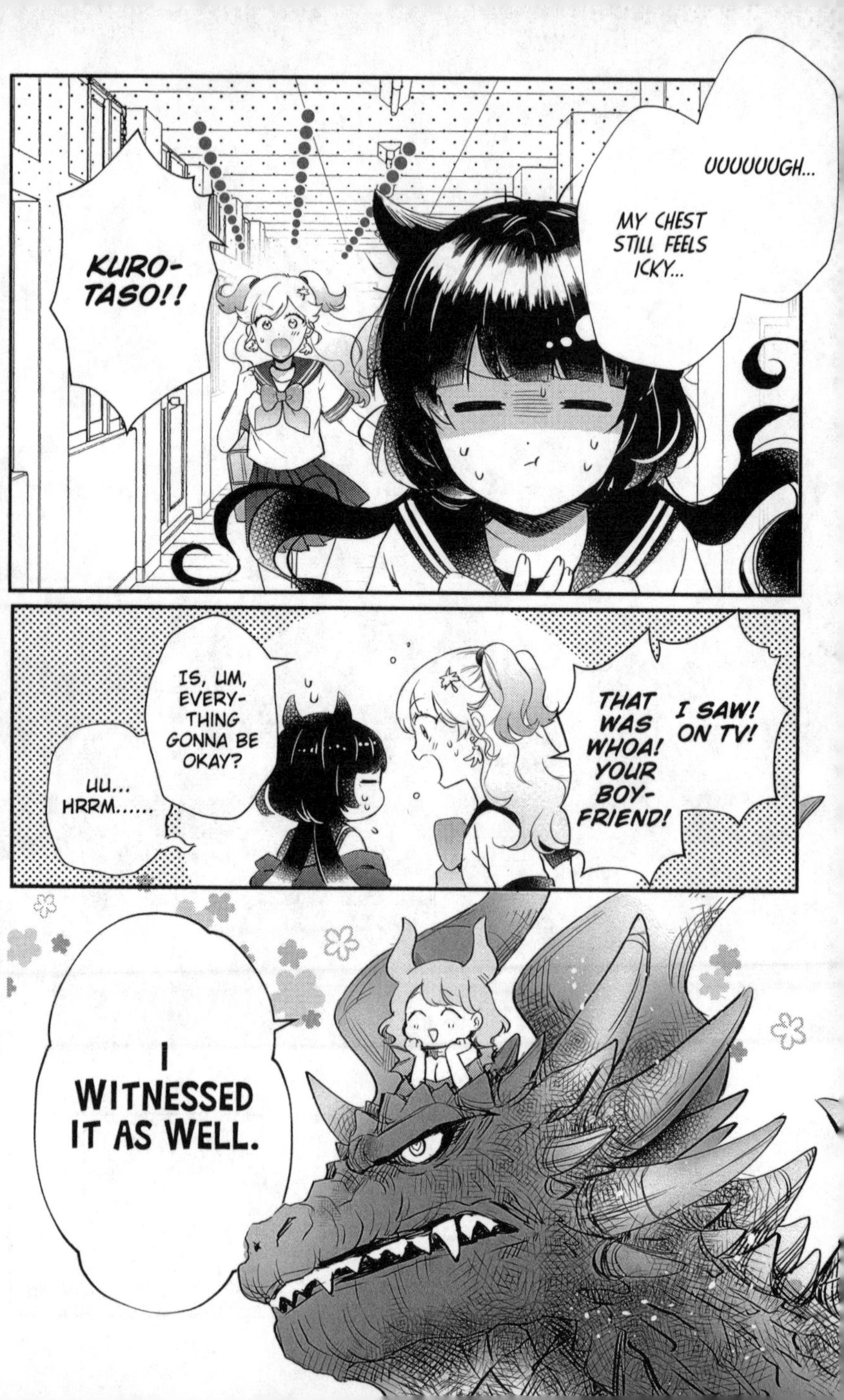
UUUUUUGH...
MY CHEST STILL FEELS ICKY...
KURO-TASO!!
I SAW! ON TV!
THAT WAS WHOA! YOUR BOY-FRIEND!
IS, UM, EVERY-THING GONNA BE OKAY?
UU... HRRM......
I WITNESSED IT AS WELL.

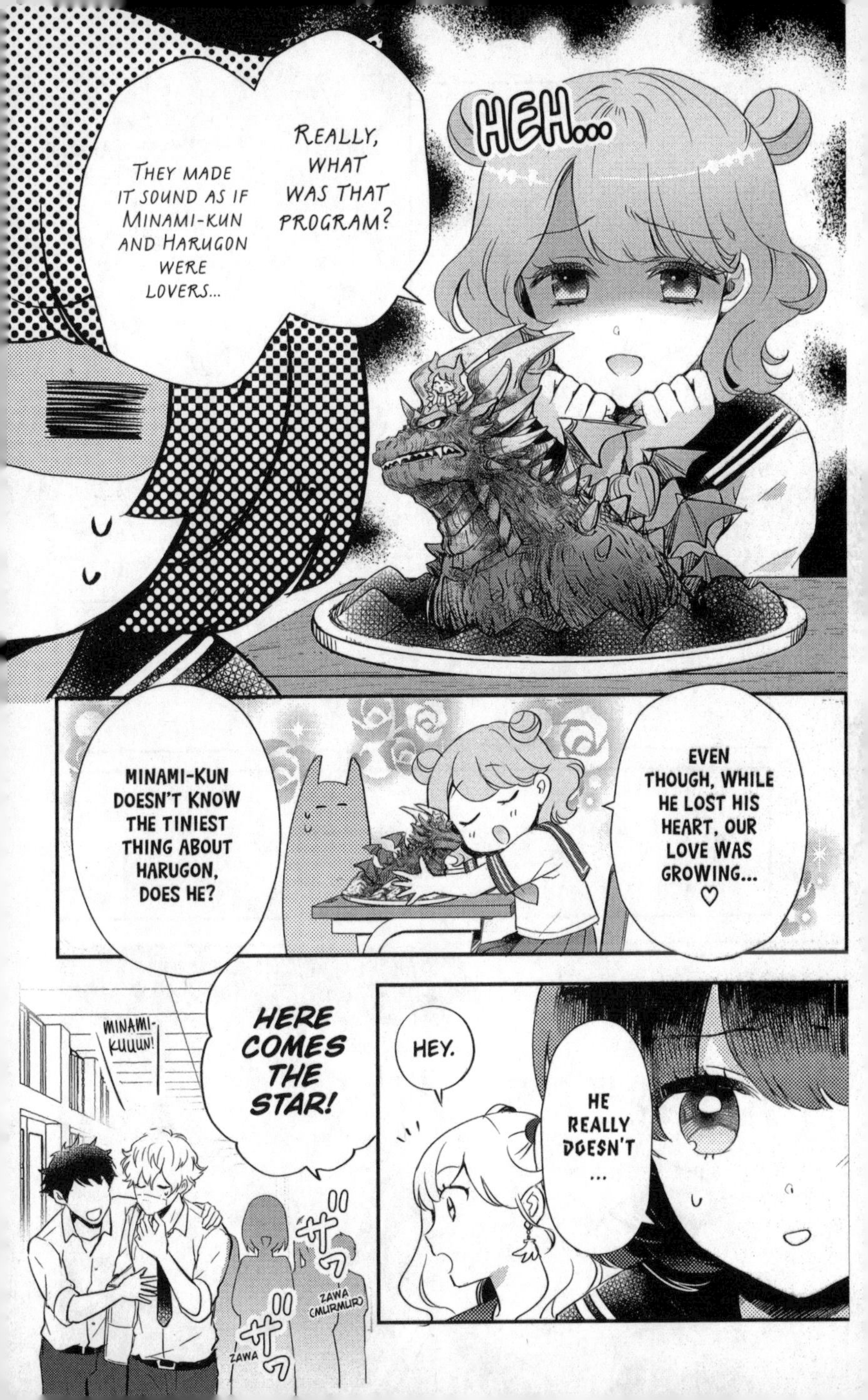
HEH...
REALLY, WHAT WAS THAT PROGRAM?
THEY MADE IT SOUND AS IF MINAMI-KUN AND HARUGON WERE LOVERS...
EVEN THOUGH, WHILE HE LOST HIS HEART, OUR LOVE WAS GROWING... ♡
MINAMI-KUN DOESN'T KNOW THE TINIEST THING ABOUT HARUGON, DOES HE?
HEY.
HE REALLY DOESN'T ...
HERE COMES THE STAR!
MINAMI-KUUUN!
ZAWA (MURMUR)
ZAWA

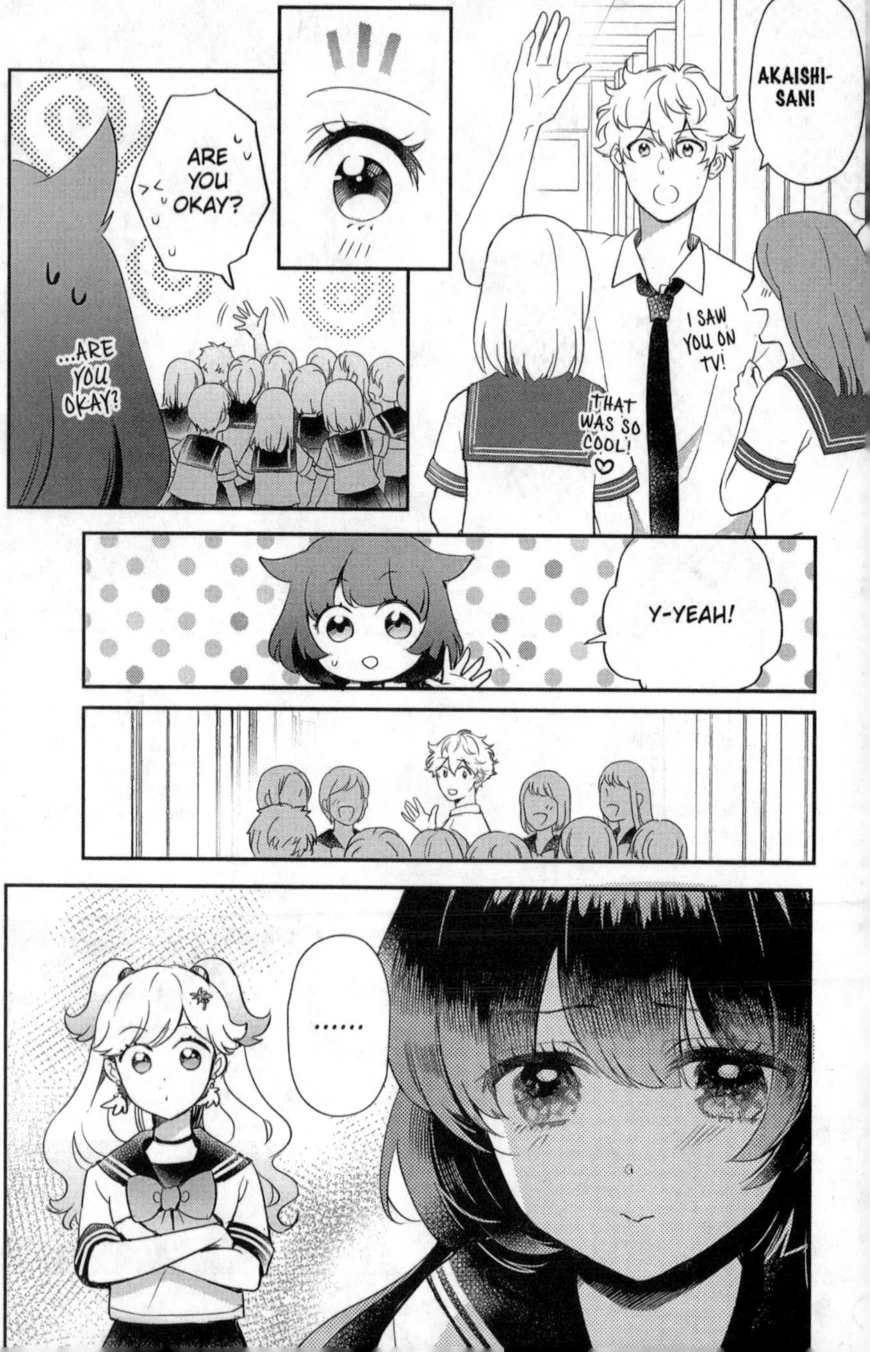
AKAISHI-SAN!
I SAW YOU ON TV!
THAT WAS SO COOL! ♡
ARE YOU OKAY?
...ARE YOU OKAY?
Y-YEAH!
......

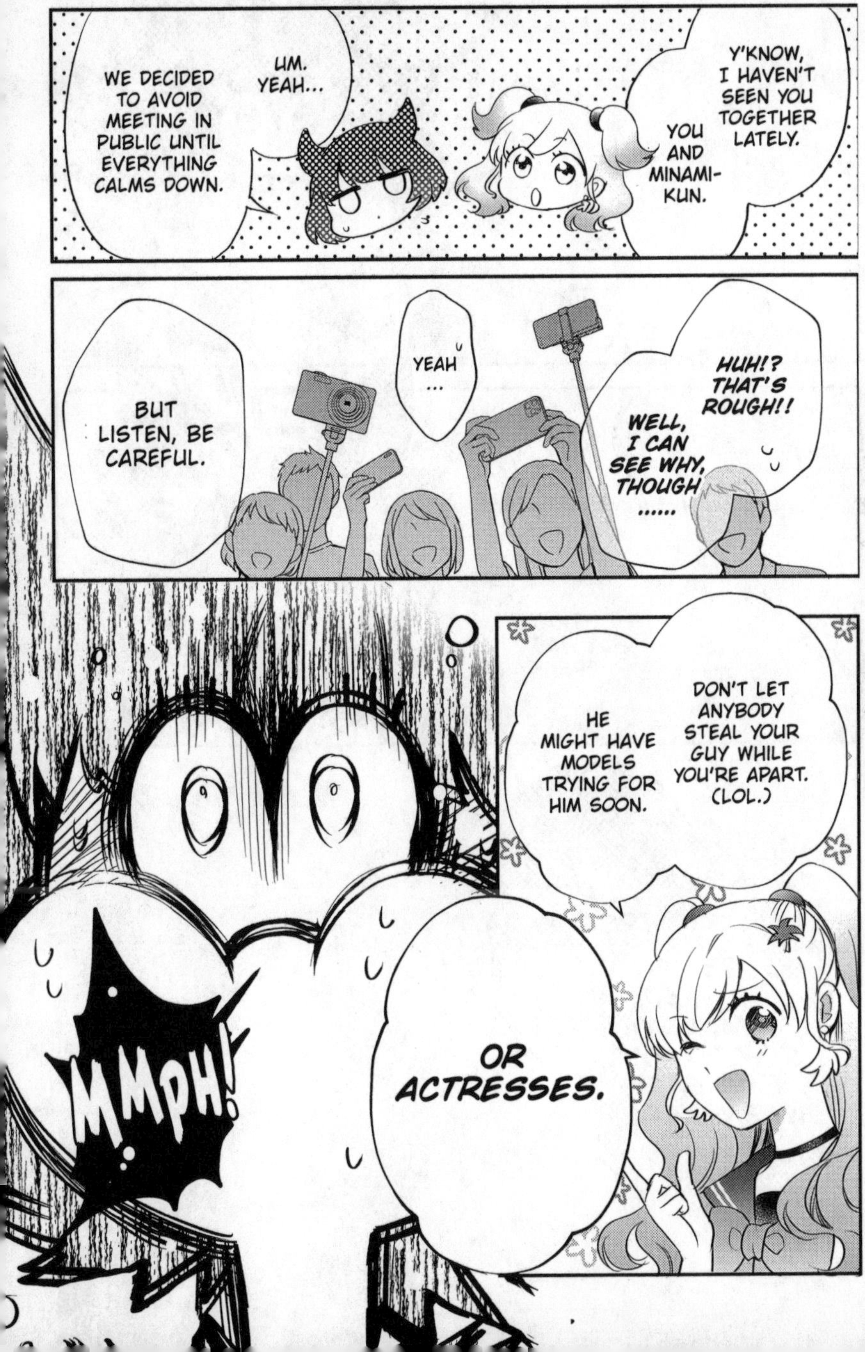
Y'KNOW, I HAVEN'T SEEN YOU TOGETHER LATELY.
YOU AND MINAMI-KUN.
UM. YEAH...
WE DECIDED TO AVOID MEETING IN PUBLIC UNTIL EVERYTHING CALMS DOWN.
HUH!? THAT'S ROUGH!!
WELL, I CAN SEE WHY, THOUGH ......
YEAH ...
BUT LISTEN, BE CAREFUL.
DON'T LET ANYBODY STEAL YOUR GUY WHILE YOU'RE APART. (LOL.)
HE MIGHT HAVE MODELS TRYING FOR HIM SOON.
OR ACTRESSES.
MMPH!

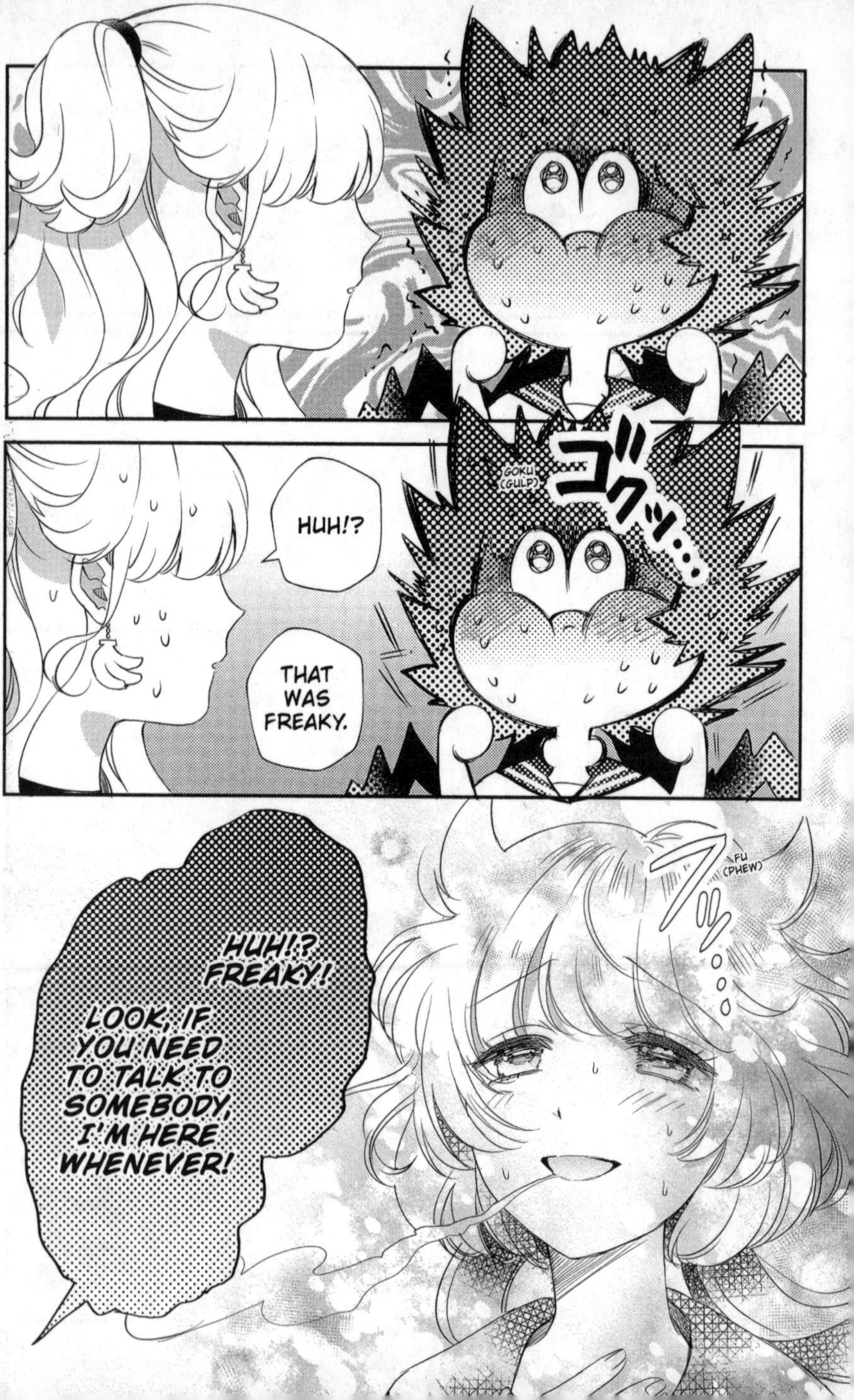
ゴクッ…
GOKU (GULP)
HUH!?
THAT WAS FREAKY.
フ〜…
FU (PHEW)
HUH!? FREAKY!
LOOK, IF YOU NEED TO TALK TO SOMEBODY, I'M HERE WHENEVER!

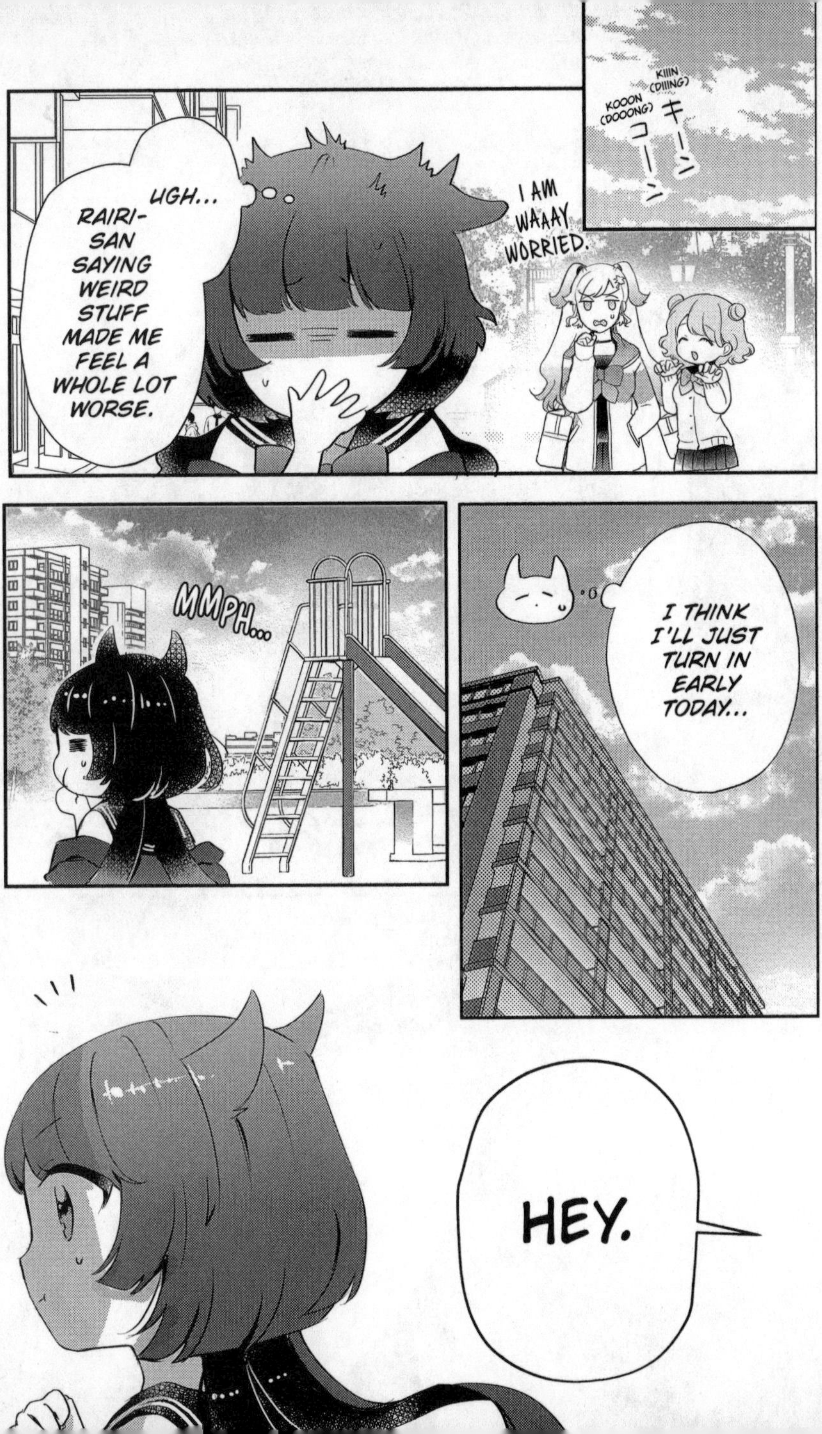
KIIIN (DIIING) キーン
KOOON (DOOONG) コーン
I AM WAAAY WORRIED.
UGH... RAIRI-SAN SAYING WEIRD STUFF MADE ME FEEL A WHOLE LOT WORSE.
I THINK I'LL JUST TURN IN EARLY TODAY...
MMPH...
HEY.

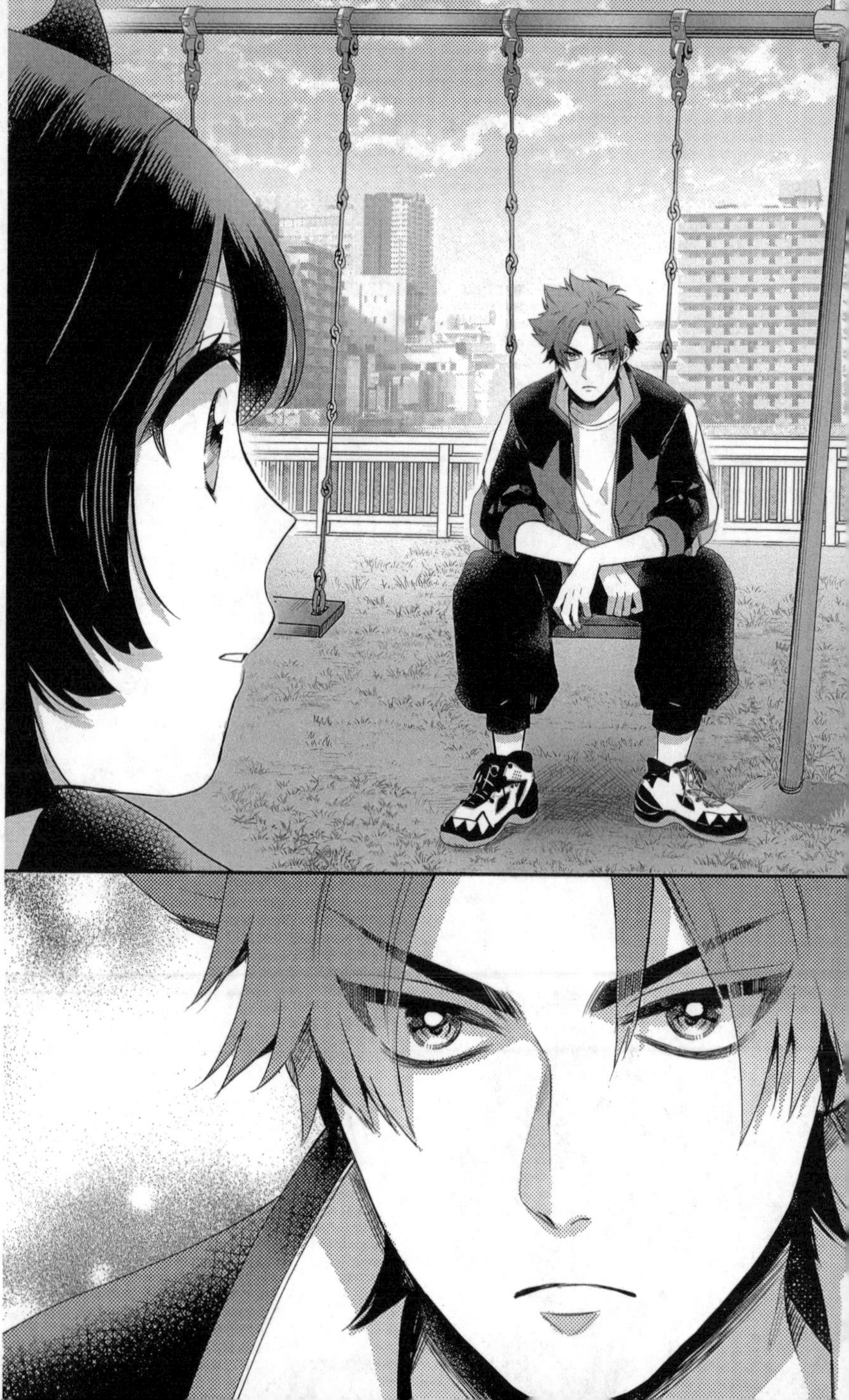

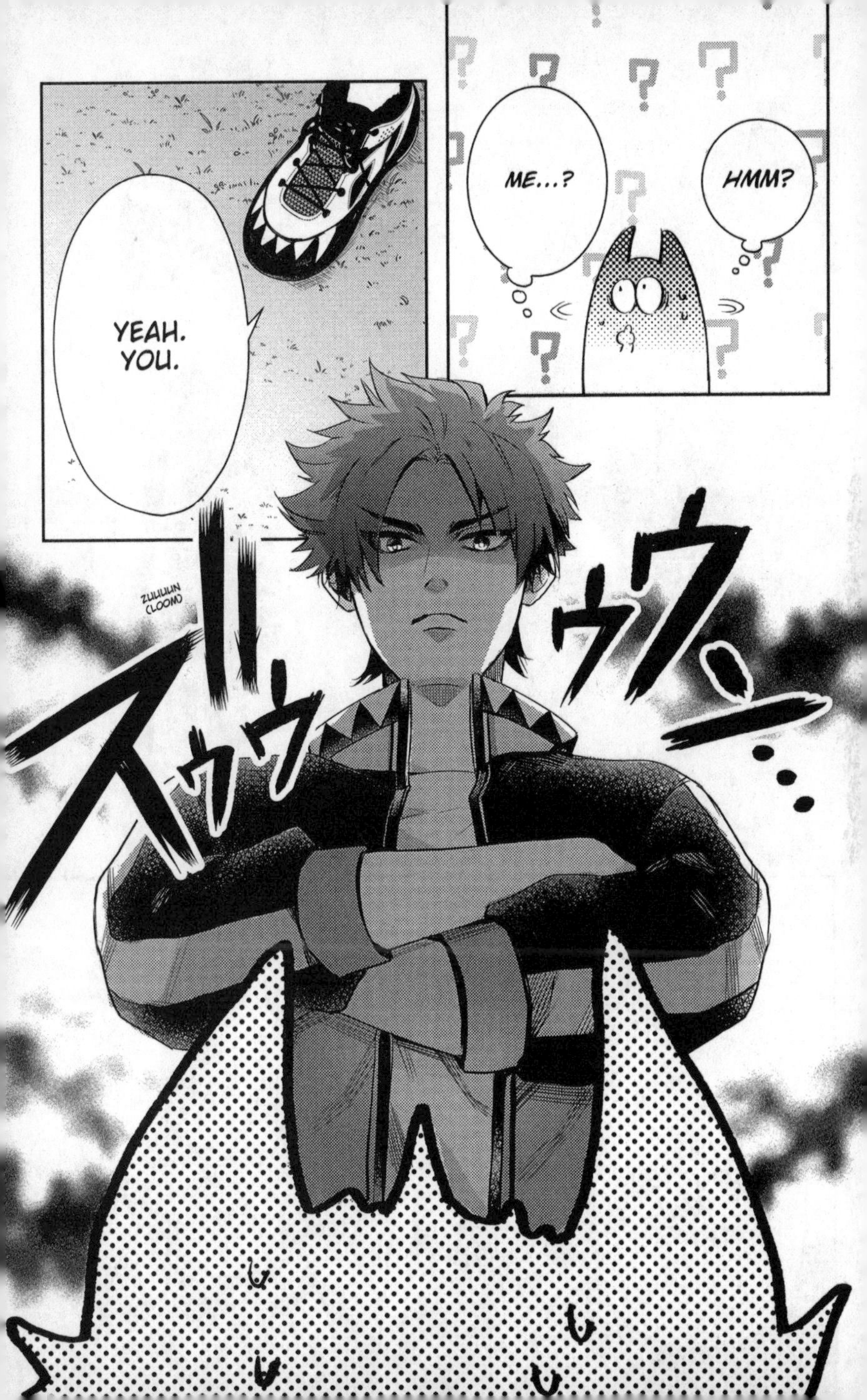
HMM?
ME...?
YEAH. YOU.
ZUUUUN (LOOM)

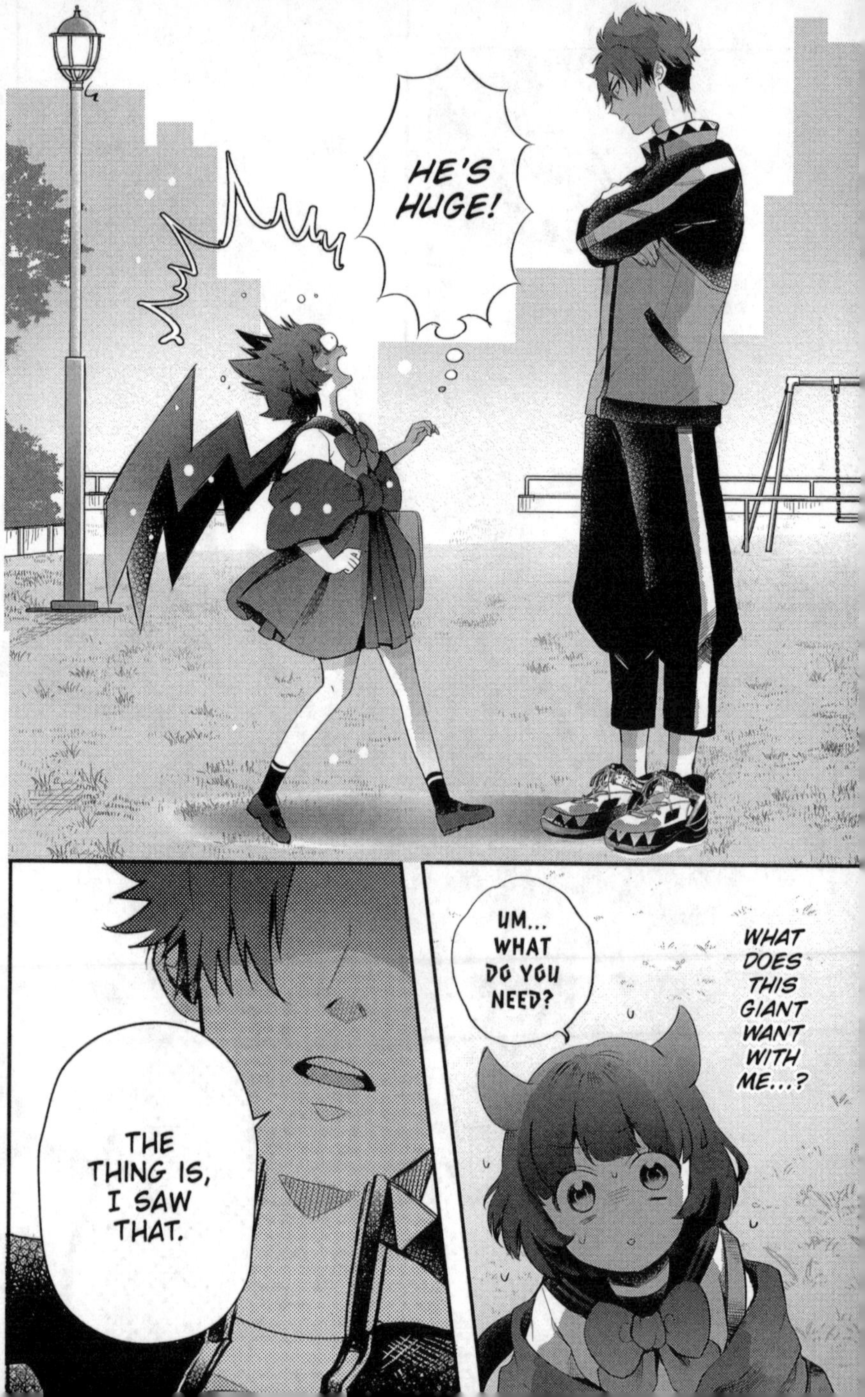
HE'S HUGE!
WHAT DOES THIS GIANT WANT WITH ME...?
UM... WHAT DO YOU NEED?
THE THING IS, I SAW THAT.

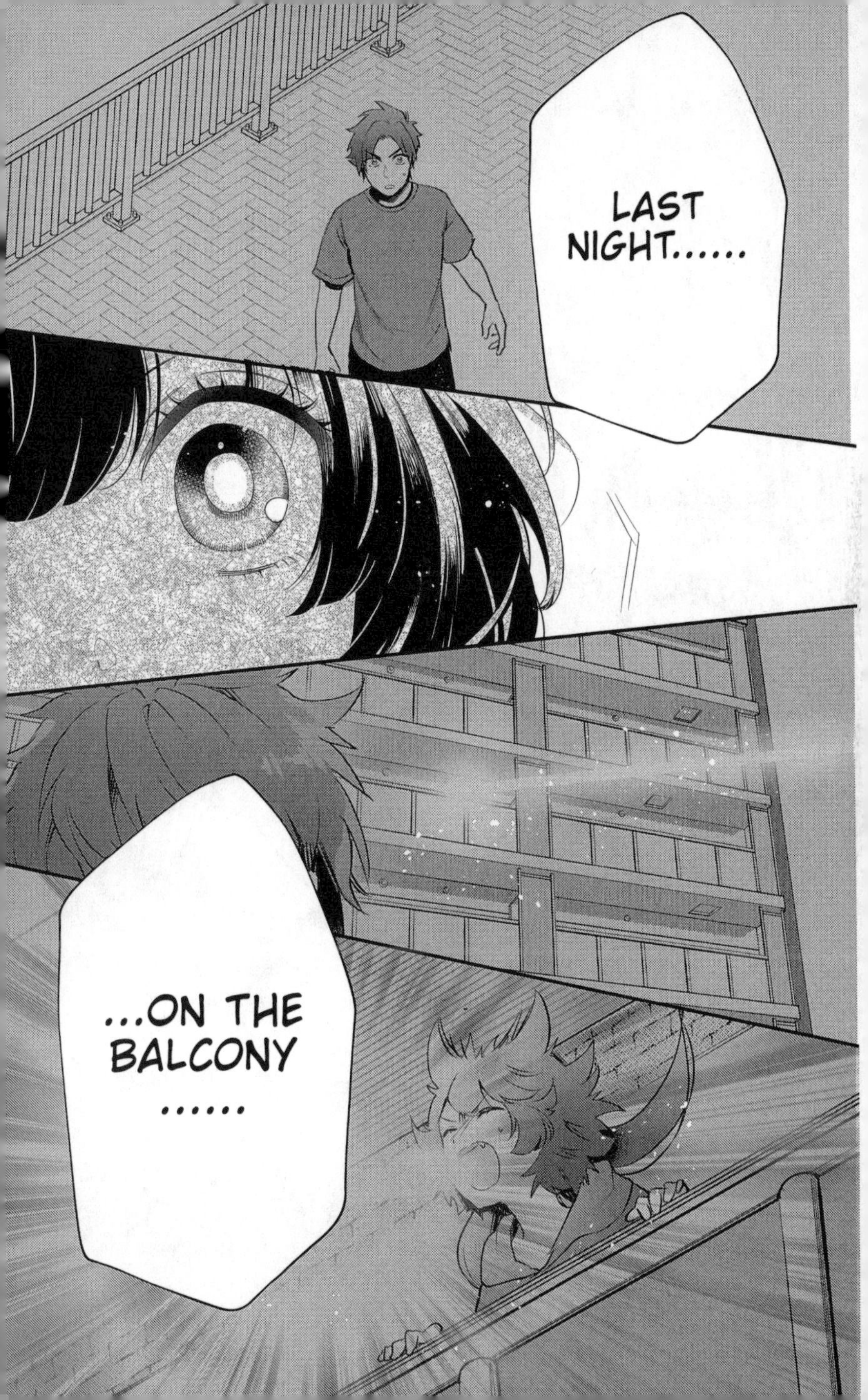
LAST NIGHT......
...ON THE BALCONY ......

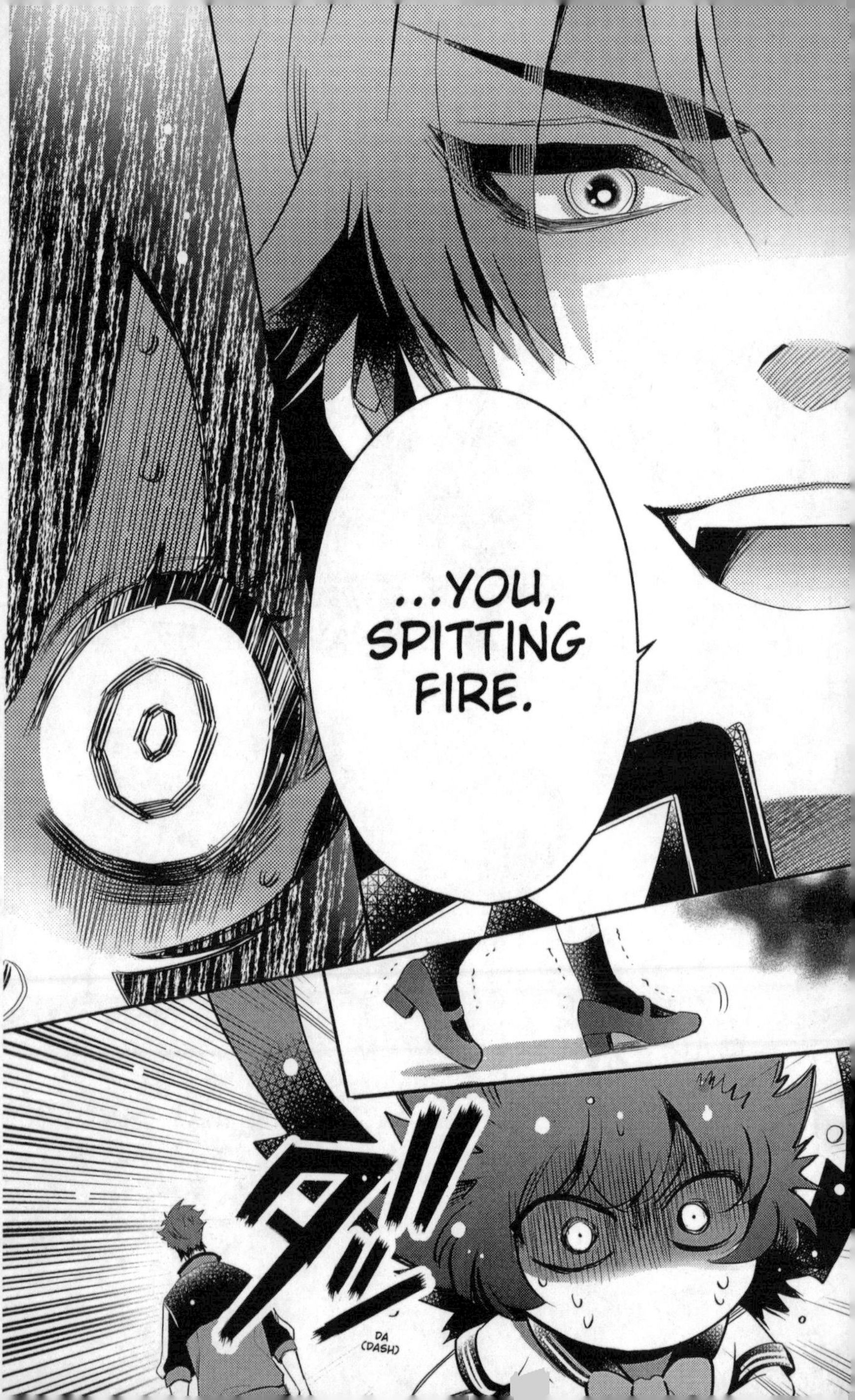
...YOU, SPITTING FIRE.
ダッ
DA (DASH)

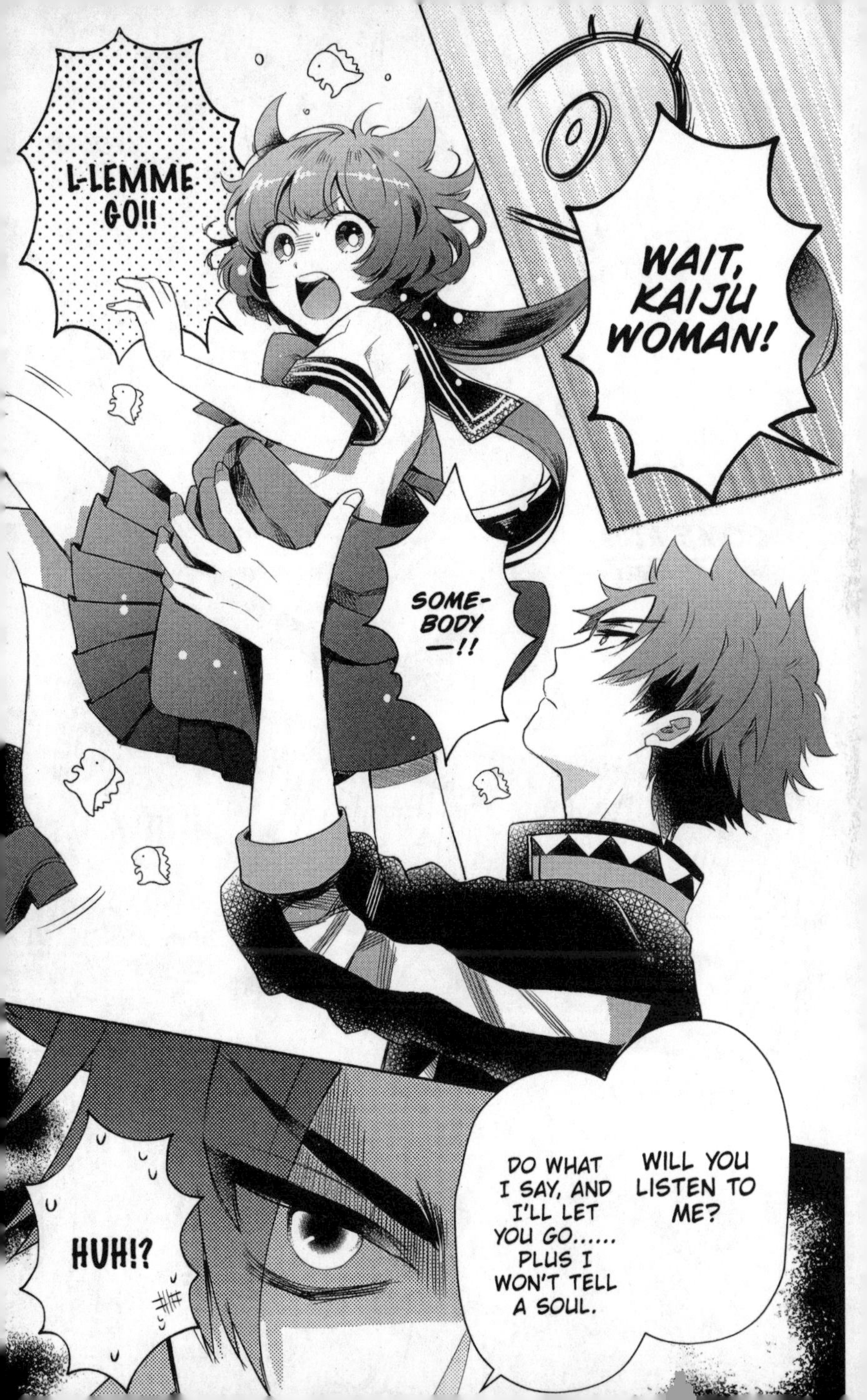
WAIT, KAIJU WOMAN!
L-LEMME GO!!
SOME-BODY—!!
WILL YOU LISTEN TO ME?
DO WHAT I SAY, AND I'LL LET YOU GO...... PLUS I WON'T TELL A SOUL.
HUH!?

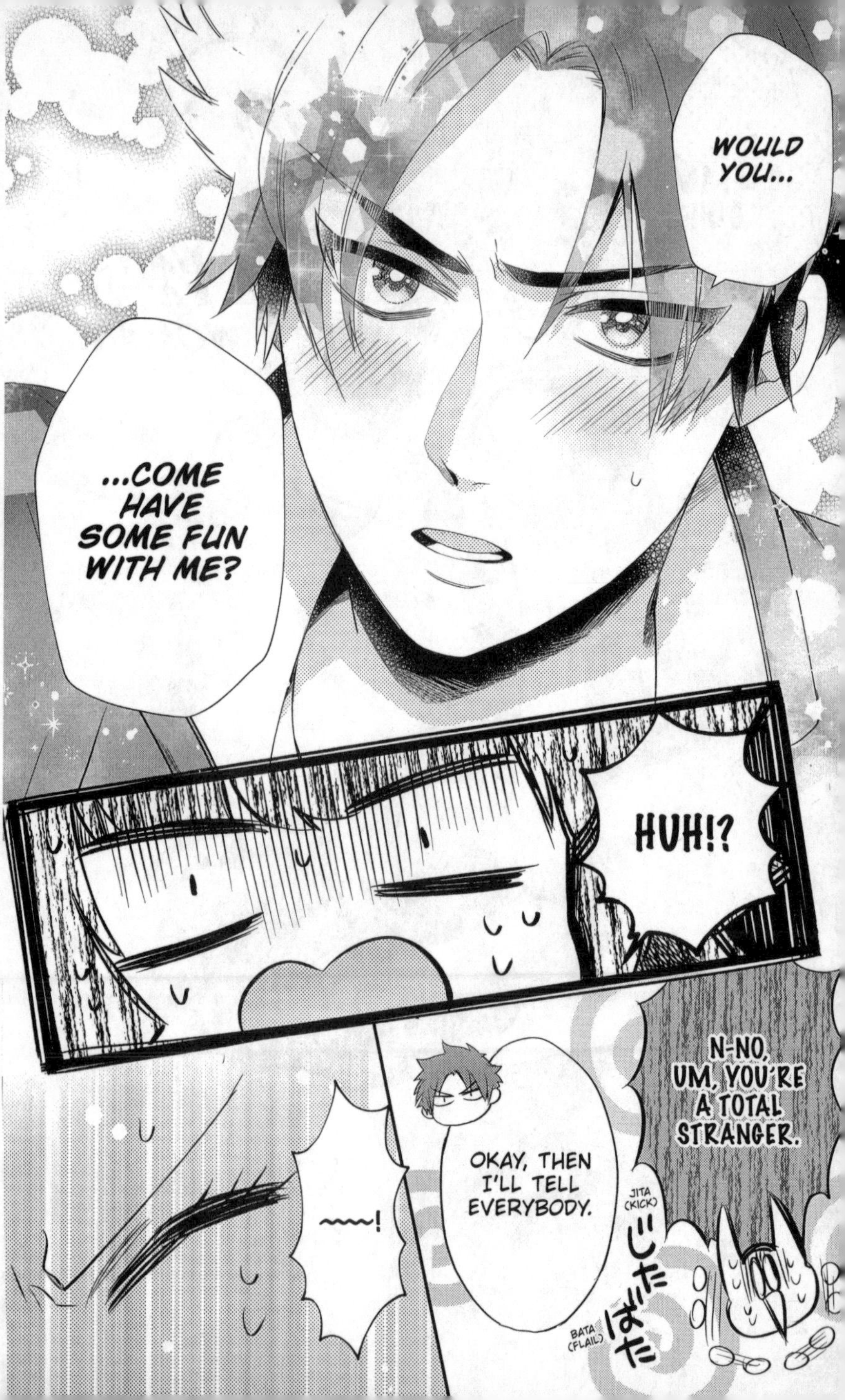

WOULD YOU...
...COME HAVE SOME FUN WITH ME?
HUH!?
N-NO, UM, YOU'RE A TOTAL STRANGER.
JITA (KICK) じた
BATA (FLAIL) ばた
OKAY, THEN I'LL TELL EVERYBODY.
~~~~!
~~~~

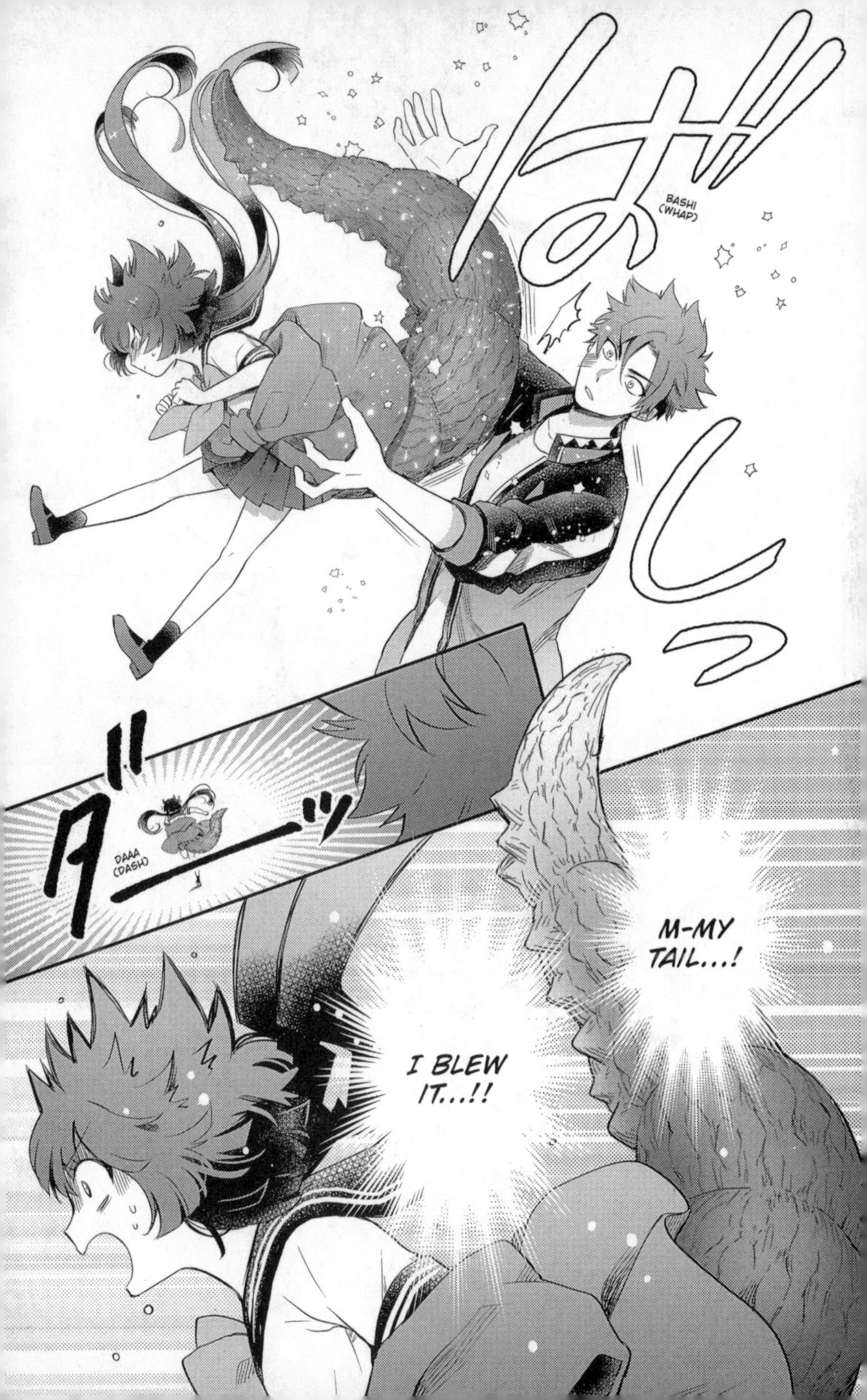
ばしっ
BASHI (WHAP)
ダーッ
DAAA (DASH)
M-MY TAIL...!
I BLEW IT...!!

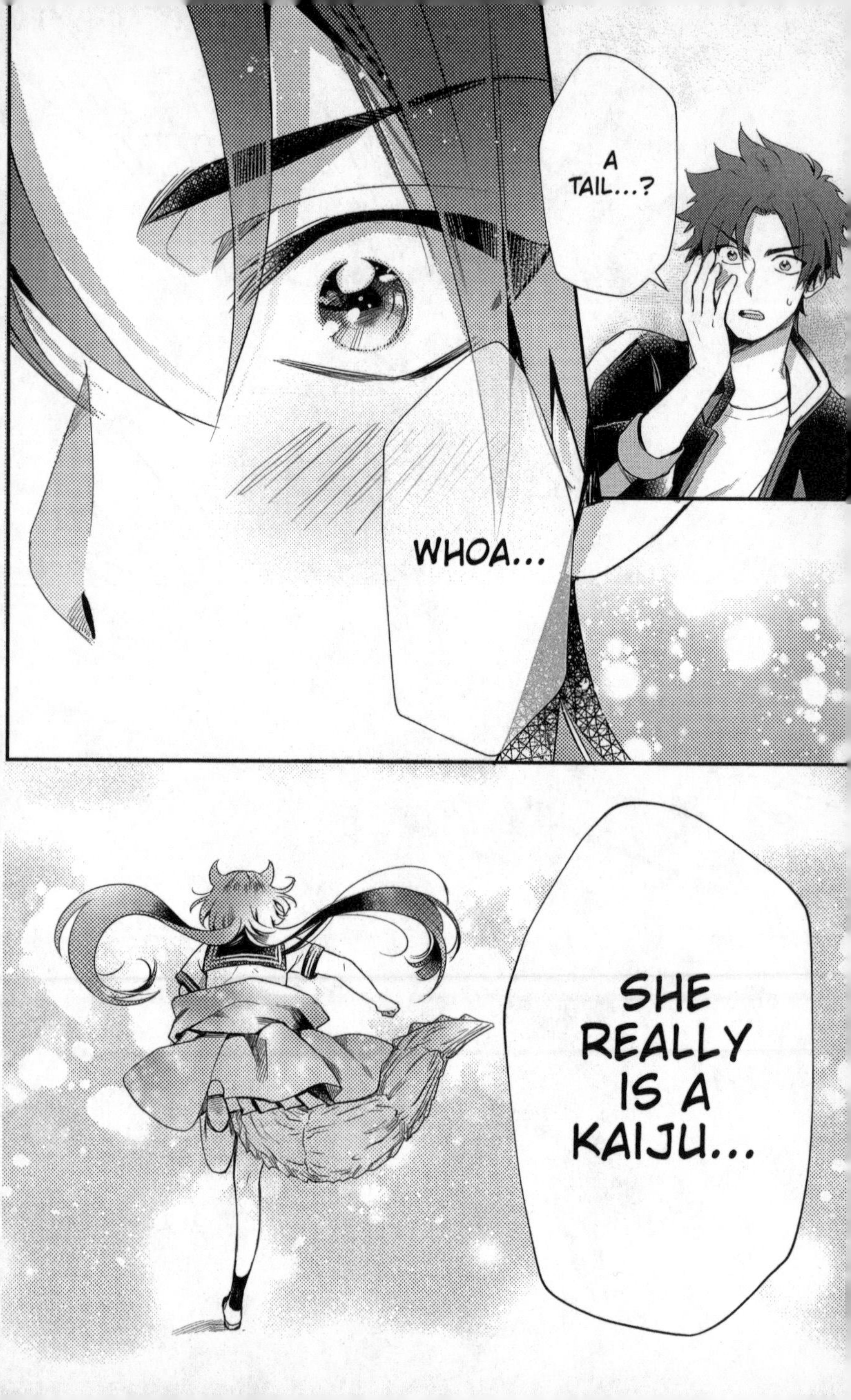
A TAIL...?
WHOA...
SHE REALLY IS A KAIJU...

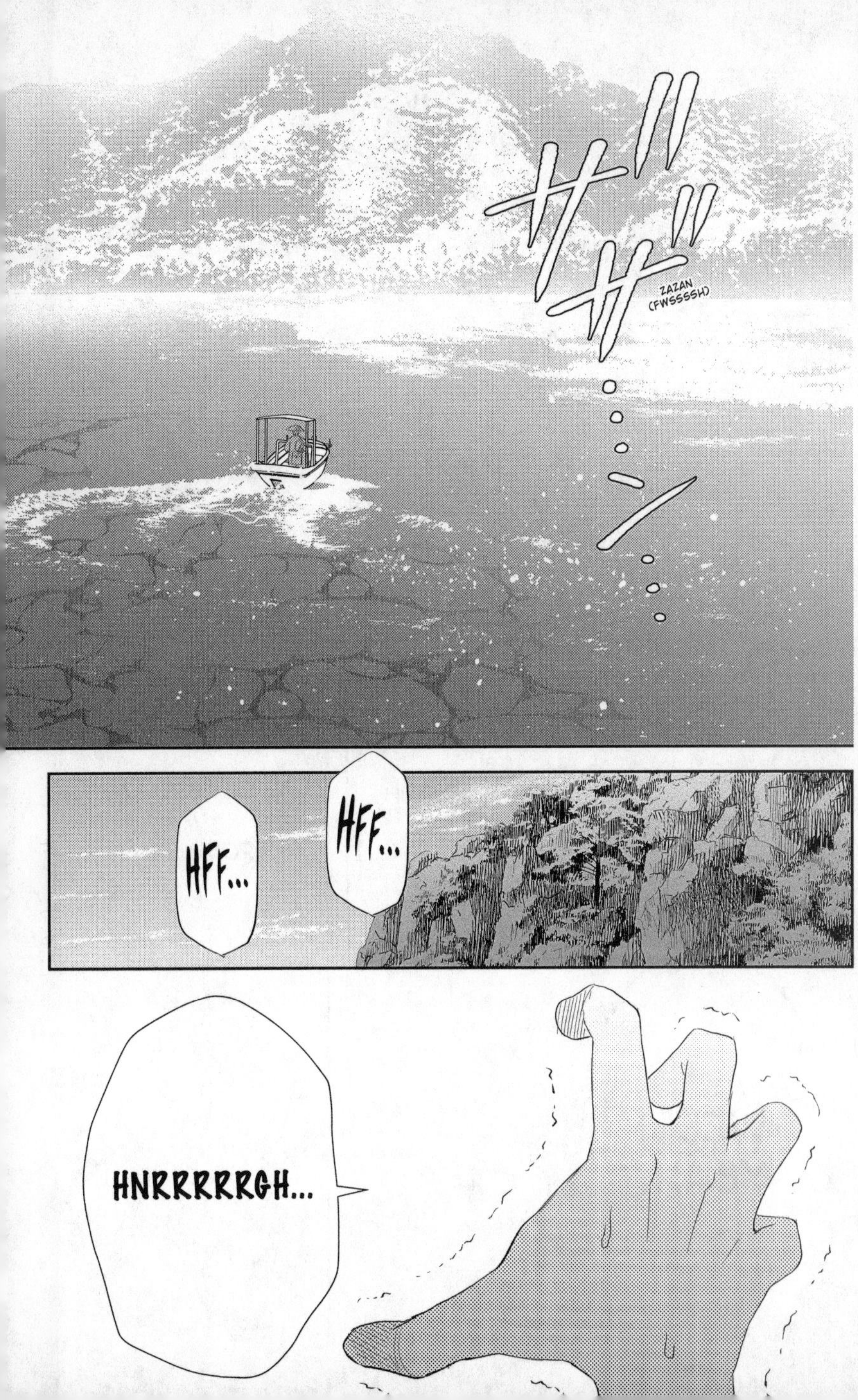
ザザ…ン
ZAZAN (FWSSSSH)
HFF...
HFF...
HNRRRRRGH...

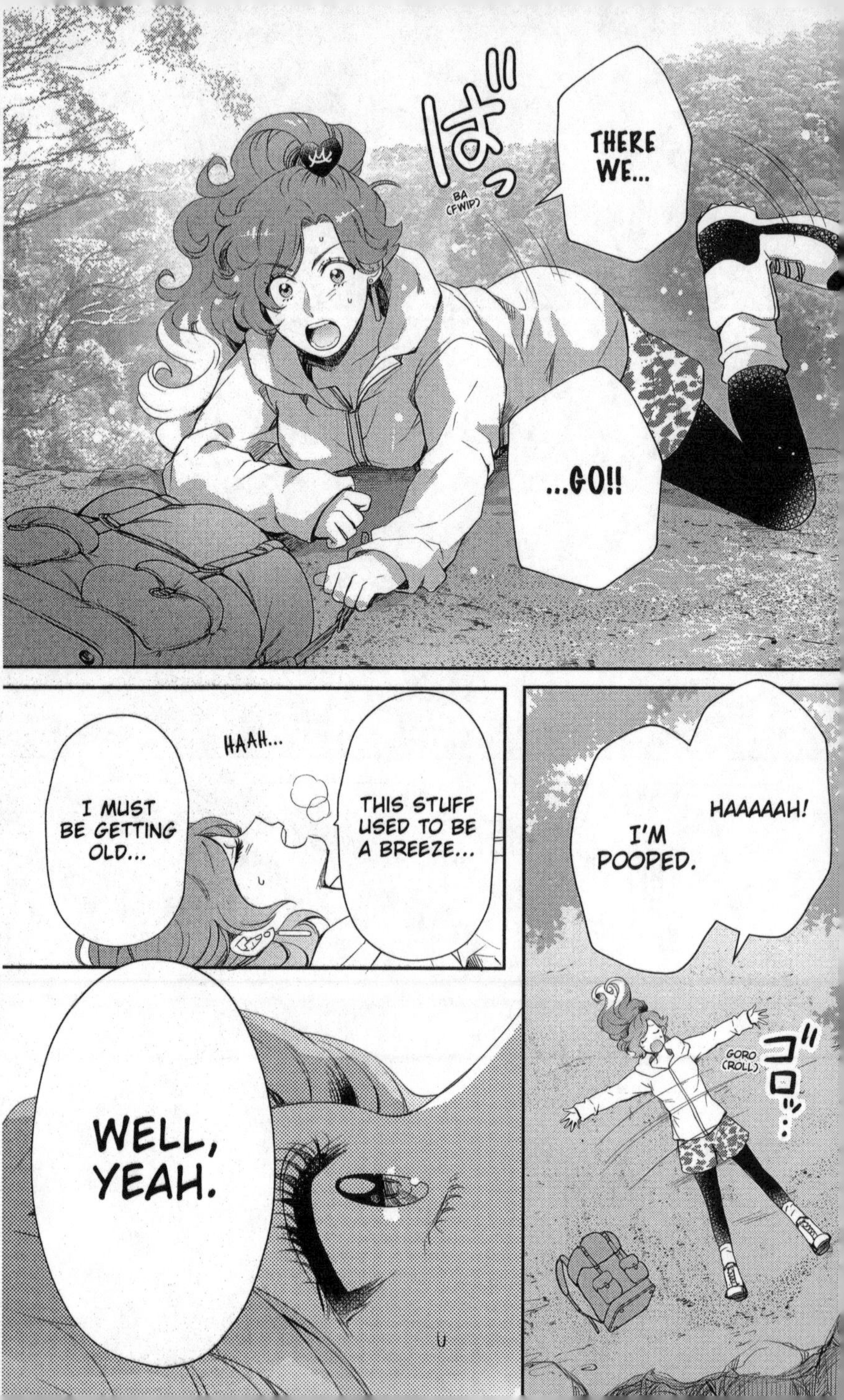

THERE WE...
ばっ
BA (FWIP)
...GO!!
HAAAAAH!
I'M POOPED.
ゴロッ
GORO (ROLL)
HAAH...
THIS STUFF USED TO BE A BREEZE...
I MUST BE GETTING OLD...
WELL, YEAH.

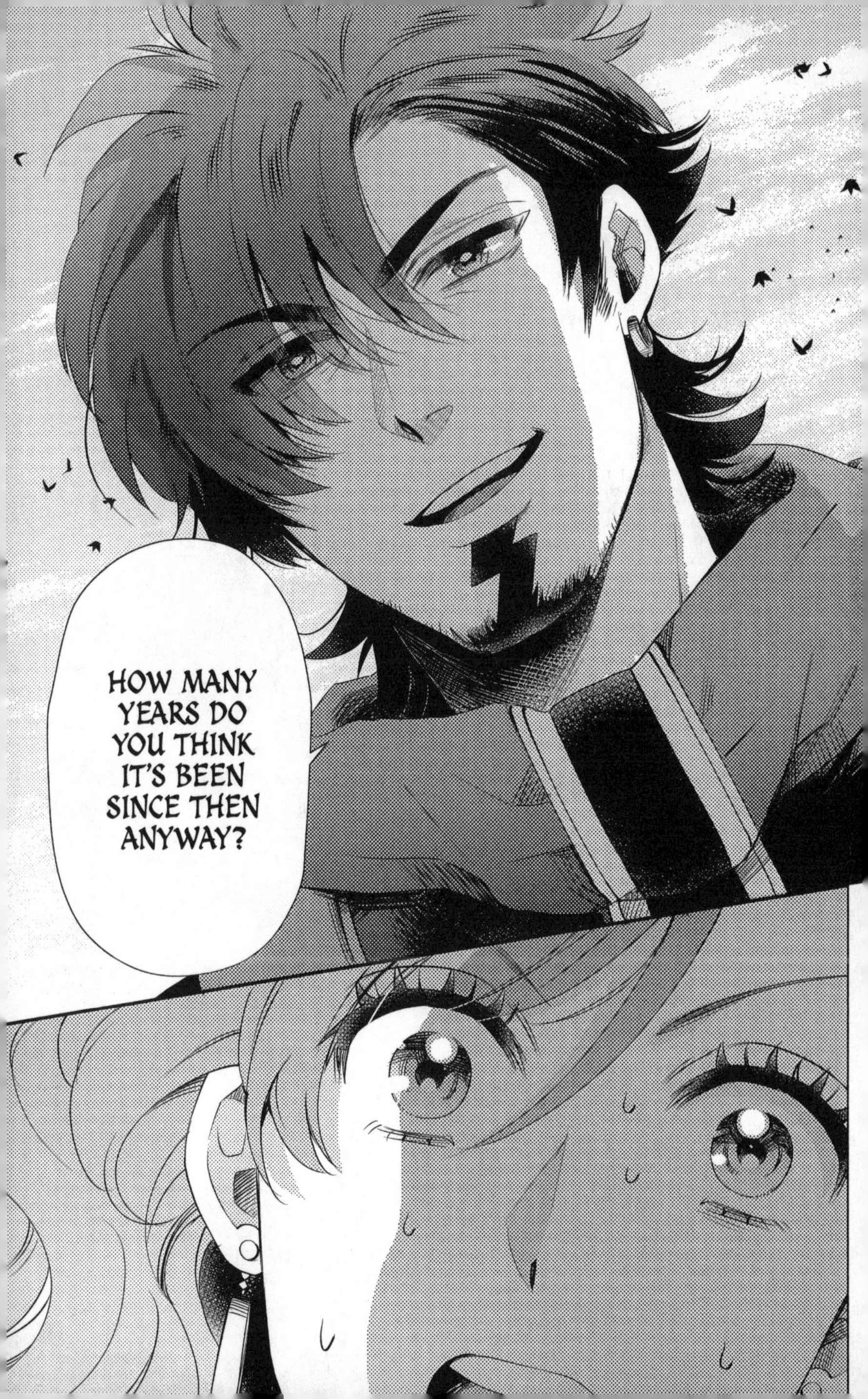
HOW MANY YEARS DO YOU THINK IT'S BEEN SINCE THEN ANYWAY?

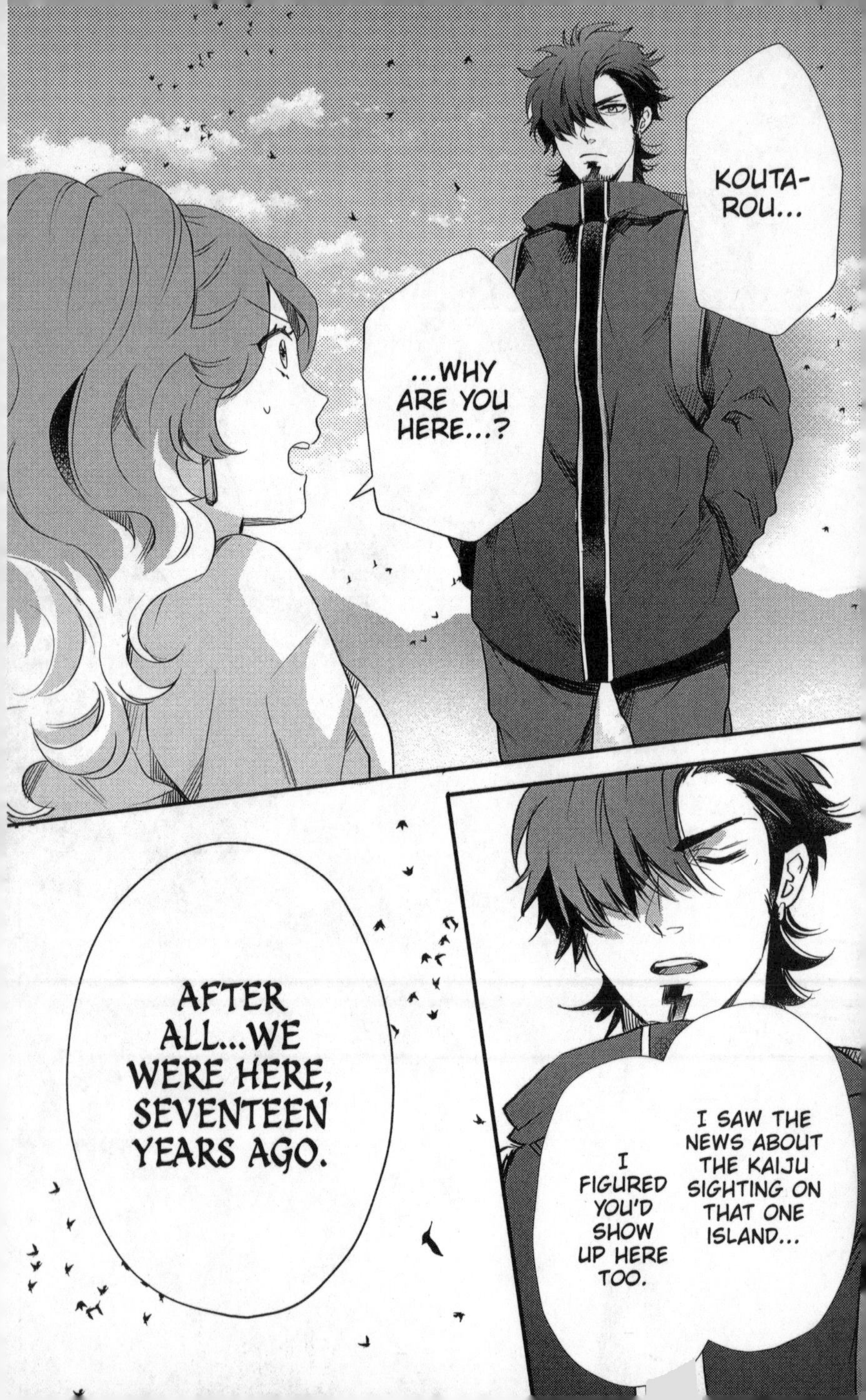
KOUTA-ROU...
...WHY ARE YOU HERE...?
I SAW THE NEWS ABOUT THE KAIJU SIGHTING ON THAT ONE ISLAND...
I FIGURED YOU'D SHOW UP HERE TOO.
AFTER ALL...WE WERE HERE, SEVENTEEN YEARS AGO.

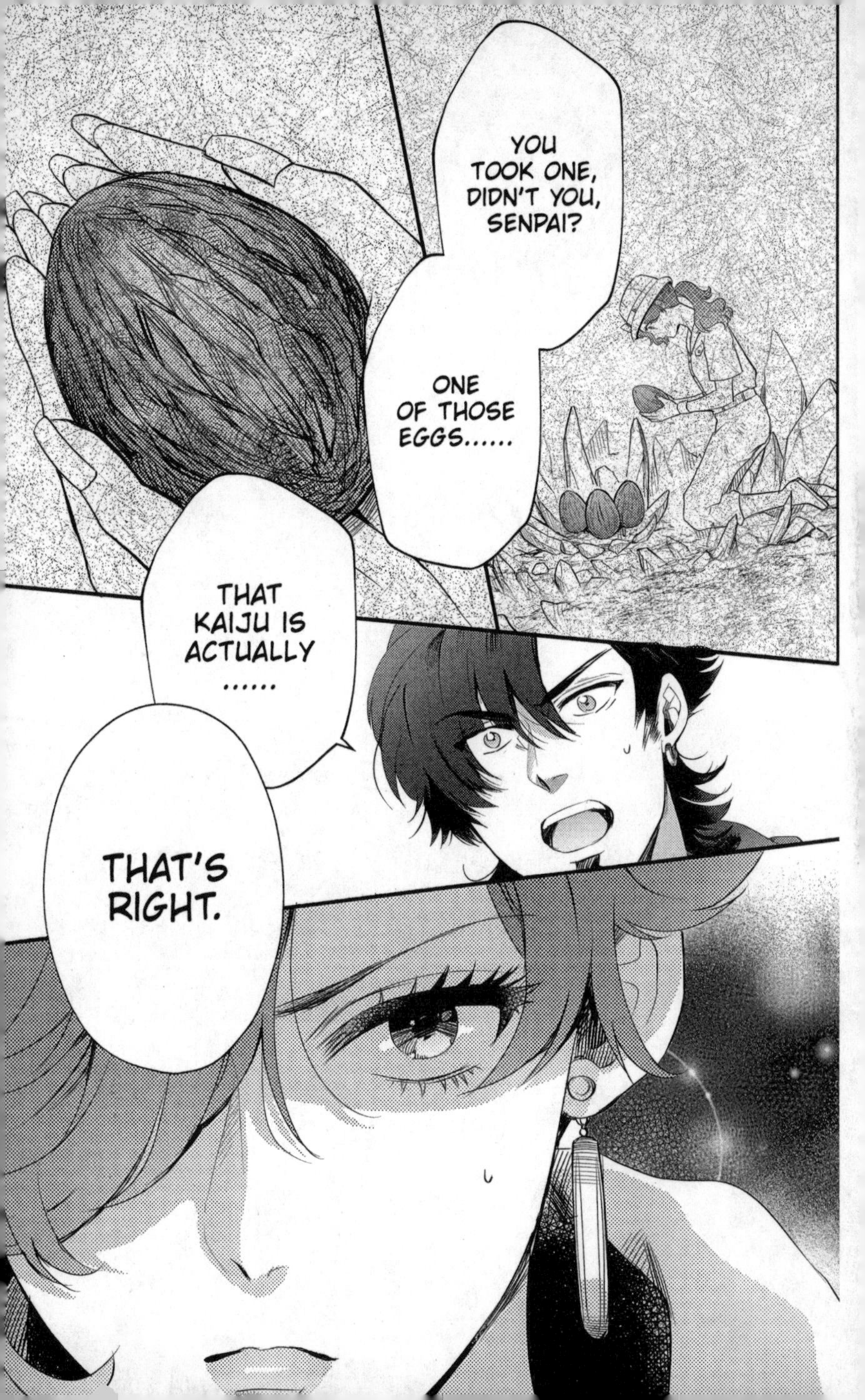
YOU TOOK ONE, DIDN'T YOU, SENPAI?
ONE OF THOSE EGGS......
THAT KAIJU IS ACTUALLY ......
THAT'S RIGHT.

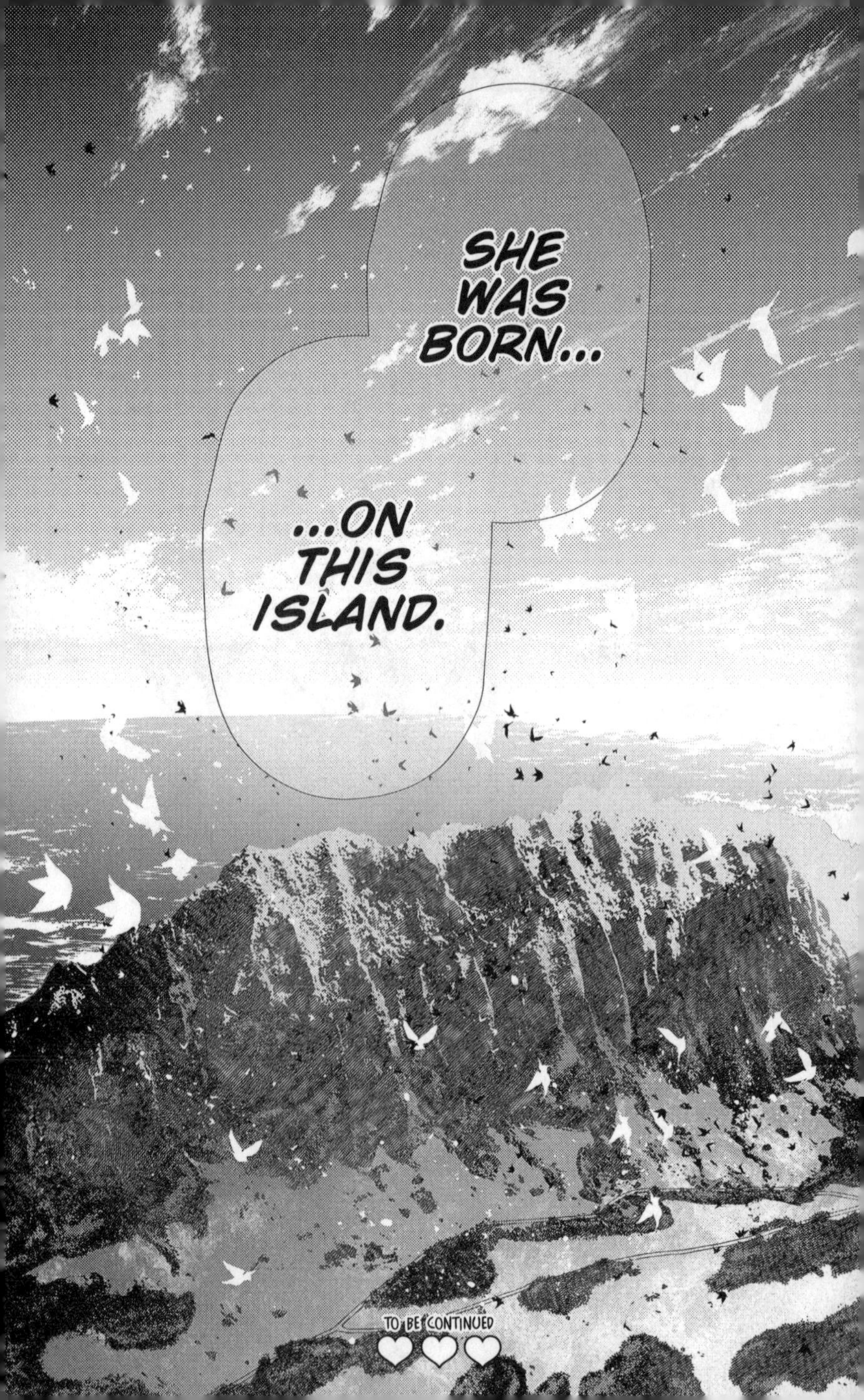
SHE WAS BORN...
...ON THIS ISLAND.
TO BE CONTINUED

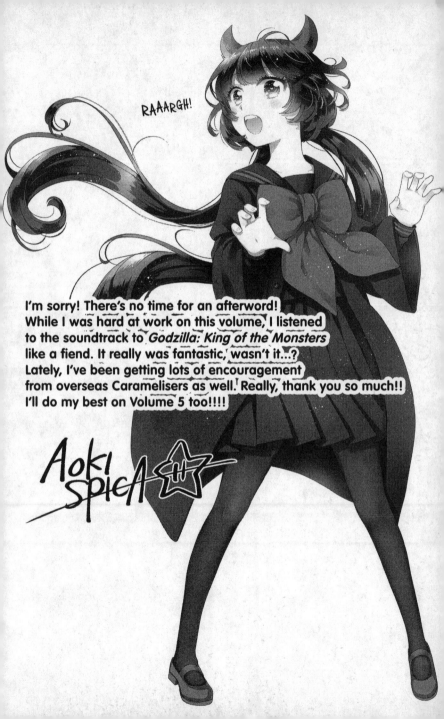

RAAARGH!

I'm sorry! There's no time for an afterword!
While I was hard at work on this volume, I listened
to the soundtrack to *Godzilla: King of the Monsters*
like a fiend. It really was fantastic, wasn't it...?
Lately, I've been getting lots of encouragement
from overseas Caramelisers as well. Really, thank you so much!!
I'll do my best on Volume 5 too!!!!

AOKI SPICA

TRANSLATION NOTES

COMMON HONORIFICS
no honorific: Indicates familiarity or closeness; if used without permission or reason, addressing someone in this manner would constitute an insult.

-*san*: The Japanese equivalent of Mr./Mrs./Miss. If a situation calls for politeness, this is the fail-safe honorific.

-*sama*: Conveys great respect; may also indicate that the social status of the speaker is lower than that of the addressee.

-*kun*: Used most often when referring to boys, this indicates affection or familiarity. Occasionally used by older men among their peers, but it may also be used by anyone referring to a person of lower standing.

-*onii-san*: A respectful way of referring to one's older brother or a young man.

-*chan*: An affectionate honorific indicating familiarity used mostly in reference to girls; also used in reference to cute persons or animals of either gender.

-*tan*: A casual honorific that expresses closeness and affection; it is similar to *chan* in that it is used in reference to cute persons.

-*taso*: A casual honorific similar to *tan*. It comes from the fact that *tan* and *taso* look nearly identical when written out in katakana. In the same vein, *tei* is another cute way of ending someone's name.

PAGE 26
In Japan, most people use last names until they have reached a level of familiarity—usually with family, close friends, or significant others—to use first names. Minami's use of Kuroe's last name, Akaishi, comes across as the two having a distant relationship.

PAGE 30
Rolled ice cream is just about what it sounds like—ice cream that is spread very thinly on an extremely cold metal plate, then rolled into tight curls with a metal spatula and served in a cup, with or without toppings.

PAGE 43
Komodo dragons actually are carnivorous, dangerous, and fast in real life, although these seem significantly bigger than the real-life version.

PAGE 135
The Sumidagawa Fireworks Festival is a fireworks festival that is held on the last Saturday in July.

KAIJU♥GIRL CARAMELISE 4

Spica Aoki

TRANSLATION: **Taylor Engel** 🐾 LETTERING: **Lys Blakeslee**

OTOMEKAIJU CARAMELISE Vol. 4
©Spica Aoki 2020
First published in Japan in 2020 by KADOKAWA CORPORATION, Tokyo.
English translation rights arranged with KADOKAWA CORPORATION,
Tokyo through TUTTLE-MORI AGENCY, INC., Tokyo.

English translation © 2021 by Yen Press, LLC

Yen Press
150 West 30th Street, 19th Floor
New York, NY 10001

Visit us at yenpress.com ♡ facebook.com/yenpress ♡
twitter.com/yenpress ♡ yenpress.tumblr.com ♡
instagram.com/yenpress

First Yen Press Edition: March 2021

Yen Press is an imprint of Yen Press, LLC.
The Yen Press name and logo are trademarks of
Yen Press, LLC.

The publisher is not responsible for websites (or
their content) that are not owned by the publisher.

Library of Congress Control Number: 2019935205

ISBNs: 978-1-9753-2275-5 (paperback)
        978-1-9753-2276-2 (ebook)

10 9 8 7 6 5 4 3 2 1

BVG

Printed in the United States of America